The Many Lives
of *The Evil Dead*

The Many Lives of *The Evil Dead*

Essays on the Cult Film Franchise

Edited by RON RIEKKI *and* JEFFREY A. SARTAIN

McFarland & Company, Inc., Publishers
Jefferson, North Carolina

ISBN (print) 978-1-4766-6871-0
ISBN (ebook) 978-1-4766-3604-7

LIBRARY OF CONGRESS CATALOGUING DATA ARE AVAILABLE

BRITISH LIBRARY CATALOGUING DATA ARE AVAILABLE

© 2019 Ron Riekki and Jeffrey A. Sartain. All rights reserved

No part of this book may be reproduced or transmitted in any form or by any means, electronic or mechanical, including photocopying or recording, or by any information storage and retrieval system, without permission in writing from the publisher.

The front cover image is of Bruce Campbell in *The Evil Dead*, 1981 (New Line Cinema/Photofest)

Printed in the United States of America

*McFarland & Company, Inc., Publishers
Box 611, Jefferson, North Carolina 28640
www.mcfarlandpub.com*

Table of Contents

Introduction	1

Part I: The Films

Deadites and the American Zombie Tradition BRANDON KEMPNER	4
"The Number One Nasty": How Britain's Most Popular Eighties Horror Was Banned SARAH CLEARY	15
Final Girl, Final Boy: Ash's Imperiled Masculinity DALE BAILEY	27
Perceptions of Paranormal Plausibility: Method and Manipulation in *The Evil Dead* LEON LEWIS	34
Naturom Demonto: How *The Evil Dead* Claims Evil for Both Literature and Cinema JOHN SEMLEY	41
Tracking Gaze, Possessing Perspective: Evil as Affect HAERIN SHIN	51
The Evil Dead and Punk Rock Cinema ALEX PITOFSKY	55
Horrid Addictions and Curious Cravings EMILY D. EDWARDS	59

Dismembering, Repeating and Working-Through: Queer
  Disability and Neoliberal Crises of Deracination
  in Sam Raimi's *Evil Dead* Trilogy
      CLAYTON J. PLAKE   70

The First Horror Film Shot in Michigan
      RON RIEKKI   82

Part II: The Franchise and Adaptations

"Don't call me Ash!": Success, the Bruce Campbell Way
      MICHAEL FUCHS and MICHAEL PHILLIPS   94

Ash vs. the Cult of Personality
      ALEX LIDDELL   109

"For God's sake, how do you stop it?!": The Powers
  and Limitations of the Deadites
      MICHAEL P. JAROS and ROBERT I. LUBLIN   120

"Shoot first, think never": Ash's Satire of Neoliberal
  Individualism
      JEFFREY A. SARTAIN   131

Franchising Fright from Film to Game
      STEFAN HALL   144

Repulsion and Convulsion in "The Splatter Zone"
      ROB ROZNOWSKI   153

Stage Horrality: *Evil Dead: The Musical* and the Theatricality
  of Embarrassment
      ANDRÉ LOISELLE   158

Deadites vs. Adaptation
      VALERIE L. GUYANT   164

Deadite Porn
      OLGA TCHEPIKOVA-TREON   172

Macduff vs. Army of Darkness
      ERIN HARRINGTON   182

Part III: Testimonials

Fake Shemping
    BILL VINCENT   188

Do the *Necronomicon*: *Evil Dead*'s Journey into the Realm
  of Musical Theater
    L. MICHAEL ELLIOTT   196

Being Linda
    BETSY BAKER   200

About the Contributors   203

Index   207

Introduction

The Many Lives of The Evil Dead: *Essays on the Cult Film Franchise* is a collection of essays from film and media scholars examining the extended legacy of one of the all-time great horror motion pictures. One of the top grossing independent films of all time, *The Evil Dead* (1981), made by Michigan natives Sam Raimi, Rob Tapert, and Bruce Campbell, sparked a worldwide cult following for a media franchise that has lasted almost four decades.

The *Evil Dead* franchise is a staple of American independent cinema and a favorite of horror fans worldwide. There have been several histories, biographies, and documentaries made about *The Evil Dead*, as well as a growing body of scholarship that has amassed since the first film's release in 1981. This book gives scholars and fans of *The Evil Dead* a wide variety of new and novel approaches to the original film, as well as the extended franchise. For convenience, we have divided the volume into three major sections.

In "The Films," authors from a variety of disciplines present ten fresh perspectives on the four feature films of the *Evil Dead* franchise, expanding on almost four decades of criticism and scholarship engendered by Raimi's original classic.

In "The Franchise and Adaptations," ten more essays discuss the wide variety of ways that the *Evil Dead* story has made its way into other media forms, including video games, stage musicals, comics, pornography, television, and more.

The final section, "Testimonials," offers a special treat for fans and scholars alike. In this section, we have offerings from three individuals involved with various productions of the *Evil Dead* franchise—Bill Vincent (Fake Shemp and one of Raimi's professors), L. Michael Elliott (musical director for *Evil Dead: The Musical*), and Betsy Baker (Linda) from *The Evil Dead*.

We want to thank all of our contributors for the opportunity to present their work in this volume. It has been a labor of love to produce a work of scholarship about an enduring franchise with so many talented, generous writers.

PART I
The Films

Deadites and the American Zombie Tradition

BRANDON KEMPNER

Are the Deadites zombies?

While the *Evil Dead* franchise makes it abundantly clear that its white-eyed antagonists are the demon-possessed dead, the Deadites have always been confused with their more popular zombie brethren.[1] *The Evil Dead* (1981) debuted shortly after George A. Romero's *Dawn of the Dead* (1978) and Lucio Fulci's *Zombi 2* (1979) pushed the zombie back into the public consciousness, and *Ash vs. Evil Dead* (2015–2018) returned to a television landscape defined by the runaway success of *The Walking Dead* (2010–). As a result, the Deadites exist in profound conversation with the zombie tradition, and this essay argues that the *Evil Dead* franchise plays up this confusion, using the unavoidable comparisons between zombies and Deadites to create new approaches to the cultural anxieties of possession, infection, and survivalism.

American zombie scholarship has blossomed over the past decade, driven by books such as Jamie Russell's *Book of the Dead: The Complete History of Zombie Cinema* (2005, revised 2014), Kyle William Bishop's *American Zombie Gothic: The Rise and Fall (and Rise) of the Walking Dead in Popular Culture* (2010), Sarah Juliet Lauro's *The Transatlantic Zombie: Slavery, Rebellion, and Living Death* (2015), and academic collections such as *Zombies Are Us: Essays on the Humanity of the Walking Dead* (2011) and *Race, Oppression and the Zombie: Essays on Cross-Cultural Appropriations of the Caribbean Tradition* (2011). These works argue that zombies operate as the ultimate metaphor for the ills and fears of society, whether capitalism, infectious diseases, or racial tensions. *The Evil Dead*, with its characteristic slapstick tone, addresses these same fears but does so in a uniquely different—and disturbing—way. While appropriations of the zombie occur across the landscape of the *Evil Dead* franchise, these cross-pollinations are most clearly visible in *Evil Dead 2* (1987) and *Ash vs. Evil Dead* (2015–2018). Since both operate as sequels in the *Evil Dead* universe, they anticipate their audiences having specific ideas about the "rules" of the zombie as well as the "rules" of the *Evil Dead* franchise itself. By undermining audience expectations about zombies being overwhelming and unconquerable, *Evil Dead 2* and *Ash vs. Evil Dead* infuse their zombie-like monsters with humor, satire, and, in the end, a triumphant optimism.

The Territory of the Zombie: Possession, Infection, Survivalism

Over the past decade, zombie scholars have argued that zombies owe their popularity and cultural significance to their flexible symbolic nature. In *American Zombie Gothic*, Bishop powerfully lays out this theoretical framework:

> the zombie functions primarily as a social and cultural metaphor, a creature that comments on the society that produced it by confronting audiences with fantastic narratives of excesses and extremes. By forcing viewers to face their greatest fears concerning life and death, health and decay, freedom and enslavement, prosperity and destruction, the zombie narrative provides an insightful look into the darkest heart of modern society as it is now or as it might quickly become [31].[2]

By focusing on the zombie's symbolic function rather than its physical characteristics, Bishop opens up a broad space for analysis. Even if the precise nature of the zombie as a "social and cultural metaphor" changes from work to work, what remains is a cluster of cultural anxieties expressed in those possessed, infectious, and violent figures. While the zombie-like monsters of *The Evil Dead* may differ in some important physical ways from ordinary zombies, they operate in an equally metaphoric fashion. If the zombie is a dark mirror of society, then the Deadites are the dark mirror of the zombie.

Scholars and film historians have long noted the essential role that Romero's *Night of the Living Dead* (1968) played in the formation of the *Evil Dead* franchise. In *The Evil Dead Companion*, Rob Tapert, one of the trio of original producers of *The Evil Dead* along with Sam Raimi and Bruce Campbell, reminisces that "I came up with information that was encouraging; some of the biggest low budget-hits had been horror movies: *Night of the Living Dead, Last House on the Left, The Texas Chain Saw Massacre*" (34). John Kenneth Muir provides further evidence of Romero's influence in *The Unseen Force: The Films of Sam Raimi*: "'We were big fans of what Romero had done with a small budget … and just one cabin,' Raimi once noted, citing *Living Dead* as an influence. The winding road, the late 1960s to early 1970s car model, and the isolated, rural location all play into a feel reminiscent of *Living Dead*" (63). Operating in the same territory as Romero's films, *The Evil Dead* employs the same central strategy of using the Deadite as a metaphor for cultural anxieties.

Despite these connections, *The Evil Dead* has been marginalized in zombie scholarship. When discussing *The Evil Dead*, Bishop notes its connection to the zombie tradition but dismisses it as mere parody. After noting "Raimi's *Evil Dead* films feature demons and possessed corpses instead of traditional zombies," Bishop writes of *Evil Dead 2*: "Rather than attempt any sociopolitical commentary, Raimi apparently just wanted extreme physical comedy, outrageous sight gags, and over-the-top special effects and gore" (187).[3] Similarly dismissive analysis, at least from the zombie perspective, can be found in Russell's *Book of the Dead*. Russell claims that *The Evil Dead* "is not strictly a zombie movie—its ghouls are dead bodies possessed by demons rather than walking corpses" (113) and that "*The Evil Dead* was so horrific it became hilarious" (113). Russell expresses doubts as to any deeper level of cultural critique in Raimi's work: "If there's a comparison to be drawn between the original *Evil Dead* series and the *Return of the Living Dead* films, it's that both indulge in a demented kind of gory comedy. Harking back to Romero's custard pie splatter in *Dawn of the Dead*, both series prove less interested in social commentary than physical comedy" (114), with any serious conversation "neutered by the desire to play everything for yucky yuk-yuk-yuks" (115).

Given this background, it should come as no surprise that serious zombie scholars have largely steered away from *The Evil Dead*. While this perspective is understandable—zombies have not, until recently, been given the kind of academic weight and seriousness they deserve—this dismissal of the *Evil Dead* franchise as brainless comedy is unfortunate. Instead of seeing *The Evil Dead*'s excesses as preventing serious cultural commentary, those excesses are more profitably read as a deliberate attempt to undermine the oppressive conventions of zombie cinema. When speaking of the "rules" of zombies, Jonathan P. Eburne argues, "The formal codes of the genre have become so familiar, so utterly knowable, as to exceed the parameters of fiction altogether. The rules, however worn out, now propose to walk among us" (394). If traditional zombie movies like *Night of the Living Dead* lay out a territory of the zombie, with specific relationships imposed between death, survivalism, and philosophy, works like *The Evil Dead* transform that territory, opening up new and liberating possibilities of thought and action. In *The Cinematic Body*, Steven Shaviro argues that the Romero zombie movies "exceed the boundaries usually assigned to mass entertainment" (100), forcing audiences outside their typical approach to American life. This same idea can be applied to the *Evil Dead* franchise: it exceeds the boundaries usually assigned to the zombie narrative. Rather than let its audience be stupefied by the fixed and stable rules of a zombie apocalypse, *The Evil Dead* constantly violates those rules, reframing them in new, exciting, and optimistic ways.

Zombie Rule #1: Possession

When modern audiences think of the zombie, they most likely think of an infectious corpse hungering for human flesh. As dominant as that image has become, it is a recent invention, created "almost single-handedly" (Bishop 94) by Romero in *Night of the Living Dead*. Before Romero, the original Haitian zombie first entered the American public's imagination with William Seabrook's travelogue *The Magic Island* (1929) and its loose movie adaptation *White Zombie* (1932).[4] In this first configuration, the zombie is a voodoo-hypnotized slave, controlled by a cruel master and rendered into a mindless automaton. These possessed zombies obey their master's will without question, losing all sense of identity. Possession here represents a profound cultural anxiety over loss of control, and this anxiety extends from the Romero films and into the *Evil Dead* franchise.

This anxiety is heightened when the zombie takes over the body of a loved one. When describing this zombie rule, Bishop identifies these zombies as "corpses raised from the dead—more significantly, they are the corpses of the *known* dead ... the zombies pursue living humans with relentless, tireless dedication and kill people mercilessly by eating them alive" (20). These "known dead" are terrifying because they are both familiar and unfamiliar, recognizable as loved ones but without "emotional capacity" (Bishop 20). They represent a mind-shattering and overwhelming fear of death and loss, best exemplified by the famous scene in *Night of the Living Dead* when a daughter eats her own parents. That horrific moment reflects the general pessimism of the film, as described here by Shaviro, "Even as dread pulses to a climax, as plans of action and escape fail, and as the characters we expect to survive are eliminated, we are denied the opportunity of imposing redemptive or compensatory meanings" (90). The zombies of *Night of the Living Dead* and the anxieties they represent are unstoppable and irresistible.

Like most zombie works, *The Evil Dead* is a franchise about possession and the "known dead." The Deadites possess human bodies, transforming them into something both familiar and unfamiliar, symbolized by those milky white eyes and their unrelenting cruelty. While *The Evil Dead* replaces the voodoo master with the demons of the *Necronomicon*, the same fundamental fear is at play here as in the original Caribbean zombie. *Evil Dead 2* dramatizes the fear of possession from the very beginning, opening with a romantic moment between Ash (Bruce Campbell) and his girlfriend Linda (Denise Bixler). After Ash unwittingly releases the Deadites, Linda is possessed immediately. Our initial glimpse of the transformed Linda shows her lurching towards Ash with the characteristic zombie walk: arms held out stiff and staggering awkwardly. Ash then decapitates her with a shovel, playing on the audience's familiarity of the "rule" of killing a zombie by destroying their brain.

Across its first fifteen minutes, *Evil Dead 2* follows the zombie "rules" faithfully, operating as a serious horror movie, complete with jump scares, ominous camera shots, and droning sound effects. The tone shifts abruptly with the return of Linda, rising zombie-like from her grave. Instead of threatening Ash like the audience must have expected, she proceeds to dance, naked, her severed head rolling across the rocks to land atop her body. Her twirling dance is an ironic mockery of the romance that came before. She taunts Ash, crying out, "Dance with me." Like any number of zombie films, Ash cowers behind a boarded-up door. In a slapstick scene, Linda reaches her arms through the wooden slats and bonks Ash's head against them. These two moments—the ridiculous dance, and the Three Stooges style head bash in a moment of pure terror—begin to demonstrate how *Evil Dead 2* breaks the zombie rules. In a traditional zombie film, the anxiety of possession is overwhelming, a fear that cannot be escaped; there are no "redemptive or compensatory meanings." In *Evil Dead 2*, the mixture of possession, humor, and violence launches Ash on a journey outside simple zombie conventions.

Knocked out by Linda, Ash recovers consciousness a few minutes later in a chair. He begins to say "Just a …" but before he can say "dream," Linda's head falls into his lap, biting his hand. In a scene of pure excess, he tries to get her off, smashing her head into everything around. The humor does not last; nothing in the *Evil Dead* franchise is that stable or that permanent, both for good and ill. After clamping her into a vice in the woodshed, the possessed head reverts back to Linda's original personality, piteously crying out, "Please, Ash. Please don't hurt me. You swore that we'd always be together. I love you." The possession resumes a moment later, with the Deadites now using Linda to taunt Ash: "Yes. Your lover is mine, and now she burns in hell." As disturbing as this moment may be, punctuated with gore as Ash destroys Linda's head with a chainsaw, there is also an excess of meaning here. In the normal zombie "rules," once a zombie, your loved one can never recover. The range of emotions presented is narrow, grim, and horrifying. In *Evil Dead 2*, the horror is still there, but the franchise now offers brief moments of recovery and flickering glimpses of possibility. Linda is herself for a moment, something that would never happen in *Night of the Living Dead*.

Something very similar concerning possession happens in the first episode of *Ash vs. Evil Dead*, "El Jefe." After Ash accidentally summons the Deadites while trying to impress a woman, the episode switches to a dramatic scene. State police officers Amanda (Jill Marie Jones) and Carson (Mike

Edward) enter an empty house, flashlights and guns at the ready. In sharp contrast to the humorous sequences that opened the episode, Amanda moves into the next room, only to find her partner staring at an empty rocking chair. A shrouded figure rises up, the same woman Ash was trying to impress with the *Necronomicon*. She goes Deadite, snapping her head around and contorting her body. Amanda shoots her several times in the chest; it does not stop her. Carson then shoots her in the head. However, the zombie rules do not apply, and the Deadite kills Carson by flinging him onto a set of antlers. Carson is resurrected as a Deadite seconds later, crawling on the ceiling and then leaping onto Amanda. *Ash vs. Evil Dead* is performing the same anxiety of losing the "known dead," someone you trust, to the undead curse. Midway through the attack, Carson returns to his old self, crying out, "Don't shoot me. Please, Amanda. I'm your friend. I need you." Then he goes Deadite again, "I need you … to die." This is the same essential moment as depicted with Linda in *Evil Dead 2*, a seesaw use of possession that both reinforces the cultural anxiety of zombies (losing your loved ones while they retain their bodies) while disturbing that moment by showing something more (humor, possibility of recovery) in the landscape of possession.

The back-and-forth of possession is one of the central ideas of the *Evil Dead* franchise. Abruptly moving from camp to horror and back to camp, *The Evil Dead* juxtaposes a wider range of emotional states than traditional zombie works. Rule-bound zombie films represent possession as overwhelming and horrifying, an anxiety that cannot be overcome, without meaning or hope. The "known dead" are lost permanently. This is not the case in *The Evil Dead*. The "known dead" are possessed, but they mock the living, and they return to cry out in horror, and, in a few rare cases, they survive their possession. When Ash is possessed in *Evil Dead 2*, it does not spell his doom. He survives, becomes himself again, and triumphs. The *Evil Dead* franchise creates this space by using the rules of the zombie and then violating them, providing its audiences with something more than the hopeless anxiety of losing your loved ones to an unstoppable possession.

Zombie Rule #2: Infection

When Romero radically reimagined the zombie in *Night of the Living Dead* and *Dawn of the Dead*, he did so by making it infectious, with a single bite capable of transforming the victim into a zombie. After Romero, the spread of zombie-ism from person to person became one of the defining zombie rules, and the anxiety surrounding infection is often greater than the fear of death. As Shaviro explains, "The dread that the zombies occasion is based more on a fear of infection than on one of annihilation" (97). Bishop expands this idea by focusing on how "Romero's conception of the zombie amplifies the mere physical horrors of death by marrying mortality with the loss of autonomy" (118). Infection means loss of control, the destruction of self-determination, and an inability to control your fate, all anxieties greater than the mere unpleasantness of being devoured by your loved ones. Death may be final and sudden, but living on as a zombie is even more horrific.

Evil Dead 2 plays on this fear of infection and the subsequent anxiety about loss of self-control in an innovative manner. *Evil Dead 2* presents the well-worn "bitten by a zombie moment" when Ash is bitten on the hand by Linda's head. In the normal zombie world, infection and loss of self would be the inevitable result. Such as scene is played out time and time again in zombie films, with the doomed victim anxiously waiting for the transformation into a mindless zombie. In a clear parody of zombie rules, only Ash's hand becomes infected, and it proceeds to attack him in one of *Evil Dead 2*'s most uproariously slapstick moments. All the same fears of loss of control are present, but now rendered ridiculous as Ash shouts: "Give me back my hand." His hand fights back, punching Ash repeatedly. Ash responds with an outraged: "Jerk. You broke my tooth." The wry humor of that line is revealing. Ash has witnessed his girlfriend come back to life, killed her with a chainsaw, and faces the near constant threat of total annihilation, but he still has time to complain about a missing tooth. While the fear of infection is usually overwhelming, there is an excess of meaning in *Evil Dead* 2, with something more happening than just fear. This possibility is reinforced when Ash cuts his hand off with the chainsaw. While the hand continues to be an antagonist, even returning in *Ash vs. Evil Dead*, losing that hand to the Deadite infection makes Ash a more powerful hero. In place of that absent hand, representing the loss of autonomy to infection, he attaches his trademark chainsaw. The traditional zombie anxiety has now been fully inverted: infection has become a benefit rather than a curse.

Ash vs. Evil Dead extends this inversion of infection in several important ways. The series takes the fear of infection to its most literal end. In the first season, Pablo (Ray Santiago) becomes infected by the *Necronomicon* itself, and the consequences of this infection play out across season 2. Pablo experiences hallucinations, flashing to visions of the book taking over his identity. In a horrific scene from Episode 2.5, "Confinement," Pablo lifts his shirt to show his pulsing, distended stomach. As Ruby (Lucy Lawless) explains in Episode 2.6, "Trapped Inside," "I've never seen this before. *The Book of the Dead*, festering inside a live human body." Ash answers with characteristic optimism: "That's good, right?" Utilizing the language of infection ("festering") and the same anxiety over the loss of autonomy ("Once the *Book* manifests completely, there'll be no Pablo"), *Ash vs. Evil Dead* has set up the classic zombie moment between when someone is bitten and when they become a zombie. Where your average zombie movie would treat this moment tragically, *Ash vs. Evil Dead* treats it as an opportunity. Not only does Ash doggedly refuse to kill Pablo, insisting that they not "overthink" the situation, but Pablo's infection becomes the critical element to defeating the demon Baal. Instead of trying to prevent or stop the infection, Ruby accelerates it, which manifests the spell they need to banish Baal onto Pablo's skin. Just like Ash replacing his hand with the chainsaw, Pablo's infection by the *Necronomicon* becomes a way of gaining power and control, not a tragic loss of autonomy.

The *Evil Dead* franchise shows that both Ash and Pablo are lucky to be infected. Without his chainsaw arm, could Ash have triumphed over the Deadites? Without the *Necronomicon* writing passages on his body, could Pablo have defeated Baal? While infection may be a source of profound anxiety when related to zombies, the *Evil Dead* franchise shows it as a surprising opportunity, as a new possibility regarding the infected dead and the possible apocalypse they represent. This, of course, ties in significantly with the fact that Ash, Pablo, and Kelly (Dana DeLorenzo) are all triumphant rather than defeated heroes. They confront the anxieties represented by the zombies and the Deadites and they find a way to overcome those fears rather than be destroyed by them.

Zombie Rule #3: Survivalism

On the surface, nothing is more hopeless than a zombie outbreak: an all-powerful tide of death that threatens—and often succeeds—in destroying society. Russell writes that the zombie "is a monster whose appearance always threatens to challenge mankind's faith in the order of the universe" (8). With this challenge, though, comes potential. The zombie threat gives people a chance to reach new heights of survivalism and competence; Bishop claims, "this terrifying breakdown of social order leads to one of the most curious allures of zombie films: their ability to fulfill survivalist fantasies" (23). Zombies represent a complete rupture from civilized society, a place where the survivors can joyfully engage in their most violent tendencies. *The Walking Dead* provides an archetypal example: series protagonist Rick is metaphorically reborn by waking up in a hospital. He quickly moves from small-time cop to a true leader, demonstrating power and competence he never knew in his former life. Rick pulls together all the instruments of survival, including various guns, tools, and even a camper—exactly the same kind of implements that Ash uses in *Ash vs. Evil Dead* when he hits the road.

From this perspective, Ash is the ultimate survivor, gleefully slicing apart Deadites with his chainsaw arm. While the classic Romero films and other zombie works often depict dire stakes, broken and traumatized heroes, and the sense that no success over the zombie horde is eventually possible,

Ash brings an optimistic violence to the table. While this triumphant tone begins in *Evil Dead 2* and *Army of Darkness*, it reaches its logical conclusion in *Ash vs. Evil Dead*. At the beginning of the series, Ash is literally stuck: his trailer is parked in a decrepit trailer park, and his life has stalled out, giving him no clear direction forward as a person. The various references to the missing 30 years of Ash's life indicate that he has done nothing but drink, hit on women, and work dead-end jobs. It is only with the return of the Deadites that he resumes his position as a "hero." Ash needs the undead threat to become his best self.

Ash's "survivalist fantasies" are as amusing as they are over-the-top. *Ash vs. Evil Dead* extends and enhances the ridiculous violence already present in earlier *Evil Dead* works. This underscores one of the most intriguing ideas present in *The Evil Dead*: that its heroes are actually happier as a result of the Deadite threat because they are able to utilize their full abilities, as violent as those may be. The climactic episode of Season 1, "The Dark One," is the clearest example of this intersection. The episode begins with an extended fight between the possessed Linda and Ash, all while Kelly attempts to rescue Pablo from the *Necronomicon*. Even amidst this violence, *Ash vs. Evil Dead* presents an opportunity for redemption and survival: "That lady has my book, and she has my Pablo. I gotta save him. I'm not losin' anybody else I care about." Ash then accomplishes exactly that. This refusal to lose, even in the face of an overwhelming threat like zombies or the Deadites, is the fundamental difference between the *Evil Dead* franchise and many other zombie works. Rather than letting the cultural anxieties represented by zombies or Deadites overwhelm him, Ash (and his audience) is invigorated by the undead threat, driving him to new heights of survival and blood-soaked violence.

The Cultural Work of The Evil Dead

The cultural work of *The Evil Dead* has always been close to the surface. Instead of reproducing the social and cultural anxieties of the typical zombie movie, as great as those contributions to the American horror genre may be, *The Evil Dead* shows that these cultural anxieties can be overcome with a chainsaw and laughter. If traditional zombies force audiences to confront their deepest fears regarding mortality, possession, and infection, *The Evil Dead* liberates a positive energy surrounding those fears, and, in doing so, forges Ash as a triumphant, rather than defeated, zombie hero. If *Night of the Living Dead* ends on a dour note, with Ben (Duane Jones) being shot through the window, confirming all our fears about race, death, and the coming apocalypse, *The Evil Dead* is surprisingly uplifting, with Ash's gore-spattered form rising above all the danger.

In the middle of *Evil Dead 2*, there is a scene of manic laughter, as the Deadites possess the entire room around Ash. Started by a mounted deer head, the whole cabin starts laughing. Instead of running in horror, Ash himself joins in, laughing along with the Deadites. The moment passes, Ash fires his shotgun again, and the battle with the dead resumes. The wild laughter of this scene sums up the unique approach of *The Evil Dead*. While your typical zombie movie, beholden to the well-established zombie rules, presents a world of fixed anxiety, where human endeavor is largely hopeless, with mere survival the best outcome, *The Evil Dead* gives us something much more optimistic. Surrounded by the anxieties that horror symbolizes, there is always the possibility for a positive outcome, even if nothing more than a moment of shared enjoyment with the Deadites. By laying down a trajectory where the anxieties represented by zombies can be overcome, *The Evil Dead* launches its undead monsters—and its audience—upon a new and more optimistic journey.

Notes

1. As examples, consider two popular internet sources. The Evil Dead Wiki defines the Deadites "as evil demonic Zombie Hybrids" while Dreadit, a popular horror subReddit with over 100,000 subscribers, lists *Evil Dead 2* as the ninth best zombie movie of all time, four spots above George A. Romero's *Day of the Dead* (1985).

2. Similar ideas about the metaphorical nature of zombies are expressed in Russell: "Growing out of a wide range of cultural anxieties—from American imperialism to domestic racial tensions, Depression-era fears about unemployment, Cold War paranoia about brainwashing, post-1960s political disenfranchisement and AIDS-era body horror—the zombie has become, as we will see, a potent symbol of the apocalypse" (8). See also McGlotten and Jones: "zombies disturb established ontological and epistemological categories, as well as hegemonic norms. Those disruptions are frequently associated with an assortment of social anxieties: about viral contagion, biological warfare, neoliberal and totalitarian securitization, environmental collapse, and capitalist end-times" (3).

3. Bishop provides a more nuanced analysis of "the comedic zombie" in *How Zombies Conquered Popular Culture*, reading *Zombieland* (2009) "as a positive social force within both the comedy and horror traditions" (43).

4. For a full history of *The Magic Island* and its influence on *White Zombie* and other Hollywood zombie movies, see Russell (9–30) and Rhodes (70–88). Lauro provides a comprehensive history of the Haitian zombie and its connections to slavery and rebellion in *The Transatlantic Zombie*.

Works Cited

Bishop, Kyle William. *American Zombie Gothic: The Rise and Fall (and Rise) of the Walking Dead in Popular Culture*. McFarland, 2010.
_____. *How Zombies Conquered Popular Culture*. McFarland, 2015.
"Confinement." *Ash vs. Evil Dead*, season 2, episode 5, Starz, 30 Oct. 2016.
"The Dark One." *Ash vs. Evil Dead*, season 1, episode 10, Starz, 2 Jan. 2016.
"Deadite." *The Evil Dead Wiki*, http://evildead.wikia.com/wiki/Deadite.
Eburne, Jonathan P. "Zombie Arts and Letters." *The Year's Work at the Zombie Research Center*, edited by Edward P. Comentale and Aaron Jaffe. Indiana University Press, 2014, pp. 389–415.
"El Jefe." *Ash vs. Evil Dead*, season 1, episode 1, Starz, 31 Oct. 2015.
Fleischer, Rueben, director. *Zombieland*. Columbia Pictures, 2009.
Fulci, Lucio, director. *Zombi 2*. Variety Film, 1979.
Halperin, Victor, director. *White Zombie*. United Artists, 1932.

Lauro, Sarah Juliet. *The Transatlantic Zombie: Slavery, Rebellion, and Living Death.* Rutgers University Press, 2015.
Moreman, Christopher M., and Cory James Rushton, editors. *Race, Oppression, and the Zombie: Essays on Cross-Cultural Appropriations of the Caribbean Tradition.* McFarland, 2011.
_____. *Zombies Are Us: Essays on the Humanity of the Walking Dead.* McFarland, 2011.
Muir, John Kenneth. *The Unseen Force: The Films of Sam Raimi.* Applause, 2004.
Raimi, Sam, director. *Army of Darkness.* Renaissance Pictures, 1992.
_____. *The Evil Dead.* Renaissance Pictures, 1981.
_____. *Evil Dead 2.* Renaissance Pictures, 1987.
Rhodes, Gary D. *White Zombie: Anatomy of a Horror Film.* McFarland, 2001.
Romero, George A., director. *Dawn of the Dead.* Laurel Group, 1978.
_____. *Day of the Dead.* Dead Films, Inc., 1985.
_____. *Night of the Living Dead.* Image Ten, 1968.
Russell, Jamie. *Book of the Dead: The Complete History of Zombie Cinema.* Titan Books, 2014.
Seabrook, William. *The Magic Island.* 1929. Dover Publications, 2016.
"Second Coming." *Ash vs. Evil Dead*, season 2, episode 10, Starz, 11 Dec. 2016.
Shaviro, Steven. *The Cinematic Body.* University of Minnesota Press, 1993.
"Top 20 Zombie Films." *Dreadit: The Horror Reddit*, reddit.com/r/horror/wiki/topzombie.
"Trapped Inside." *Ash vs. Evil Dead*, season 2, episode 6, Starz, 6 Nov. 2016.
The Walking Dead. Developed by Frank Darabont, AMC, 2010.
Warren, Bill. *The Evil Dead Companion.* St. Martin's Griffin, 2000.

"The Number One Nasty"
How Britain's Most Popular Eighties Horror Was Banned

Sarah Cleary

> "We're going to get you.
> We're going to get you.
> Not another peep.
> Time to go to sleep."
> —Linda, *The Evil Dead* (1981)

 Maligned by some of the most powerful voices of eighties Britain, a new threat invaded the country's homes that supposedly threatened to corrupt and demoralize an entire generation of British children from the ostensible sanctuary of their parents' living rooms. Taking on the guise of horror videotapes of assorted quality and extremity, a whole host of titles, dubbed in the popular press as "Video Nasties," were imbued with an almost supernatural resonance allegedly capable of harm. Yet a close reading of this period in British film history tells an interesting tale of how an inherently problematic narrative of harm concerning these films was spun within a thorny multidimensional spectacle, facilitated by a complex web of state intervention, political scapegoating and profiteering, media sensationalism, and taste-based assumptions masquerading as moral concerns. In early eighties Britain, the video nasties were "Enemy Number One," and Sam Raimi's debut feature *The Evil Dead* (1981) was heralded as "The Number One Nasty" (Mathews 42).

 While paying close attention to the social and political climate that facilitated the development of the video nasty controversy, I concentrate on how one text and the particular manner in which it earned its rather dubious moniker of the "number one nasty" seemed to embody the entire video nasty controversy. While this is neither a full exploration of the video nasties period, nor an extensive examination of the films themselves, placing the locus of attention on a text such as *The Evil Dead* provides not only an overview of the period in question but also seeks to highlight the more nuanced aspects of how a film which was lauded as being the most watched horror of 1984 came to be banned.[1]

Background to the Video Nasty Controversy

As popular in the UK as it was in the U.S., JVC's VCR exploded onto the consumer market and in just a few years between 1979 and 1982 the video retail had grown from a "fledgling business to a massive, totally unregulated industry" (Wingrove and Morris 10). Video rental shops sprung up throughout the country, offering everything from the most visceral and sexually explicit of films from directors such as Meir Zarchi's *I Spit on Your Grave* (1978) and Abel Ferrara's *The Driller Killer* (1979), to the most chaste of Hollywood family entertainment. Never seen before on cinema or domestic screens, British audiences had access to a glut of violent and gory horror that had escaped any formal rating or censorship. For some, this oversight in the regulation of films available to the British public was a major cause for concern. Speaking in 1979, the year the VCR was launched in the UK, the British Board of Film Classification (BBFC) director James Ferman, foreshadowing the video nasty controversy four years later, stated:

> Audiences in Britain never see the worst the world's filmmakers have to offer. Films glorifying rape, the torture of naked women, the degradation of adolescent girls, the infliction of serious bodily harm through easily copied weapons, the casual slaughter of animals—such things are habitually cut or rejected in the British cinema. If they were permitted, I believe the public would demand that the police and the courts and Parliament take a far tougher line with cinema than they have so far [66].

As a means of evading state intervention, in November 1981 the British Videogram Association (BVA) entered into negotiations with the BBFC. Within a year, both organizations were efficiently working quite well together and had drawn up a self-policing code of practice (Mathews 239). By the following year, however, any voluntary control the BVA believed they held over the distribution and classification of videotapes was effectively taken out of their hands and placed within state control.

As the home video rental market was emerging as an extremely popular form of entertainment, 1979 would prove a pivotal year in British politics as the Tory conservative party took power and dominated internal and external policy for the next eleven years. Drawing a line between the previous governments' failures and Thatcher's rise to Prime Minister, Nigel Wingrove and Marc Morris observe how this assent was "supported by a loose collective of radical right-wing theorists, from politicians and think tanks ... to media tycoons like Rupert Murdoch who, through his chosen mouthpiece *The Sun*, would be an invaluable champion of Thatcherite values" (Wingrove and Morris 9). Another member of this loose collective was National Viewers' and Listeners' Association, (NVLA) founder and prominent anti-nasty campaigner Mary Whitehouse, who would remain a prominent figure in both securing the Video Recordings Act and vilifying video nasties in the press.

In complement to such alliances, Thatcher's Conservative Government was also determined to preserve its reputation as "the tough law and order party" (Barker 11) in light of social upheaval in early eighties Britain. "One very effective way to do that," according to Martin Barker, was "to mount a major moral campaign against something which no one worth noticing would be expected to defend. The video nasties issue could help launder the Governments' law and order image—at little cost" (12). As a result of such an alliance, Thatcher was perceived as an advocate of traditional moral values, while Whitehouse had secured influential political support. Moreover, four years later, in June 1983, when Thatcher's government faced a general election, using the apparent video nasty "crisis" as a platform for social reform would arguably prove one of the most strategic political campaigns ever mounted in the UK. Promising to tackle one of "the most serious ... problems" apparently affecting the British public, legislation would be introduced to stop the "dangerous spread of violent and obscene video cassettes" (Barker 12). Such unprecedented legislation would eventually become the Video Recordings Act of 1984. It is no coincidence that the necessity to regulate and eventually restrain what up until then had been a relatively cooperative relationship between video distributors, the British Videogram Association, and video vendors, fell within the same period as the 1983 Tory re-election campaign.

The term "nasty," according to Kim Newman, was appropriated from literary jargon used to describe horror authors such as James Herbert and Guy Smith (Newman 134). Though the term has often been attributed originally to Whitehouse, both Chas Critcher (2009) and Julian Petley (2011) identified the first use of the term in an article published on May 23, 1982, in *The Sunday Times*.[2] Hot on the heels of the *Daily Mail*'s explosive article "The Secret Video Show," which outlined the alleged dangers of the domestic video, *The Sunday Times* followed suit with its own sensational exposé; "How High Street Horror is Invading the Home." Apparently using the term "nasty" for the first time, journalist Peter Chippendale recalled his experience of a visit to a video trade fair, where certain titles were referred to as "nasties." Clumped together regardless of genre, age, or quality, Kate Egan argues how the "'video nasty' titles weren't predominantly grouped together because they shared common thematic and formal characteristics" (Egan, *Trash or Treasure*, 3). Instead they were categorized "by pure historical coincidence—specifically, by dint of the fact that they all happened to be released on video during the pre–VCR era in Britain" (Egan, *Trash or Treasure*, 3). Egan's point that these films were all released to the British public at the same time is central to understanding, at least in part, the reaction to these films. Though many of these titles were upwards of twenty years old by the time they came under the eagle eye of the DPP, for a new technological generation of home-movie viewers, these films were reborn. Unlike the American horror comics of the fifties, which had caused similar backlash from various divergent groups in Britain,[3] these horror titles were neither bound by nation or narrative. What they did share was a collective impulse that sought, both consciously and unconsciously, to undermine the sovereignty of established norms and tastes upheld by previous generations. Perhaps because of this maverick idealism, many of these films were acutely self-conscious of how bad they were. This was often the allure. Yet for its detractors, the video nasty represented a "veritable cornucopia of sleaze," specializing in "sadism, mutilation and cannibalism," which in direct conflict with the Obscene Publications Act of 1959 allegedly had the "tendency to deprave and corrupt, or make morally bad, a significant proportion of the *likely* audience" (Wingrove and Morris 11).[4]

As a point of origin of the video nasty controversy, Wingrove and Morris cite a series of complaints to the Advertising Standards Authority (ASA) and the British Videogram Association in 1981 in relation to a number of imported horror videos. Amongst the offending titles were *Cannibal Holocaust* (1980), *The Driller Killer* (1979), and *SS Experiment Camp* (1976). Interestingly however, not all of these complaints came from anti-nasty sources; John Martin cites an instance whereby UK distributors for *Cannibal Holocaust* Go Video decided to "anonymously" tip off Mary Whitehouse in relation to the horrors in their film. "Nobody had heard of *Cannibal Holocaust*," claimed Martin, "Once she got in on the act I couldn't run off enough copies to meet the demand" (Martin 45). Although this reputedly improved sales, such marketing ploys eventually singled out the film as a primary target for protestors. Little did they know just how well that marketing ploy would work, for just under two years later artwork from *Cannibal Holocaust* that featured a crude drawing of a "primitive" male tearing at bloodied guts became the banner image for the *Daily Mail*'s "Ban the Sadist Videos!" campaign.

While it was the use of gory and sensational cover artwork that initially grabbed the attention of anti-nasty campaigners early on, numerous critics have argued that the video nasty controversy was partly the result of imperialist anxiety that had lingered in the British psyche since the horror comic ban some thirty years previously. Whether it was jazz music, rock 'n' roll, or horror comic books, James Kendrick notes that all these "transgressive American cultural products "[have] been heavily scrutinized by British authorities and moral reformers, thus lending credence to the notion that the United

Sates is a corrupting influence in British cultural life" (171). A telling indictment of such a view is found in Caetlin Benson-Allott's *Killer Tapes and Shattered Screens* (2013). Referencing Kendrick, Benson-Allott aligns the video nasty controversy with the preservation of national identity; "conservative British lobby groups pushed the Thatcher government to crack down on 'video nasties' and 'ban the sadist videos' they suspected of Americanizing British youth" (73). Nonetheless, contrary to Benson-Allott who seems to dismiss the political and indeed economical context of eighties Britain in which the video nasty controversy first erupted, I wouldn't be as inclined to postulate imperialist anxiety as the sole reason behind the affair. Firstly, this threat was neither as concentrated as the one represented by "American" comics and music as many of the titles were not originally distributed from America and, secondly, the video nasty controversy was a much more complex amalgam of numerous political and social factors, which capitalized on a narrative of harm sensationalized by the press.

Even though the same titles were available on video in the U.S., nothing comparable to the moral outcry ensued upon their release. With rising unemployment, exacerbated by the downsizing of industrial factories and mines throughout the country, a war that divided both public and political opinion,[5] and increasing civil unrest[6] video nasties not only became a scapegoat for larger, more complex concerns, which could not be "legislated" away as easily. In other words, as Barker maintains, these horror films became "general purpose explanations of moral decline" for eighties Britain. One of the most contentious issues for Barker during this era was of course the protection of children, a crusade he argues, "dissolves away when we start investigating the campaign" (7). "What we are left with," Barker wrote, was a "politically motivated rhetoric which systematically distorts the meaning and nature of the videos themselves" (7). Summarizing the position of the anti-video nasty campaigners, he mused sardonically that these nasties could

> damage their minds, soil their souls, inducing a sick love of violence, sadistic sex, torture, maiming, cannibalism—in fact there is apparently nothing at all outside their revolting purview. By letting children see them we may well be depraving a minority, if not more, and turning them into society's future murders and rapists. No society is worth a grain of salt if it does not protect its children—and the video nasties represent the most urgent danger to them for a very long time [7].

It is no coincidence that the necessity to regulate and eventually restrain what up until then had been a relatively cooperative relationship between video distributors, the BVA, and video vendors, fell within the same period as the 1983 Tory re-election campaign.

As early as May 1982, *The Sunday Times* had commented upon the concern expressed by Scotland Yard's operational head of Obscene Publications, Peter Kruger, over the use of videos "in the home" which were "beyond the bounds of decency." Broadsheets such as *The Sunday Times* and the more liberal leaning *The Guardian*, which typically advocated a more measured and calculated approach to any hysteria, decided to essentially exploit any newsworthy feature surrounding the case. With a subtle degree of chagrin betrayed within his emphasis on the egalitarianism of the video market, Chippendale raged how it was despicable that "uncensored horror video cassettes, *available to anyone of any age,* have arrived in Britain's high street stores."

Out of all the newspapers, it was to be the British tabloid the *Daily Mail* whose torch burned brightest for the anti-nasty campaign. On the same day as the video trade press published the DPP infamous list of seventy-two video nasty titles, thirty-nine of which (including *The Evil Dead*) went on to be prosecuted under the Obscene Publications Act of 1959, Thatcher, now three weeks into her second term of office, drew reference to the video nasty situation, stating how she recognized the "great concern caused by the matter." She declared, "It is not enough to have voluntary legislation. We must bring in a law to regulate the matter" (Barker 10). Confident of Tory assistance and approval, that same day the *Daily Mail* began their "Ban the Sadist Videos!" campaign, the overtly sensational headline: "Rape of Our Children's Minds."

The Evil Dead

While Stephen King's remarks at the 1982 Cannes Film Festival that *The Evil Dead* was "the most furiously original horror film" of 1982 catapulted Raimi's debut feature into the limelight (Martin 71); if it wasn't for the enthusiasm of a young British film distributor, *The Evil Dead* may never have been such an integral feature of the video nasties campaign. Purchasing the rights to the film at the American Film Market in March 1982, Stephen Woolley of Palace Pictures, claimed that he was first startled by "the graphicness of the violence," but after a while he was equally struck by the its "humor and most importantly by the quality of the filming and editing" (Woolley). Upon purchasing the rights, Woolley and his partner Nik Powell embarked upon a rather fearsome marketing campaign. Citing Joan Hawkins, Egan remarks how both the more specialist genre fan and more mainstream audiences could appreciate the text as it seemed to straddle an unusual position from the perspective of a horror film in that it could be seen to flirt "with the possibility of existing simultaneously as high and low art" (Egan, *The Evil Dead*, 23). Aside from its controversy in the press, arguably the most effective aspects of the marketing campaign were the striking promotional imagery designed by twenty-year-old Graham Humphreys. Unlike its glossy American counterpart, Humphreys conveyed a much more punk aesthetic, (Humphreys

2003) emulating its more manic, frenetic, and, indeed, contemporary qualities, capturing the zeitgeist of early eighties underground cinema. With a nod to the film's indie/slasher heritage within his aberrant use of coloring and visceral splatter, the present and future of horror is also clearly alluded to in the form of the videocassette reels taking center position as blood spirals from each of the spools.

While in retrospect it is easy to identify *The Evil Dead* as an integral text synonymous with advances in the horror genre from both a technological and cultural perspective, that is not to say that the film was a hit with all critics at the time of its release. Oliver James writing for *The Observer* lamented how "The screenplay is all effects and no story"; while fearing for the nation's pockets, Linsay Mackie for the *Glasgow Herald* declared, "*The Evil Dead* takes no interest whatsoever in psychology, except maybe in the psychology of people who will give up their own money to watch other people rot to bits in front of their very eyes." Regardless, Palace saw something in *The Evil Dead* that not only singled it out as a superior text but also rather ironically seemed to both encapsulate all the other texts of its time, as well as tap into a culture that sought to rebuke the status quo. Taking the unusual steps of releasing the film theatrically and on video simultaneously in February 1983, the film was granted the ubiquitous X certificate, which drew attention to its more nefarious aspects, yet still operated in accordance with the voluntary BVA system, with eighteen cuts totaling fifty-six seconds.[7]

One of the greatest ironies of *The Evil Dead* within the context of its release in Britain was that it could not have come at a better time as horror spectatorship was on the rise owing in part to a surge in foreign titles and ease at which these once hard to come by films were now attained. In *Film and Video Censorship in Contemporary Britain*, Julian Petley cites a What Video/Popular Video survey conducted in 1982 that places horror films above all other genres as the most popular rentals (47). Subsequently, *The Evil Dead* went on to gross over £100,000 in box-office takings in the film's first week of release, becoming the highest rented video in the UK in 1983 (Egan, *Trash or Treasure*, 26). Yet for all their efforts and popularity, *The Evil Dead* was maligned in the press as the quintessential video nasty. It was becoming quite clear that a war was being waged against films such as *The Evil Dead* by opportunists and moral guardians, who ostensibly looked towards them as an embodiment of the fictional evil they sought to represent. Imbued by moral crusaders with a degenerate agency, *The Evil Dead* was positioned at a "border of symbolic dissolution," where fact and fiction are perceived as fungible (Martin and Savoy vii). Consequently, where some saw entertainment, others saw evil.

"Number One Nasty"

The Evil Dead's popularity was a double-edged sword for Palace. While its reputation secured the company's position as one of Britain's leading film distributors and forged the way for others to seek out obscure titles similar in tone and quality, as a high profile film it was also susceptible to attack, eventually being singled out as the "number one nasty," an accolade originally ascribed by Whitehouse, though she had admitted in an interview that she had not seen the film herself. "I have never seen a video nasty. I wouldn't.... I don't need to see visually what I know is in that film" (Whitehouse). Yet her patrician ideals and indeterminable belief in "common sense" allowed her to make assumptions about films such as *The Evil Dead*, assumptions quickly acted upon by the press and opportunistic politicians. While the rumblings of disquiet towards video nasties were beginning to be heard in the early years of the decade, as Barker observes, up until the 1983 general election, the conservative government had been content to allow the video industry to self-regulate. Yet against the backdrop of an increasingly frantic press, moral campaigners such as Whitehouse who sought out these "merchants of menace" continued to add to the melting pot of hysteria.

While *The Evil Dead* was BBFC approved playing in over 190 cinemas throughout the UK, within a month of release in February 1983, compelled by the recent "panic," Manchester police seized copies of the film on VHS. Considered something of a knee-jerk reaction, copies were returned with apologies as it was initially believed that the VHS version of the films contained content somehow more illicit. However, amidst the confusion of this time, with no coherent guidelines other than the Obscene Publications Act of 1959 to act upon, the head of the Obscene Publications Unit, Peter Kruger was granted permission by the DPP to apply for a warrant under the act. In essence, this gave the police the authority to confiscate *any* videos they determined were in conflict with the act and prosecute individuals involved within the distribution of such videos. Extremely ad hoc in nature, what was confiscated throughout these raids was at the discretion of the chief constable in charge. In view of the fact Palace Video was responsible for the distribution of the most popular horror of 1983, it wasn't long before they too were raided. In other areas across Britain, video shop owners were being raided and indeed prosecuted for holding obscene items such as *The Evil Dead*. Instead of incurring further costs in court, many shop owners simply pled guilty instead of defending the titles. However, bearing in mind the work that Palace had put into one of the most popular videos, they were not prepared to lie down as easily.

Just one month after *The Evil Dead* appeared on the DPP list of films liable to be confiscated and prosecuted (a list published in the *Daily Mail* campaign article of June 30, 1983),[8] in an attempt to clarify their position in a test case at Snaresbrook Courts, Palace Pictures subsided the costs of a group of video shops known as the Barker group who had been raided in April of 1983. Spaced out over four months, Palace went as far as to fly Raimi over to testify in defense of the film, though he never actually testified. *The Evil Dead* was eventually acquitted in this case and went on to be vindicated in numerous courts up and down the county. Before long, *The Evil Dead* was once again under the spotlight, but this time it was not the seller but the distributor Nik Powell along with his companies Palace Video and Palace Virgin & Gold Distribution who were charged with distributing "obscene articles" in conflict with Section 2 of the Obscene Publications Act (Martin 73). Fortunately for Powell and Palace, *The Evil Dead* was once again acquitted on July 25, 1985. Judge Stableford, in an unprecedented move, awarded the defendant costs of £20,000, as he believed that the DPP had acted inappropriately in continuing to charge a title that had been only found guilty of obscenity in two out of forty cases (Martin 73). Expressing his delight at the outcome, Powell stated how he wished the "DPP will now do the honorable thing and drop any further prosecutions, allowing *The Evil Dead* to be certified in line with the terms of the Video Recordings Act" (Martin 75). Contrary to Powell's hope that *The Evil Dead* would receive a certificate having finally come off the list in September 1985, it would take a further five years before *The Evil Dead* received its BBFC rating. Attempting to explain the delay while it had been removed from the list, the BBFC remained somewhat concerned about "the acceptability of the video version in its current form." "Of greatest concern [according to the BBFC] was that regardless of the verdict at Snaresbrook, the film had nonetheless been found obscene by other courts around the country. Under the terms of its designation under the Video Recordings Act, the BBFC was obliged to avoid classifying any material that might be found obscene" ("Evil Dead Case Study"). While these hearings were overwhelmingly in favor of *The Evil Dead*, closer to the truth perhaps may be the acknowledgment of *The Evil Dead* as something of a *bête noire* for the BBFC. Approved upon release, it had become one of the most contentious texts of the decade and given the climate of the mid-eighties, the BBFC were hesitant to release a title that had been at the center of so much controversy.

Finally rated in 1990, almost a decade had elapsed since its initial release. Nevertheless, in a post–VRA climate additional cuts were made to the film, further to the ones that appeared in 1983. These supplementary cuts included the now infamous arboreal assault whereby a character is held down and molested by the possessed forest. The consequences of this meant that the 1990 release was now cut by 1 minute 55 seconds. Seeking to test the waters of a newly liberalized and revamped BBFC, Film4's Adam Roberts in March of 2001 submitted an uncut American print of *The Evil Dead* for VRA classification, whereupon it was granted an 18 rating in its uncut form for home video and DVD audiences. According to the BBFC, they believed that "that standards had changed since 1990 (and certainly since 1982) and that modern audiences were more accustomed to the excesses of horror films. Compared to films like *Scream*, *The Evil Dead* now looked rather tame" ("Evil Dead Case Study").

Such an estimation is overwhelmingly problematic. In the early eighties, horror films *were* the standard and considering how popular both *The Evil Dead* and "video nasties" in general were, audiences were indeed becoming more and more accustomed to the "excesses." In 1983, the viewing public had already spoken and they wanted horror. Instead, a small minority of people acting as moral guardians found allies in a political climate that wished to not only scapegoat a sundry of social issues and impose restrictions upon an industry that had operated independent of state intervention. While all the time the press sought to capitalize on these issues, exaggerating claims, publishing false information, and ultimately orchestrating what seemed like a moral panic amongst its readers when in fact at its core the video nasty debacle was neither about morals or panic but a desire to police taste, political profiteering, and media sensationalism.

Conclusion

As a dynamic yet marginal form, the genre of horror has always enjoyed quite a dexterous versatility towards emerging technologies that perhaps in themselves were viewed with suspicion. From Penny Dreadfuls, to horror comics, VHS to video games, horror has been at the forefront of each new form of media, as its detractors were equally on hand to denounce both the mode and the medium. The controversy surrounding video nasties was symbolic of both technological and cultural changes in the UK that politicians and moralists sought to suppress through an elusive narrative of harm. Fortunately, the VRA and the various amendments made to it did not succeed in dampening interest in horror films or in fact the *Evil Dead* franchise, as the box office receipts for its latest reimagining, *Evil Dead* (2013) and ratings for the spin off series *Ash vs. Evil Dead* (2015–2018) can attest. Considered nothing more than a scare tactic to deflect complex social problems and police social mores, "The real problem," as Raimi explained,

> is not a movie like *The Evil Dead*, because it's not really important whether it is seen. The real problem is, once the people allow the censors to determine what is right and wrong for them, once they've given them that power, who's to say that a politically disturbing picture that differs from the views of the censors politically shouldn't be censored? The people of Britain shouldn't allow them the power because soon they'll find out that other rights are being taken away from them one by one, till they don't have the right to speak at all [qtd. in Martin 75].

Regularly in the guise of a liminal form of entertainment such as horror, with each generation comes a new bogeyman. Similar to Raimi's Kandarian Demon, this bogeyman in the eighties was seemingly able to imbue these films with a form of "evil" capable of corrupting the nation. But similar to the Kandarian Demon, this bogeyman was indeed fictional; a manufactured trope derived from a narrative of harm.

NOTES

1. Further reading on video nasties: Barker, M., editor. *The Video Nasties: Freedom and Censorship in the Media* (1984); Barker, M., and Petley, J., editors. *Ill Effects: The media/violence debate* (2001); Critcher, C. *Moral Panics and the Media* (2003); Petley, J. *Film and Video Censorship in Modern Britain* (2011); Petley, J. "'Are we Insane?' The 'Video Nasty' Moral Panic" in *Moral Panics in the Contemporary World* (73–100); Springhall, J. *Youth Popular Culture and Moral Panics. Penny Gaffs to Gangster-Rap 1830–1996* (1998).
2. See Jeffery Sconce's *Sleaze Artists: Cinema at the Margins of Taste, Style, and Politics* (185) and Robert Cetti's *Offensive to a Reasonable Adult: Film Censorship and Classification in Secular Australia* (57).
3. See Martin Barker's *A Haunt of Fears: The Strange History of the British Horror Comics Campaign* (1984).
4. Video Recordings Act 1984. Emphasis mine.
5. For more on this period in British history see David Yates' *Bomb Alley: Falkland Islands 1982* (2006), Christopher Hilton's *Ordinary Heroes: Untold Stories from the Falklands Campaign* (2012), and Jimmy Burns' *The Land That Lost Its Heroes: How Argentina Lost the Falklands War* (2012).
6. See Graham Stewart. *Bang! A History of Britain in the 1980s* (2013) for a comprehensive overview of the period.
7. Edits included "reducing the number of blows with an axe, reducing the length of an eye gouging, and reducing the number of times that a pencil was twisted into a person's leg" ("Evil Dead Case Study").
8. That article listed the 52 films officially named by the DPP, and *The Evil Dead* was among them. This became known as the DPP video nasties list, which was modified monthly as prosecutions failed or were dropped. It contained as many as 79 separate titles at one point, but had settled on 39 by December 1985.

WORKS CITED

Barker, Martin. *A Haunt of Fears. The Strange History of the British Horror Comics Campaign.* Pluto Press, 1984.
Benson-Allott, Caetlin. *Killer Tapes and Shattered Screens: Video Spectatorship from VHS to File Sharing.* University of California Press, 2013.
Chippendale, Peter. "How High Street Horror Is Invading the Home." *The Sunday Times,* 23 May 1982.
Critcher, Cas. *Moral Panics and the Media.* Open University Press, 2003.
Egan, Kate. *The Evil Dead.* Wallflower Press, 2011.
_____. *Trash or Treasure. Censorship and the Changing Meanings of the Video Nasties.* Manchester University Press, 2007.
"The Evil Dead." *Book of the Dead: The Definitive Evil Dead Website,* bookofthedead.ws.
"The Evil Dead Case Study." *British Board of Film Classification (BBFC),* bbfc.co.uk/case-studies/evil-dead.
Ferman, James. "Censorship Today." *Films Illustrated,* October 1979, pp. 62–67.
Humphreys, Graham. "Dead Good Marketing." *The Evil Dead Trilogy DVD.* Anchor Bay Entertainment UK, 2003.
James, Oliver. "The Evil Dead." *Observer,* 18 April 1982.
Kendrick, James. "Social Panics, Transnationalism, and 'The Video Nasty.'" *Horror Film: Cre-*

ating and Marketing Fear, edited by Steffen Hantke. University of Mississippi Press, 2004.
Mackie, Linsay. "Evil Dead." *Glasgow Herald*, 17 January 1983, pp. C8.
Martin, John. *Seduction of the Gullible: The Truth Behind the Video Nasty*. Procrustes Press, 1997.
Mathews, Tom D. *Censored: What They Didn't Allow You to See, and Why—The Story of Film Censorship in Britain*. Chatto & Windus, 1994.
Miles, Tim. "Rape of Young Minds." *Daily Mail*, 24 November 1983.
Newman, Kim. "Journal of the Plague Years." *Screen Violence*, edited by Karl French. Bloomsbury, 1996.
Petley, Julian. *Film and Video Censorship in Contemporary Britain*. Edinburgh University Press, 2011.
Raimi, Sam, director. *The Evil Dead*. Renaissance Pictures, 1981.
Savoy, Eric. "Introduction." *American Gothic: New Interventions in a National Narrative*, edited by Robert Martin and Eric Savoy. University of Iowa Press, 1998.
Whitehouse, Mary. "Interview." *Ban the Sadist Videos*. Anchor Bay Entertainment UK, 2005.
Wingrove, Nigel, and Marc Morris. *The Art of the Nasty*. FAB Press, 2009.
Woolley, Stephen. "Discovering The Evil Dead." *The Evil Dead Full Uncut Version DVD*. Anchor Bay Entertainment UK, 2002.

Final Girl, Final Boy
Ash's Imperiled Masculinity
DALE BAILEY

Sam Raimi's *The Evil Dead* (1981) burst unrated into wide release on American movie screens in 1983, allowing viewers nationwide to share the experience of Stephen King, who had seen the film a year earlier at the Cannes Film Festival. To many of them, it must have seemed, as King called it in the November 1982 issue of *The Twilight Zone Magazine*, like "the most ferociously original horror film" of the year (20). Like many critics, King cites as evidence the fiendish originality of Raimi's camera work, and the buckets of blood he spills, which transcend mere horror movie gore in almost comic abundance.

Yet, as King himself acknowledges, Raimi's film is deeply indebted to a number of precursors (21). In *The Evil Dead Companion*, Bill Warren reports that Raimi, his producer, Rob Tapert, and his lead actor, Bruce Campbell, conducted a careful survey of the genre, studying films such as *The Texas Chainsaw Massacre* (1974), *The Hills Have Eyes* (1977), and *Halloween* (1978), before undertaking their own venture into the horror arena (33–36).[1] *The Evil Dead* borrows liberally from these and other predecessors. The claustrophobic setting, a rural cabin cut off from the outside world, suggests the abandoned house of George Romero's drive-in classic *Night of the Living Dead* (1968). The idea of possession, down to its associated tropes, descends from William Friedkin's adaptation of William Peter Blatty's novel, *The Exorcist* (1971). And the *Naturom Demonto*, the ancient Sumerian volume that unleashes *The Evil Dead*'s demonic forces, alludes at least in part to the *Necronomicon*, the forbidden volume of arcane lore created by early–20th-century horror writer H.P. Lovecraft. Indeed, it can be argued that *The Evil Dead* is even less "ferociously original" than this mishmash of influences would suggest. The slasher film, perhaps the most formulaic incarnation of the American horror movie, ruled the box office during the brief period between John Carpenter's *Halloween* (1978) and Wes Craven's *A Nightmare on Elm Street* (1984). *The Evil Dead* went into wide release at the height of this boom and has strong affinities with the form. Yes, it is a story of possession by Sumerian demons, but scratch the surface and what you discover comes very close to a slasher film in Sumerian drag.

The Evil Dead *as Slasher Movie*

In her classic study *Men, Women, and Chainsaws: Gender in the Modern Horror Film*, Carol J. Clover describes both the slasher film's structure and its five basic elements: the killer, the Terrible Place, the use of weapons, the victims, and the Final Girl. Structurally, the purest examples of the slasher film, like many horror movies, adhere to a very simple formula. A group of teenagers is isolated in an ominous setting (an abandoned summer camp, an empty carnival funhouse), there to be picked off one by one by a psychopathic killer. The appeal of this simple structure arises from its particular deployment of Clover's elements. The psychopathic killer, almost always employing a variety of murderous tools (the more novel the better), spends the first two thirds of the movie dispatching his victims, most of whom seem to deserve it in some way or other (they are smoking pot or having premarital sex or otherwise violating social prohibitions).[2] This pattern escalates through the discovery of said victims until finally the sole survivor—a plucky, vice-free "victim-hero" that Clover calls the Final Girl (it is always a girl)—turns the tables on the killer. The bloody chess match between them comprises the film's final act.

Despite this primitive plot, however, the slasher film's vision of gender is complex. As Clover argues, the murderer is often "a male in gender distress" who is "propelled by psychosexual fury" (27). Even more important, are Clover's contentions about the Final Girl and the degree of audience identification she engages. In the first two thirds of the film, she argues, the primarily male adolescent audience[3] almost always adopts the camera's male gaze (which usually coincides with that of the killer); in the final third, however, as the Final Girl shifts from victim to hero, she becomes the character with whom the male audience tends to identify. In either case, killer or Final Girl, sexual identity is complicated by gendered behavior. As Clover puts it,

> Sex, in this universe, proceeds from gender, not the other way around. A figure does not cry and cower because she is a woman; she is a woman because she cries and cowers. And a figure is not a psychokiller because he is a man; he is a man because he is a psychokiller ... [T]he perceived nature of the function generates the characters that will represent it [13].

In short, the audience's masculine identity is explicitly preserved by its emotional engagement with gender-amorphous characters: the gender-confused psychopath and the gender-shifting Final Girl, who in the last act of a slasher film, takes on the aggressive, violent gender identity we associate with men.

Such are the conventions and implications of the slasher film that reigned when *The Evil Dead* debuted. Raimi often subverts these elements, but, with one important exception, he rarely violates them. Clover's killer, for instance, is a lone wolf. Raimi displaces this minatory figure with a rotating cast of four teenagers, a murderous indignity the film's protagonist, Ash (Campbell), is alone spared. They are not driven by any explicitly "psychosexual fury," but by demonic possession. However the narrative structure—the stalking and destruction (here figured as possession) of the murderer's victims—remains the same, as does the reliance on "intimate" weapons. Few guns show up in slasher films (Ash's shotgun is a crucial exception) and when they do they tend to misfire or otherwise malfunction.

For its part, Raimi's cabin in the woods, with its history of demonic possession, is clearly a Terrible Place where "human crimes and perversions have transpired" (Clover 31). And his crudely drawn characters—two teenage couples, Ash and Linda, and Scott and Shelly, plus Ash's virginal sister, Cheryl—are slasher archetypes.

Cheryl—like Ash's shotgun—is especially important, since she represents the first radical departure from the slasher formula. As Clover points out, "The practiced viewer distinguishes [the Final Girl] from her friends minutes into the film. She is the Girl Scout, the bookworm, the mechanic. Unlike her girlfriends … she is not sexually active" (39). Cheryl fits this profile almost perfectly. As the only member of the group without a romantic partner, Cheryl is at least symbolically virginal (and, as far as we can ascertain, literally), and her interests are wholesome (she is a budding artist). So it comes as a shock when she is raped by the animate forest and the first to become possessed (to die, in the coded language of the film). When she winds up locked in the cellar, cackling demonically through a crack in the trapdoor, the viewer is left with a key question. Failing Cheryl, whom are we to identify as the Final Girl? Neither Linda nor Shelly, both romantically involved, seems to fit the bill. Since that is the extent of the female cast, we have to wonder if *The Evil Dead* offers us a Final Girl at all.

Ash as Final Boy

The answer is that it does and does not. To be sure, there is no Final Girl in biological terms. But Clover's injunction that sex in a slasher film proceeds from gendered behavior rather than vice versa is all important here, for the film *does* reverse gender polarities; however, it does so by feminizing its central character, Ash—or Ashley, as Cheryl calls him, in keeping with one of the key Final Girl conventions. Their names—Clover mentions Marti, Terri, Will, and Joey, among others—place them in an androgynous space that the gendered action of their final confrontation with the killer resolves as masculine, thereby enabling their primarily male audience to identify with them (40).

It is telling, then, that, as Bruce Campbell reports, Raimi "felt that [making the protagonist a man instead of a woman] could make [the film] even more horrifying; if you could reduce a man to scrambling and screaming ... it would be even more horrifying than a woman doing that" (Warren 36–37). Campbell's use of the word "reduce" highlights the gender politics of the slasher movie. The male-gendered woman—the Final Girl—does more than expose the complex shift of the male audience's gender identification; it reflects important social changes that had empowered women in the personal and professional world. Two decades previously, in the patriarchal world of Hitchcock's *Psycho* (1960), the prototype of the slasher film, the germinal Final Girl (Lila Crane) had to be rescued by a male protector (Sam Loomis). By the time *Halloween* debuted in 1978, the Final Girl could rescue herself. Donald Pleasence's patriarchal psychiatrist (also named, in apparent homage, Sam Loomis), the presumptive rescuer, arrives on the scene after Jamie Lee Curtis's Laurie Strode has already defeated Michael Myers (to the extent the quasi-supernatural Shape, as the credits style him, can be defeated).[4]

Ash(ley), the Final Boy of *The Evil Dead*, exposes the flip side of the coin: masculine anxiety, and ambivalence, about the female-gendered man in the dawning era of a "sensitive" model of masculinity. As Sally Robinson says of shifting gender mores in the 1970s, "[t]he truism that men aren't 'allowed' to cry and thus to release pent-up emotions is central to the men's liberationists' construction of blocked masculinity" (210). This new template for masculinity challenged an American cinematic tradition that had long equated patriarchal power—and masculine heroism—with the capacity for violence, and the willingness to use it. Critic Joan Mellen notes that Hollywood had since the 1920s endorsed an ideal of "a male superior to women, defiant, assertive, and utterly fearless" (3), later pointing out that "[f]ilm after film has insisted that the masculine male is he who acts—and kills—without a moment's thought" (9). Seventies-era male liberationist Marc Feigen Fasteau adds that the "capacity, even affinity, for violence ... is supposed to represent the primal untamed base of masculinity" (144).

By this standard, Ash, the Final Boy and presumptive hero of *The Evil Dead*, is an almost complete failure. In the film's opening shots, he appears in the backseat of his own car—like the gun, a cherished emblem of American masculine autonomy—and, metaphorically, he's rarely in the driver's seat after that. Rather, he is continually under attack by a trio of demon-possessed women who can be seen as the fearful personification of the newly empowered woman who was challenging the patriarchy in multiple cultural arenas. His responses to those attacks do not by any means measure up to masculine convention. He stands by in impotence, holding an axe—the phallic symbolism is not subtle—as Shelly attacks Scott. Later, though he knows that only "bodily dismemberment" can protect him from Linda, who has in turn been possessed, sentiment prevents him from using the chainsaw (also phallic) he finds in the woodshed. When he finally *does* decapitate Linda, he does so by instinct rather than by intent.

In a slasher film, the proactive Final Girl increasingly assumes masculine characteristics. She overcomes the killer through courage and ingenuity. She keeps her head in a crisis. By contrast, Ash, the Final Boy, is almost entirely *re*active. Rather than keep his head in extremis, he descends into madness. He cannot find shells for his shotgun, again emphasizing his phallic impotence, and when he does find them, he cannot use the weapon effectively. In short, he is feminized throughout the film.

Scott, on the other hand, reacts to distaff aggression in conventionally masculine ways. He dismembers Shelly with the axe Ash cannot bring himself to use, buries her despite Ash's sentimental (i.e. feminine) protests—"We can't bury Shelly. She's our friend" (the best laugh line in the film)—and strikes off courageously into the woods alone. Despite these heroic measures, however, Scott winds up possessed, aligned with Ash's female attackers, complicating the easy reading of the film tendered by *Slant* reviewer Ed Gonzalez, who argues that Ash "is horrordom's most memorable wuss" and that "Raimi actively teases his protagonist for *not* being a man." Similarly, *Ms. Magazine* blogger Holly L. Derr argues, "Ash is clearly at a disadvantage due to his sentimental connection to his girlfriend and his sister," concluding that the movie teaches Ash "that he has to be ruthless."

In fact, in its ambivalence about the competing paradigms of masculinity, *The Evil Dead*'s vision of gender is more complex than either Gonzalez or Derr allow. If Ash is found wanting for a dearth of masculinity, Scott is punished for its excess. This ambivalence is expressed in three scenes that explicitly feminize Ash. In the first, we see Ash at his most sentimental, shyly proffering a gift—a tiny magnifying glass on a silver chain—to Linda. As they kiss, we see them through the window from the voyeuristic perspective of the demonic Force that prowls the woods (the POV camera is another echo of the slasher film). It watches them until the kiss breaks, and then circles the cabin to peer through another window into the bedroom Scott and Shelly share. Inside, Shelly takes off her blouse, briefly exposing her breasts, as if to contrast the feminized sentimentality Ash and Linda share with the socially prohibited sexual impulse the slasher film vicariously allows us to enjoy, because it simultaneously punishes it.[5] It is no wonder that Shelly precedes Linda in possession: Shelly is the more clearly sexual being. "You can never have sex," Randy proclaims of slasher films in Wes Craven's meta-slasher *Scream* (1996). "Sex equals death." Ash's sexual innocence, like that of the Final Girl he is modeled on, saves him. He is feminized as she is masculinized. In both cases, the shifting gender dynamic leads to salvation.

The film's ambivalence about this new model of sensitive masculinity is shown in the second scene, when Ash chains Linda down in the woodshed and prepares to dismember her with the chainsaw. Just as he brings the saw to bear, his gaze falls upon the tiny magnifying glass. Unable to complete his gory task, he throws the chainsaw aside and leans over Linda's body. "Oh, Linda," he weeps, cast once again in an emotionally sensitive feminine role— a role the film's plot this time calls into question, for in his decision to bury Linda intact, Ash not only unleashes much of the havoc that consumes the rest of the movie, but drives himself to the brink of insanity and beyond. If he had possessed Scott's masculine instinct to primal savagery, he might well have salvaged his sanity. In this case, Ash's sentimental failure to act contributes directly to his psychological disintegration.

The conflict between these competing paradigms of masculinity is resolved in the third scene, which casts Ash as feminized action hero. As the now-possessed corpse of Scott hangs on to his knees and the still-possessed Cheryl beats him with a poker, Ash uses the magnifying glass, the sentimental symbol of his feminine self, as the instrument of his salvation. The Final Girl takes on a gender-masculine role. Ash's Final Boy assumes a gendered synthesis of male and female. For virtually the first time in the film he takes responsibility for his own preservation (male action), using the magnifying glass (female sentiment) on its chain to drag the Sumerian Book of the Dead into reach so that he can cast it into the fire. As the book burns, Cheryl and Scott collapse and decay, their demons exorcised.[6]

The viewer's anxieties about masculine identity are (temporarily) exorcised, as well. In an age of heightened gender anxiety, *The Evil Dead* reinvents the slasher archetype of the Final Girl, replacing it with a Final Boy that offers up a synthesis of masculine and feminine gender roles for a new era of female empowerment. Like most horror movies, *The Evil Dead* is an artifact of its cultural moment, an expression, perhaps unconscious, of the zeitgeist. Despite the praise for originality the film has so often received, it is in its influences and structure a decidedly conventional work—little more than a slasher flick leavened with a sprinkle of Lovecraft and a spritz of William Peter Blatty. Yet for all its conventionality, the movie breaks new ground in an era when gender roles were profoundly in question. It reverses the slasher formula by feminizing its Final Boy, and making his feminine sentimentality—his urge to preserve the symbol of his love with Linda—the vehicle of his ultimate salvation. In a world where women were increasingly masculine, the movie concludes, it might not be so bad if men were a little bit more feminine—and in that vision *The Evil Dead* is ferociously original, after all.

NOTES

1. A poster for *The Hills Have Eyes* adorns the cellar wall of the backwoods Tennessee cabin where *The Evil Dead*'s horrors begin, and the set is decorated with folk-art made of bones and feathers, in homage to Tobe Hooper's *Chainsaw*.

2. An example: in *Friday the 13th* (1980), Kevin Bacon lights a joint, lays back on his bed, and gets an arrow jammed through his throat—*from underneath the mattress*—for his troubles.

3. No hard data exists to support this assumption, but my experience coincides with that of Clover (6–7) and John Cawelti, who notes, "horror seems especially fascinating to the young and relatively unsophisticated" (48).

4. "It was the boogeyman," Curtis says in the film's final moments, to which Pleasence responds, "As a matter of fact, it was."

5. Noël Carroll, following psychoanalyst Ernst Jones, calls this dynamic attraction-repulsion: "The products of the dream-work are said to be often simultaneously attractive and repellent, insofar as they function to enunciate both a wish and its inhibition" (169).

6. In the end, as Ash exits the cabin into the breaking dawn, the demonic Force that haunts the woods hurtles down upon him, sealing his doom (barring the inevitable sequels). In this moment the film succumbs to (a) horror movie conventions that call for a final twist, and (b) a lingering ambivalence about the new masculinity. The gender-synthesized man cannot be suffered to survive. The culture—and maybe Raimi himself—had yet to catch up with the film's gender-amorphous vision of masculinity.

WORKS CITED

Carroll, Noël. *The Philosophy of Horror or Paradoxes of the Heart*. Routledge, 1990.
Cawelti, John G. *Adventure, Mystery, and Romance: Formula Stories as Art and Popular Culture*. University of Chicago Press, 1976.
Clover, Carol J. *Men, Women, and Chainsaws: Gender in the Modern Horror Film*. Princeton University Press, 1992.
Derr, Holly L. "The New Evil Dead. Another Lesson in Masculinity. And Tree Rape." *Ms. Magazine Blog*, 17 Apr. 2013, msmagazine.com/blog/2013/04/17/the-new-evil-dead-another-lesson-in-masculinity-and-tree-rape/.
Fasteau, Marc Feigen. *The Male Machine*. McGraw-Hill, 1974.
Gonzalez, Ed. "Review of *The Evil Dead*." *Slant Magazine*, 6 Mar. 2002, slantmagazine.com/film/review/the-evil-dead.
King, Stephen. "*The Evil Dead*: Why You Haven't Seen It Yet … and Why You Ought To." *Rod Serling's The Twilight Zone Magazine*, Nov. 1982, pp. 20–22.
Mellen, Joan. *Big Bad Wolves: Masculinity in the American Film*. Pantheon Books, 1977.
Raimi, Sam, director. *The Evil Dead*. Renaissance Pictures, 1981.
Robinson, Sally. "Men's Liberation, Men's Wounds: Emotion, Sexuality, and the Reconstruction of Masculinity in the 1970s." *Boys Don't Cry? Rethinking Narratives of Masculinity and Emotion in the U.S.*, edited by Milette Shamir and Jennifer Travis. Columbia University Press, 2002.
Warren, Bill. *The Evil Dead Companion*. St. Martin's Griffin, 2000.

Perceptions of Paranormal Plausibility
Method and Manipulation in The Evil Dead

Leon Lewis

"Art attracts us only by what it reveals of our secret self."
—Jean-Luc Godard

The horror film has been a part of the cinematic cosmos since its inception. Georges Méliès's *Le Manoir du diable*, released in the United States in 1896 as *The Haunted Castle*, is a three-minute excursion into the supernatural, the beginning of a line leading toward feature-length "dark melodramas" (the term "horror" was not utilized until the 1930s) like the still striking German Expressionist *The Cabinet of Dr. Caligari* (1920). Conventional critical commentary indicated an uncertainty about how to categorize that film and other innovative uses of what are now recognized as horror motifs, resulting in a genre, which, according to Walter Lacqueur, "led nowhere." What might have been lacking was a film theorist with the particular capacity to respond to and describe the singular inventions of the nascent genre. The laudatory reviews of Sam Raimi's *The Evil Dead* (1981) upon its release were the work of cineastes and aficionados of the genre, an example of a century long difficulty in discerning the qualities of cinematic skill exhibited by what has been a strain of filmmaking as much independent venture as studio supported production.

The German psychologist Hugo Münsterberg was already enthralled by the rapidly evolving art of film when he was invited by William James to join the faculty at Harvard in 1889, where he had the opportunity to examine the development of film from "Edison's half-minute show to *The Birth of a Nation*" (2). Dependent more on his training as a psychologist to search for universal elements of cinematic achievement rather than the kind of detailed consideration of a film resembling the methods of a modern critic, Münsterberg's range of viewing is apparent in his astute references to highlights of the early cinema, such as "the noise when Charley [sic] Chaplin falls downstairs" (88); or appreciation of *"Neptune's Daughter,* the mermaids in the surf " (89); or his recognition that "Near the end of the Theda Bara edition of *Carmen* the scene changes" (45). His pioneering theoretical exploration, *The Photoplay: A Psychological Study* (1916), might have been recognized by both practitioners and theorists of the medium as a visionary document if Münsterberg had not already been severely criticized for his misguided attempts to argue for a German-American unity of purpose at the moment when World War I had engulfed the western world. Ignored by critics for much of the twentieth century, the republication with a discerning Foreword by Richard Griffith of Münsterberg's monograph in 1969 resulted in a rediscovery of what James Monaco called "a sophisticated theory of film psychology that conceives of film as an active process—a strongly mental activity—in which the observer is a partner with the filmmaker" (Monaco 440).

The central concept of Münsterberg's monograph is his contention that the essence of cinematic "reality" is "shaped by the inner movement of the mind" (Münsterberg 441). He insisted that what he called "the photoplay" (the era's standard term for the succession of images on the screen) offers a field in which "We do not see objective reality but a product of our own mind." (Münsterberg 441). Comparing film with the theatrical presentations, he felt that "In every respect the film play is further from the physical reality than the drama and in every respect this greater distance from the physical world brings it nearer to the mental world" (Münsterberg 412). He was convinced that while the photoplay is a projection on a flat screen, it "strongly suggests to us the actual depth of the real world" (Münsterberg 414). Recognizing the ways in which film can bend, stretch, reverse, slow down and compress temporal apprehension, "Time is left behind," and, "the freedom of the mind has triumphed," thus establishing a psychological reality that is a product of "the free play of our mental experiences" (Münsterberg 414). Münsterberg died in 1916, the year his book was published, quite possibly due to the extreme stress that his political advocacy had led to. Consequently, his theories remain as an intriguing proposition that he never supported with a close critique of a film; however, the resonance of his reflections is evident in the assertions of filmmakers like Jean-Luc Godard whose life and work have transformed the cinema in ways that Münsterberg might have endorsed. As Godard, in one of his characteristic propositions put it, "The cinema is not an art which films life: the cinema is something between art and life," and in close accordance with one of Münsterberg's central tenets, "Art attracts us only by what it reveals of our secret self," quoting Alfred North Whitehead in an essay "Les Amis du Cinéma" in 1952.

Because Münsterberg was writing in the early stages of cinematic invention, his theories might be more appropriately applied to the kind of filmmaking that did not have access to either the technical apparatus of the modern era or the economic support associated with studio productions. The primal conditions of filmmaking that Sam Raimi and company confronted when they began work on *The Evil Dead* in 1979 resembled the operative circumstances of many of the filmmakers Münsterberg studied, and the relative lack of constricting expectations were a source of liberation for their creative instincts as well as an opportunity for the improvisation of extremely low-tech solutions to problems that arose during the process of production. When *The Evil Dead* was released in 1981, it was hardly noticed by most film commentators and critics. David Bordwell and Kristin Thompson's influential *Film History: An Introduction* (1994) does not mention the film, nor does Robert Sklar's *Film: An International History of the Medium* (1993). It is not listed in the "Horror" section of the nearly comprehensive *Facets* catalogue in 1996. By 2003, it is included in Leonard Maltin's *Movie and Video Guide* (**1/2; "Wildly stylish, ultra-low-budget"), Maltin citing the wide release date of 1983, the year after *E. T.* (1982), and *Poltergeist* (1982); however, Stephen King's now oft-cited encomium in *The Twilight Zone Magazine* "The most ferociously original horror film of 1982 ... beyond doubt," is a better indicator of the immediate impact of the film for connoisseurs of the genre much more alert to a brilliantly radical as well as classically responsive utilization of its defining elements.

Münsterberg's approach to film is in accord with the Modernist movement circa the first decades of the 1900s that Hugh Kenner called "by tacit definition international, and no one worked in the country of his birth" (Kenner *xii*). Highlighting radical innovations in the arts, Kenner delineated how

> Painters dispensed with Newton's 3-D space, musicians worked with interdicted intervals; the poem, novel folded time up on time, tongue upon tongue. Polyglot masterpieces were stress-tested to validate new systems of connectedness, so that the reader's mind can jump aligned gaps... [Kenner *xiii*].

His description of key instances of Modernist invention is applicable to the kinds of cinematic innovation that Münsterberg was identifying as the essence of film—space, time, and an apprehension of existence revealed primarily through the narrative consciousness of the main characters as in James Joyce's *Ulysses* (1922) or Virginia Woolf's *To the Lighthouse* (1927). These were the features of film that, Münsterberg argued, separated film from the other dramatic arts. In the defining chapter of his book, "The Means of the Photoplay," he declares, "We must enter with our own impulses into the will of every element, into the meaning of every line and color and form, every word and tone and note," so that "the photoplay succeeds in overcoming reality" (Münsterberg 411).

Or, as in Raimi's work, the "photoplay" is designed to create its own version of a tangible, perceptible and ultimately plausible *reality* for the characters and the viewer. How Raimi does this is dependent on two fundamental precepts of the psychological discipline that formed Münsterberg's thesis— the sensory responsiveness inherent in human physiology and the primitive but metaphorically applicable concept of the four "elements" that constitute the phenomenal world—Earth, Air, Fire, and Water. Restricted by the means literally at hand during the later stages of production (i.e., his garage and its contents), Raimi was compelled to concentrate on the most basic aspects of his equipment and the most forceful expression of emotions of his actors. In accepting a necessary reduction in resources, Raimi was also removing an accumulation of associations and expectations which permitted him to work with a *tabula rasa*, a true white screen open for images, much like the white canvas that Lily Briscoe in Woolf's *To the Lighthouse* faced with apprehension and exultation. Just as Briscoe understood the ways in which the first brushstroke would set a path to be pursued, Raimi knew that the ethos of his opening sequence would be crucial in establishing the ambience of the world he was invoking. For painter and filmmaker, the establishment of an aura of understanding invited the viewer into the evolving region of existence. Consequently, Raimi constructed his *mise-en-scène* as a function of location, utilizing the landscape near Morristown, Tennessee—the site of the exterior scenes—since "cinema setting can come to the forefront ... not only as a container for human events but [when it] can dynamically enter the narrative action," as Bordwell and Thompson explain in their discussion of *Film Art* (121). Developing this insight, Bordwell and Thompson observe, "Confining the cinema to some notion of realism would impoverish [*mise-en-scène*]. The technique has the power to transcend normal conceptions of reality" (119) in accord with Münsterberg's contention that "The massive outer world has lost its weight, been freed from space, time, and causality, and has been clothed in the forms of our consciousness" (Münsterberg 416). For Raimi, the natural world is depicted as an interactive entity immediately impacting the ways in which the characters construe the *reality* that absorbs them.

The opening sequence carries the viewer toward a primeval setting, the recording consciousness of the camera moving into and across liquid suffused terrain, a gliding motion unlike human peregrination. Far from the civilized city, it is reminiscent of the country of *The Cabinet of Dr. Caligari*, jagged, diagonal lines rather than rectangular right angles cutting space into trapezoidal shapes. There is no solid ground to stand on. The earth has been intermingled with fluid, anticipating the profusion of fluids from various sources that engulf the screen. The essential element at the start is Water.

Utilizing the classic editing method of crosscutting, the narrative focus shifts to young adults also moving through the landscape, mobile rather than ambulatory, their vehicle crossing suspect terrain. The ground (Earth) they depend on for safe passage is flawed and uncertain like the rotted timber on the bridge that separates them from safety. The bridge is a kind of archetypal antecedent reflecting the futility of resisting the ruins wrought by a cosmos that mocks human effort at permanence. When the travelers reach their destination, the cabin that they enter will be insufficient to provide the shelter they need when the elemental forces surrounding the cabin on every side begin to register the upheaval provoked by the approach of the demon spirits. The meteorological phenomena occurring—lightning (Fire) and turbulence (Air)—are an atmospheric expression of the forces overrunning and transforming the normally placid world of the characters. Within the cabin itself, glasses are raised in expectations of a liquid benediction, the remnants of customary behavior about to be drastically altered. The cellar beneath the earth's surface is not a safe storage area; it is more like the jar of Pandora, which when opened unleashes forbidden forces. The dripping liquid below is like a ruptured vein, and when the Deadites summoned by the incantation of Sumerian burial practices emerge, the flashes of lightning accompanying the storm are akin to the fire that fuels the creative/destructive energy employed by scientists like Dr. Frankenstein seeking to generate life.

Thrust into an environment that becomes increasingly unnerving, the responses of the characters are registered through the ways in which Raimi concentrates on their sensory, visceral reactions. Raimi's employment of vividly physical manifestations of psychic distress is similar to the fascination with the body, skin, and organ that David Cronenberg was exploring in films of the era like *The Brood* (1979), *Scanners* (1981), and *Videodrome* (1983). Following a pattern of facial expression indicative of initial cognition, Raimi shows what the character sees, then how he or she reacts, then how what has been seen becomes a proximate agent affecting the character's physical self. The early brilliance of Raimi's grasp of cinematic possibility is evident in the stunning "Violated by Woods" scene where a young woman, emblematic of the potential for normal life, at the threshold of a procreative path toward the continuance of the race, is captured, ensnared and subjugated to a sexual assault by something unidentifiable and mysterious. It is the nature of this *mystery*, this *thing* that is at stake in terms of the "reality" of the characters and the environment in which they are situated. As a shadow obscures the limited light of the full moon, the woman, wandering in the wilderness, is caught and brought down to the earth by the limb-like tendrils of an indistinct vegetative force. Her struggles to escape from the entwining bounds are constructed in the pattern of a classic montage; rapid cuts from her face to her legs are intermixed POV shots from the "something" that is controlling the attack, a visual correlative akin to Dylan Thomas's "The force that through the green fuse drives the flower," although somewhat more sinister than Thomas's poem of that title (Thomas 77). The tempo of the cuts is increased, the camera moving closer to the woman, until a rush of extreme close-ups of gnashing teeth accompanied by shrieks brings the scene to an ambiguous climax.

Her explanation of her terror is met by a reasonable response: "Trees do not attack." But what have we just seen? The woman was able to rip away the roots which could have been dense foliage and fallen branches. Could it be that the entire scene was a product of a psychic illusion triggered by the disconcerting phenomena leading up to this scene? The convulsive intensity of the woman's reactions makes her explanation convincing, but the skepticism of her friends instills a degree of doubt that the viewer might share. For several moments, it is still possible to dismiss almost everything as a result of a fervent hyper-imaginative construction of what will eventually yield to a rational analysis of unsettling but ultimately understandable atmospheric and terrestrial activity. Then, a demon spirit enters the cabin. It is eventually pushed back down into the pit, chains locked on the trapdoor, and earth shoveled over the entrance to seal the cellar. The characters are still acting as if the intrusion is a version of a crazed rustic threatening the visitors from the civilized city. Will their efforts be sufficient to restrain the subterranean impulse surging upward? Of course not; and now the film is ready to unleash the evil dead into the "normal" world that Raimi, in accord with Münsterberg's incisive, prescient explanation of "the photoplay," has established as ground where the paranormal becomes manifest in a thoroughly convincing element of a plausible reality.

Although Raimi is enlarging the parameters of the genre, there are inescapable tropes so fundamental that they have become a part of the cultural cosmos beyond the cinematic ventures that shaped them. As the forces of evil emerge, the core query that the film will address is *What* (are they) and *Why* (are they appearing now). Stephen King, in his urtext, *Danse Macabre*, published in the year of *The Evil Dead*'s premiere, asserted that "It doesn't end with the Thing, the Vampire, and the Werewolf," but these archetypes "account for a large bloc of modern horror fiction" (77). Elements of each entity are fashioned into the formation of the evil dead. While maintaining the connection to the central narrative thread joining the characters who are threatened with the mysterious force that endangers them, Raimi engages an overarching meta-narrative strain reaching back to classic earlier manifestations of similar forces. *Gojira* (1954), successful as a monster film when it was released, has accumulated an additional cultural resonance due to the increasing understanding that the trauma of nuclear devastation was being expressed in the manifestation of the monster. King accurately identifies "fears for the ecology" (King 161) as a distinctive factor in films developed in the seventies, a parallel to the incipient awareness of environmental desecration prominent in books like Edward Abbey's *The Monkey Wrench Gang* (1975) and William Kotzwinkle's *Dr. Rat* (1976) appearing during the years the genesis of *The Evil Dead* took place.

Without unduly emphasizing these archetypal issues, Raimi has enabled the viewer to begin to wonder if there is some human responsibility for the appearance of the evil dead. Could these young adults, a generation after the cultural chasm that opened in the 1960s, represent some sort of immoral behavior counter to established religious mores now subject to punishment from a displeased divine entity? And, at least since the Greek myth of Pandora who unwisely but inevitably opened the jar of spirits, there have been cautionary fables about what humans must not do. Yet, if there is no way to escape once the evil spirits have been released, what choice is there but to resist, if one can. The longing for a heroic human figure, fearless as Daedalus, resourceful as Odysseus, persistent as Sisyphus, is an enduring archetype, and might Ash Williams (Bruce Campbell), a regular guy like any of us, have the capacity to resist evil, to strive to rescue his friends and to overcome the rampant horror? Raimi was tending in this direction with *Spider Man* (2002), and this is the archetypal heroism Raimi and crew are evoking as the desperate struggle for survival begins, taking the viewer into a region of altered reality where the paranormal has become the operative normal for the duration of the film.

WORKS CITED

Bordwell, David, and Kristin Thompson. *Film Art: An Introduction*. McGraw-Hill, 1994.
Godard, Jean-Luc. "What Is Cinema." *Les Amis du Cinéma*, October 1952.
Kenner, Hugh. *A Homemade World: The American Modernist Writers*. William Morrow, 1975.
King, Stephen. *Danse Macabre*. Berkley Books, 1982.
_____. "*The Evil Dead*: Why You Haven't Seen It Yet ... and Why You Ought To." *Rod Serling's The Twilight Zone Magazine*, Nov. 1982, pp. 20–22.
Laqueur, Walter. *Weimar: A Cultural History*. Perigee, 1980.
Maltin, Leonard. *Movie & Video Guide, 2003 Edition*. Signet/Penguin, 2002.
Monaco, James. *How to Read a Film*. Oxford University Press, 1977.
Münsterberg, Hugo. "The Means of the Photoplay." *The Film: A Psychological Study*. Dover, 1970, pp. 73–82.
Raimi, Sam, director. *The Evil Dead*. Renaissance Pictures, 1981.
Sklar, Robert. *Film Art: An International History of the Medium*. Prentice-Hall, 1993.
Thomas, Dylan. *The Poems of Dylan Thomas*. New Directions, 1971.

Naturom Demonto
How The Evil Dead *Claims Evil for Both Literature and Cinema*

John Semley

> "The stronger the evil, the stronger the film."
> —Alfred Hitchcock

In his 1957 tract *Literature and Evil,* the French novelist-philosopher Georges Bataille struck back against Jean-Paul Sartre's then-voguish proclamation of the moral function of the novel, famously claiming literature for capital-e Evil. And so did Sam Raimi, by creating a lively (and violent, and often very funny) case for literary Evil, while simultaneously prefiguring the capacity for that same Evil that, many have argued, lays dormant in cinema itself, like a restlessly slumbering ghoul yearning to break free.

Cinema, and horror cinema in particular, boasts plenty of stories about evil books: books that carry the potential to infect the reader, to incite riots or, in the case of Raimi's *Evil Dead* films, manifest evil, wickedness, plain badness in more literal ways—by directly attacking people, snapping at their fingers with spiky fangs hewn from their flesh-bound covers. Images of evil books, and mass-consuming mobs driven mad by them, offer a corrective to a longstanding suspicion towards the moving image itself: its power, its potency, its ability to rouse and corrupt the viewer.

In some quarters, this conservative attitude greeted 1981's *The Evil Dead* upon its release. In the U.S., the film received an X rating. In other countries, it was banned altogether. In the United Kingdom, the film was released at the height of the "video nasty" book of the early 1980s. Though the colloquial "video nasty" designation was typically reserved for pornographic films— which, *The Evil Dead,* despite a particularly memorable and upsetting early scene of an actress being violently penetrated by the tendrils of a fiendish tree, most certainly was not—Raimi's movie was condemned for its excessive violence, gore, and splatter, earning it the title of "Number One Nasty" (a nod to both its perceived offensiveness and its impressive video sales). But the reactionary "think of the children!" moralism that may dictate the censorship of a mostly harmless, tongue-in-cheek, no-budget horror film proceeds from deeper rooted feeling: a profound distrust of the moving image itself.

This chapter will look at the distrust of the moving image, its historical and theoretical basis, and explore the tension between the perceived evil of both motion pictures and of literature—an evil that, in both cases, arises from the inherent qualities of the mediums themselves. In doing so, I will discuss how Sam Raimi's *Evil Dead* films reclaim literature for Evil, albeit in a way that betrays the cinema's capacity for that same Evil.

In "Upon Leaving the Movie Theater," Roland Barthes recounts the experience of someone (really himself) tottering out of the cinema. He describes a sensation of numbness, of tiredness, a feeling not unlike being snapped out of hypnosis. "And from hypnosis, that old psychoanalytic saw which psychoanalysis disdains, he seeks the oldest of its powers: the cure" (1). Barthes's reflection is awash with negative language. The moving image is "a lure" (3) that attracts our "stupefied gaze" (2). Movies induce "filmic paralysis" and "cinematographic hypnosis" (3). The moviegoer is ensnared, seized by the image.

This rhetoric of what I will call *cine-negativity* is abundant in the literature and theory of the medium. In his 1984 lecture, "The Evil Demon of Images," Jean Baudrillard bore into the "diabolic seduction of images" (13). For Baudrillard, the capacity for "media images"—chief among them, the cinematic image—to diabolically seduce its beholder was tied directly to their fidelity, their apparent conformity to realism, to the "real world" (13). "There is in this conformity," says Baudrillard, "a force of seduction in the literal sense of the word, a force of diversion, distortion, capture and ironic fascination" (14–15).

The moving image, then, is not just seductive and diverting, but destructive, lulling the viewer into a state of stupefied, paralytic conformity. I am reminded of David Foster Wallace's *Infinite Jest*. The novel deals (in part) with a videocassette deemed lethally entertaining: so seductive that it quite literally paralyzes the viewer into nothing but watching it, and watching it, and watching it again, until such a time as they die of malnutrition in a pile of their own excrement, as in the case of the victim early in the novel who is discovered by his wife, plopped in a soiled recliner, staring deep into his TV set. As his wife notes, "the expression on his rictus of a face nevertheless appeared very positive, ecstatic, even, you could say" (79). The video itself, also called *Infinite Jest*, is described only fragmentally, but prefigures an incredibly beautiful woman apologizing profusely into a wobbly camera mounted on baby's crib, speaking into what's described as a "neonatal lens" (222). The description of this imagined technology recalls Georges Bataille's threefold connection between literature, childhood and Evil, where literature pits the "innocent sovereignty" (Bataille 12) of childhood against the reason and proscribed rationality of adulthood. In Wallace's book, a work of cinema (or experimental video, anyway) expressed an Evil that, qua Bataille, had been uniquely claimed for literature.

There is a firm historical basis for cine-negativity, one which Tom Gunning outlines in "Flickers: On Cinema's Power for Evil." Gunning, like Barthes and Baudrillard, investigates the "essential suspicion of cinema" (21)—misgivings not just about the kinds of stories of narratives conveyed on screen (pornography, romantic gangster myths, hyper-violent horror stories) but of the very nature of that conveyance itself. It is not one or another cinematic narrative, but *cinema itself* that is suspect, maybe even out-and-out evil.

As Gunning notes, it was not until 1952 that the United States guaranteed First Amendment protections to motion pictures (22). A unanimous 1915 Supreme Court ruling deciding *Mutual Film Corp v. Industrial Commission of Ohio*, ruled that "the exhibition of moving pictures is a business, pure and simple, originated and conducted for profit, like other spectacles, not to be regarded, nor intended to be regarded by the Ohio Constitution, we think, as part of the press of the country, or as organs of public opinion" (McKenna). But more than legalizing censorship of motion pictures and motion picture exhibition, or proclaiming (rather sensibly) that the film industry is foremost an *industry*, *Mutual Film Corp v. Industrial Commission of Ohio* alluded to the cinema's capacity for evil. "Their power of amusement," read Justice Joseph McKenna's decision, "make them the more insidious in corruption by a pretense of worthy purpose or if they should degenerate from worthy purpose. Indeed, we may go beyond that possibility. They take their attraction from the general interest, eager and wholesome it may be, in their subjects, but a prurient interest may be excited and appealed to" (McKenna). In this period, there seemed to be widely held (and court-ordered) belief that "the medium of motion pictures, with its newfound power of attraction, could overwhelm rational thought" (Gunning 35). Film, in its very essence, held the power to overthrow rationality, and warp the mind.

In this instance, contra Barthes and Baudrillard, it is not the cinema's capacity to lull us into conformity that renders it dangerous. Rather, it is the medium's "prurient" tendencies toward excitement and sensation. As Gunning notes, such judgments were irrevocably tied to considerations of class in the early twentieth century, with a popular emerging entertainment like the cinema threatening to undermine the social control of white Protestant males (24), if only by promising women, children, and the working immigrant classes a sense of spiked, socially unacceptable excitement. This idea stands opposed to Wallace's forewarning estimation of cinematic—and, perhaps especially, televisual—entertainment as being gravely absorbing and self-destructive in its ability to pacify the audience into a state of passive, dead-eyed conformity (a state Baudrillard likens to operations of ideology itself). The historical determinants for the essentialist argument in favor of cinema's power for evil are rooted in its power to rouse and energize an audience, even to the point of hazard—or madness.

Horror cinema is awash with narratives that underline this essentialist evil of the moving image. David Cronenberg's *Videodrome* (1983), a prototypical example of what is sometimes called "media horror," seems to anticipate Baudrillard's thesis on the corrupting power of images. When Baudrillard says that everyday waking life "has become cinematic and televisual" (16) he sounds not only quintessentially Baudrillardian, but seems to echo the loopy, McLuhanist grandiloquence of *Videodrome*'s Professor Brian O'Blivian (Jack Creley), who claimed that "television is reality, and reality less than television." *Videodrome*'s attitude towards the diabolism if the media image is twofold: at once sensationalist (with a bootleg TV station exciting night owl audience with images of extreme sex and violence) and conformist (using that bootleg signal to induce brain tumors in the viewer, rendering the public complacent in order to weaken opposition to a new media power bloc).

John Carpenter seems similarly obsessed with potential of the media image, positive and negative. In *They Live* (1988), television signals are used to disseminate conformist subliminal directives to "Obey," "Marry And Reproduce," etc., sent out by a ruling extraterrestrial elite. In *Prince of Darkness* (1987), TV news broadcasts are relayed back through time, transmitted in the form of dreams, in order to help the film's cast of heroic physics grad students thwart a satanic apocalypse. In *Cigarette Burns* (2005), his first entry into the Showtime cable network's *Master of Horror* anthology series, Carpenter seems to be copping *Infinite Jest*, telling the story of broker of rare film prints (Norman Reedus) tracking down a copy of an elusive film, *La Fine Absolue du Monde*, renowned for inciting homicidal riots whenever its screened.

Likewise, in Lamberto Bava's *Demons* (1985), a disturbing horror movie screened in a Berlin cinema seems to infect its audience, transforming them into murderous monsters resembling the ones projected on the movie screen. In the sequel, *Demons 2* (1986), the events of the first film are recast as a film-within-a-film, which itself serves to contaminate anyone who watches it on television. This notion of the Evil Image replicating is most conspicuously expressed in Hideo Nakata's 1998 cult Japanese horror film *Ringu*, in which a gothic ancestral curse is spread, virus-like, through bootleg videotapes—perhaps cinema's plainest articulation of what Matt Hills describes as "the powers of symbol-carrying media to virally 'infect' their audiences" (167).

The Evil Image is a keystone of horror cinema, and particularly media horror. And understandably so. This notion that moving images exude such a powerful and corruptive influence is at once flattering to filmmakers who trade in the sensationalism of gory slasher flicks, as well as viewers able to resist such a sensationalist sway. Yet there is within this strain of horror cinema a tendency, at once competing and complimentary, to depict not films, but books, as fundamentally evil.

As Gunning acknowledges, when Bataille argued that literature was Evil, he was referring to literary narratives themselves. "Evil is something literature expresses," writes Gunning. "It does not inhere in the very signifiers of the text, the materiality and perceptual qualities of literature." For Gunning, this distinguishes the evil of literature to the evil of the moving image. Literature can *express* evil. Cinema *is* evil.

Certain strains of horror cinema, however, seem to advocate for a more essentialist view of literary evil—chief amongst is Sam Raimi's *The Evil Dead* (1981). There are plenty of examples of films which express the corruptive power of evil, from Dario Argento's *Tenebre* (1982), a late cycle *giallo* picture about a serial killer whose particular M.O. is inspired by a blockbuster thriller novel, to Carpenter's *In the Mouth of Madness* (1994), in which the latest work Stephen King–styled superstar horror writer is driving the public into a murderous frenzy. But Raimi's film (and, in different respects, its two sequels, and its contemporary remake) distinguishes itself from these other films, in which the potential for madness and destruction is conveyed through literature. In *The Evil Dead*, it's a book itself—the *Naturom Demonto*—that appears to be wicked: bound in human flesh, printed in human blood, and containing invocations to ancient, soul-destroying Sumerian spirits that can be awakened when uttered.

The Evil Dead's "book of the dead" has its own referents in actuality—or something like it. The *Necronomicon*, in name and description, derives from the writings of horror author H.P. Lovecraft, whose particular métier was man's confrontation with unnamable, unfathomable evils. A fictional work of demonology, magic (or *magick*), and history of ancient spirits and Old Gods, the *Necronomicon* has since entrenched itself as a popular trope in horror fiction. According to the Lovecraftian mythos, "the book contains the formulae for evoking incredible things into visible appearance, beings and monsters which dwell in the Abyss, and Outer Space, of the human psyche" (Simon xv). Lovecraft himself encouraged the widespread use of his idea in fiction of the genre, believing that recurrent allusions to the *Necronomicon* would foster "a background of evil verisimilitude" (quoted in De Camp 101), a term which naturally calls to mind Baudrillard's description of the "collusion between images and life" (27), and the manner in which imagined systems come to ruthlessly define, or usurp, reality. For Lovecraft, encouraging this shared lore gave credence to the notion that Lovecraft's imagined volume was, indeed, a real book.

And indeed, the Avon Books paperback edition of the *Necronomicon* goes through great pains to pass itself off as a genuine artifact, despite its fairly widespread availability.[1] Compiled with extensive prefatory notes, including English translations of "common" Sumerian words and phrases, this edition traces the origin of the manuscript itself, indexing instances of madness and annihilation that have befallen those responsible for it. "A great deal of misfortune accompanied the publication of this book," writes the editor identified only as "Simon." "At one point, an unscrupulous publisher from the West Coast took a copy of the initial preface and some of the miscellaneous pages in translation ... and went off, and has not been heard from again" (xxxi). This aura of danger makes even commercial paperback editions of the *Necronomicon*, seem somehow dangerous and evil—printed with figurative, if not literal, human blood.

Across subsequent *Evil Dead* films, the slapstick sequel *Evil Dead 2: Dead By Dawn* (1987) and the comic-horror medieval fantasy *Army of Darkness* (1992), writer/director Raimi and co-writer Scott Spiegel supplied plenty of images of the *Necronomicon* as being, in itself, violent. In *Army of Darkness*, the book (and imitations of it) are brought to life, the fleshy, faces on their covers attempting to bite the hand of the series' hapless hero, Ash Williams (Bruce Campbell). In its original iteration, *The Evil Dead* effectively dovetails two of the philosophic and historical strands discussed above. It is a film about the essential evil of books, or the written (and spoken) word, that renders this evil through the spiked sensationalism particular to the cinematic medium/apparatus.

To understand precisely how *The Evil Dead* director Sam Raimi prefigures this evil of the cinematic apparatus itself, it is important to understand how the process of viewer identification functions in the horror cinema of its era. In her seminal text on gender in the horror film, *Men, Women and Chainsaws*, Carol J. Clover posits an effectively simple equation for understanding viewer identification, particularly in the American "slasher" film cycle of the late 1970s and early 1980s. As she writes, "Point of view = identification" (45). In other words, seeing through a character's eyes (as suggested by and embodied in the camera itself) creates a strong sense of psychological linkage between the viewer and that character. Or in the case of *The Evil Dead*, not really a "character" in any meaningful, traditional sense, so much as perspectival embodiment of Evil itself.

In the slasher cycle Clover describes (*Halloween* [1978], *The Texas Chain-*

saw Massacre [1974], *Friday the 13th Part II* [1981], and other similarly structured films that see a lumbering psycho-killer stalking and chopping a group of lithesome, sexually active teen victims), the pattern of identification shifts. First, the presumed viewer (a teenaged male, typically) is drawn into identification with the film's killer, yoked into their point-of-view via the sorts of first person shots that have become a hallmark of the genre. This POV is, initially, unclaimed: the viewer has no idea who the killer is, or what he (or she, but usually he) looks like. There is, typically, no reverse-shot to unveil the killer.

Take, for example, the opening sequence of John Carpenter's *Halloween*, a film that essentially struck the boilerplate for a decade-plus of slasher imitators. The film opens from the squat perspective of a child, as seen through one of those constricting, cheapo plastic Halloween masks. The child totters through the house, retrieves a knife from the kitchen and heads upstairs to murder his sister, who has just engaged in a (notably protracted) sex act. As the sister screams, Carpenter's camera does not cut to her perspective, instead staying locked inside of the mask as the child's breathing becomes more labored, disturbingly excited at the thrill of murdering his sibling. It is not until the child exits the house and is greeted by his parents that we see him, Michael Myers, the central monster of the *Halloween* film and its string of sequels, remakes, and so on. The first-person Steadicam cinematography cuts to a lavish crane shot, as the camera pulls out to reveal the young killer, clad in a clown costume, his parents, and the sleepy suburban Illinois neighborhood where his reign(s) of terror will continue to unfold.

Raimi's *The Evil Dead* is not a typical slasher movie. Functionally and aesthetically, it is more of a generic convergence of the teen slasher and the hyper-gory zombie movies of George Romero, Lucio Fulci, et al. In *The Evil Dead*, a group of young adults vacationing in a ramshackle cabin in the woods are essentially haunted down and possessed by a roving demonic spirit, largely as a pretense for sequences of explosive splatter, gory mutilation and the expulsion of abject fluids and all kinds of propulsive arterial flow. The most distinctive aesthetic/formal feature in Raimi's low budget artillery is his use of jittery tracking shots.

In his autobiography, *The Evil Dead* star Bruce Campbell describes the invention of what would become the film's trademark camera technique. "The next invention-of-necessity was the Shaky Cam," writes Campbell. "This was the polar opposite of its big budget (hence completely unavailable to us) brother, the Steadi-Cam [sic]. Our version was merely a three-foot hunk of two-by-six board with the camera bolted in the middle. The cameraman slapped on a wide-angle lens, grabbed the board at either end and ran like hell. On film, the end result was an evil, roaming entity that could leap tall shrubs in a single bound" (174).

These "Shaky Cam" sequences distinguish themselves from the first-person "I–Camera" (Clover 45) of the traditional slasher film in that the POV is *never* claimed. There is no psycho killer on the other end of the camera, only the "evil, roaming entity" that Campbell describes. In effect, the POV belongs to the camera, the cinematic apparatus, itself. The ability to instill fear in the viewer, to elicit shock and sensation, is, in *The Evil Dead*, prefigured as the stuff of cinema itself. If the early killer-POV shots in slasher films of the *Halloween* template stage and, qua Clover, complicate the operations of the "male gaze," in which the gaze of the camera itself works to objectify the female victims (and victim-heroes) of the slasher film, then the forever-unclaimed-POVs of *The Evil Dead* posit something different: A purely cinematic gaze, not an "I–Camera" but a "Camera-Eye."

It is a perspective that renders the camera, and its movements, totally embodied, animate, and even demonic, in and of themselves. As the Shaky Cam barrels through the woods surrounding the cabin in *The Evil Dead*, branches and tree boughs are pushed out of the way, twigs snap, windows break. Midway through the film, when Ash shovels dirt onto a friend's corpse, the soil covers the lens of the camera itself, gradually occluding the low-angle shot until the viewer sees nothing but smothering darkness. It is as if, by covering the lens, the machinery of cinema itself, the threat will be obviated in turn. Borrowing again from the slasher, with its stock cliffhanger of a supposedly-felled killer's hand twitching or eye opening in order to suggest unfinished business (usually in the form of a sequel), *The Evil Dead* ends with demonic Camera-Eye rushing through the remains of the ramshackle cabin to seize upon the film's final survivor, Campbell's Ash.

This idea of the "Camera-Eye" is meant to evoke Dziga Vertov's "Kino-Eye" (sometimes "Cine-Eye," in English), an idea developed in "From Kino-Eye to Radio-Eye." For Vertov, the movie camera, the cinema, and particularly the process of montage editing, was of responding to and ordering the commotion and pandemonium of life in the early 20th century. "Kino-Eye," writes Vertov, "plunges into the chaos of life to find in life itself the response to an assigned theme. To find the resultant force amongst the million phenomena related to the given theme" (88). As Annette Michelson notes in the introduction to the collected volume *Kino-Eye: The Writings of Dziga Vertov*, this notion emerged from Vertov's constructivist politics, his "ideological concern for the role of art as an agent of human perfectibility, a belief in social transformation as the means for producing a transformation of consciousness" (xxv).

The roving, demonic Camera-Eye of *The Evil Dead* serves an opposing function, embodying the concern expressed by Gunning that the cinema, through its sheer sensationalism, carried the capacity to "overwhelm rational thought" in its viewer. In the *Evil Dead* films, as in Bava's *Demons* diptych, the cinema transforms consciousness, and the social fabric—albeit in a twisted realization of Vertov's constructivist reveries. In *The Evil Dead*, the Camera-Eye, as embodiment of the cinema and its apparatus, seizes upon its human and transforms them into yellow-eyed, grinning ghouls, given to pitchy shrieking and hyper-violence. They are the warped personification (or demonification) of evil as "a power exceeding and possibly overwhelming reason" (Gunning 35) that Gunning describes. A similar thing happens in Bava's *Demons* films, where the on-screen action of a given film comes to "infect" the audience, a nightmare of the sort of imitative mimesis of reality that Vertov's montage-based Kino-Eye stood staunchly against. These films likewise allegorize—if not *realize*—Baudrillard's anxiety over the media image's "conformity" to realism and, again, the "collusion" between images and reality: across both, the endgame is essentially the substitution of humanity as we know it for its diabolic doppelganger.

Yet unlike Bava's movies, which are essentially cheapo parables of the destructive power of the mimetic media image (cynically couched in violent, destructive narratives of gore and exploitation), Raimi's film stages the mythic-literary evil of the *Necronomicon* cinematically. In this respect, *The Evil Dead* essentially dovetails the competing, often antagonistic, relationship between literature and film, regarding their capacity for Evil. The evil book of Raimi's film is ostensibly an incarnation of literary evil, of the sort of corruptive, soul-polluting books prefigured in films like Argento's *Tenebre* and Carpenter's *In the Mouth of Madness*. Yet *The Evil Dead* distinguishes itself from these films—as well as other films dealing with the evil of the moving image, such as *Ringu* or the *Demons* films—by expressing this evil through the practice, the technological apparatus, of cinema itself. In the one-upping fracas between Bataille and Baudrillard, literature and cinema, Sam Raimi splits the difference between the two traditions, boldly claiming Evil for both.

NOTES

1. I bought my copy, if I remember correctly, not in some dingy, subterranean occult bookstore staffed by a hunched clerk chuffing on an opium pipe, but in the Astrology section of a Chapters—an all-but-extinct chain bookseller in Canada, which also peddles in Starbucks caramel latte preparations and impulse buy Norah Jones CDs.

WORKS CITED

Barthes, Roland. "Upon Leaving the Movie Theater." *Cinematographic Apparatus: Selected Writings*, edited by Therese Hak Kyung Cha, translated by Bertrand Augst and Susan White. Tanam, 1980, pp. 1–4.
Bataille, Georges. *Literature and Evil*. 1957. Penguin Classics, 2012.
Baudrillard, Jean. *The Evil Demon of Images*. Power Institute of Fine Arts, 1987.
Bava, Lamberto, director. *Demons*. Ascot Films, 1985.
_____. *Demons II*. Artists Entertainment Group, 1986.
Campbell, Bruce. *If Chins Could Kill: Confessions of a B Movie Actor*. L.A. Weekly Books, 2002.

Carter, Lin. "Introduction." *Literary Swordsmen and Sorcerers: The Makers of Heroic Fantasy*, by L. Sprague De Camp. Arkham House, 1976, pp. xi-xiv.
Carpenter, John, director. *Halloween*. Columbia Pictures, 1978.
_____. *In the Mouth of Madness*. New Line Cinema, 1994.
_____. "John Carpenter's Cigarette Burns." *Masters of Horror*, Showtime, 16 Dec. 2005.
_____. *Prince of Darkness*. Universal Pictures, 1987.
_____. *They Live*. Universal Pictures, 1988.
Clover, Carol J. *Men, Women and Chainsaws: Gender in the Modern Horror Film*. Princeton University Press, 1992.
Cronenberg, David, director. *Videodrome*. Universal Pictures, 1983.
Gunning, Tom. "Flickers: On Cinema's Power for Evil." *Bad: Infamy, Darkness, Evil and Slime on Screen*, edited by Murray Pomerance. State University of New York Press, 2004, pp. 21–38.
Hills, Matt. "Ringing the Changes: Cult Distinctions and Cultural Differences in US Fans' Readings of Japanese Horror Cinema." *Japanese Horror Cinema*, edited by Jay McRoy. Edinburgh University Press, 2006, pp. 161–174.
Michaels, Annette. "Introduction." *Kino-Eye: The Writings of Dziga Vertov*, translated by Kevin O'Brien. University of California Press, 1984.
"Mutual Film Corp. v. Industrial Commission of Ohio." 236 U.S. 230, Supreme Court of the United States of America, 1915.
Nakata, Hideo, director. *Ringu*. Ace Pictures, 1998.
Raimi, Sam, director. *Army of Darkness*. Renaissance Pictures, 1992.
_____. *The Evil Dead*. Renaissance Pictures, 1981.
_____. *Evil Dead 2*. Renaissance Pictures, 1987.
Simon. "Preface to the Second Edition." *Necronomicon*. Avon Books, pp. xi-lv.
Wallace, David Foster. *Infinite Jest*. 1996. Back Bay Books, 2006.

Tracking Gaze, Possessing Perspective
Evil as Affect
Haerin Shin

The Evil Dead (1981) marks the advent of a new era for horror spectatorship, whereby the dread of sheer materiality bursts forth right in, and more notably, through the face of the viewer. Listening in on the incantation as the sonorous voice awakens the frame in ominous tremors, and riding the camera as it glides through the woods towards its hapless victims and finally jumps aboard their bodies, the viewers are drawn to inhabit the force of the narrative, becoming the very materiality that constitutes the meat of the terror invoked by the film. The true innovation of the famous track shot in the first installment of the *Evil Dead* franchise must, in this light, be attributed to the dynamic sense of movement and organic dread it incites, as many commentators have acknowledged, as well as its performative inversion of the concept, experience, and presence of evil in the medium of film. Evil, in *The Evil Dead*, is an affect that invokes and heralds the performativity of spectatorship in its trifecta: perspective, perception, and action that precede, and in turn provide, the hermeneutic ground for the ethical axiology of ill will in its exhibition. Spectatorship, by way of "Evil," becomes a crucial node that constitutes the performativity of the genre as character, in addition to the acting bodies on the screen.

Since its release in 1981, *The Evil Dead* has grown into an iconic cult piece that effectively embodies the dream of many horror film aficionados. Bringing together the comical elements of parodic splashers, relentless slashers, low-budget grotesqueries that probe into the quirkiest recesses of viewers' fears in body horror, and even serving as one of the successful precursors of the living dead frenzy the media appears to be reveling in of late, the *Evil*

Dead franchise succinctly captures the very gist of all the bumps and spooks that haunt in the night with its title alone. "Evil" is not only an abstraction but a concrete experience that propels the performative aspect of horror, and "Dead" is the ultimate product of the said evil, or, perhaps the very body of liminality whereby ethical, physical, and existential transgressions occur. All the bad stuff that terrorizes in horror films happens for a reason, however absurd (according to the unique internal logic of the narrative structure) it may be. Malevolence is perpetrated by someone or something with a clear desire to commit acts the receiver perceives as harm, given the ethical nature of the designation evil. The axiological (and therefore seemingly more immaterial than material) flavor embedded in the term "evil" stands in contrast to the corporeal crudeness the word "dead" alludes to, adding the psychological depth and foresight Ann Radcliffe sought in aesthetically sophisticated tales of fear in her hierarchy of terror and horror (41–50). Stephen King, an enthusiastic advocate of *The Evil Dead* and a faithful successor of Radcliffe's theory, addends "revulsion" as the third, most embodied and crass rhetoric of dread (25–28). Considering how the Dead (or perhaps more reminiscent of Romero's living dead, as possessed/philosophically zombified) victims of the ancient evil force in the film principally rely on abject bodies that ooze repulsive fluids, whip around twisted limbs, and emit beastly gargles, the visceral body is unquestionably a central and most effective characteristic of the film, if not entirely terrible or horrible in the way Radcliffe or King may have preferred due to its near-comical exaggeration.

Even in the eyes of those who prefer more intricate psychological thrillers minus the gore, or rather, *through* the very eyes of every spectator regardless of their intentions or taste, *The Evil Dead* delivers the height of fear in light of, or against, the ethical premise the modifier "evil" in its title carries; corruption occurs not only as the result of some arcane malice but almost as a force of nature, more akin to raw experience that precedes interpretation or agency. Moreover, its instantiation does not take form in the actions we see on the screen (the product of calculated performativity), but by and in the very present-progressive presence and engagement of the spectators. Here I am not referring to the truism that representation comes alive through the eye of the beholder; in the case of *The Evil Dead*, Evil with an uppercase "E" is an affect, with the viewers as its host. Evil, through the bodily aspect of revulsion in the film, achieves the state of affection that mediates the presence of ill-will and the material (both the living and the non-human entities used to torture them) occupants of the narrative, refusing to be subsumed under (and even preceding) the specific ordeals, emotions, desires, and intentions of the human characters or the supernatural force that takes control over their minds and bodies.

The opening shot makes it clear that the viewing experience is a most affective one that invokes non-conscious experiences falling in line with Brian Massumi's appropriative definition of affect ("prepersonal intensity corresponding to the passage from one experiential state of the body to another and implying an augmentation or diminution in that body's capacity to act" [xvii]), instead of the distanced gaze Walter Benjamin associated with the cinematic medium[1] or the "hot," visually dominant tunnel-absorption Marshall McLuhan attributed to film spectatorship.[2] The camera zooms over desolate waters, perspectivizing and perceptively performing the central hero and agent of the film (the intentional "evil" with a lowercase "e," and the viewers as its executor) with the track-shot-turned-POV-shot by the simplest maneuvers such as tilting orientations. Gliding along with the whooshing sounds of the wind on the soundtrack, audiences get the feeling that their eyes are feeling out the terrain as the perspective quizzically approaches random tree stumps and narrowly avoids them at the last minute, almost as if considering and marking its location, packing it in store for later use (which, as it turns out, proves to be a fruitful reconnaissance when we later arrive at the famous tree-rape scene). The evil force's gaze distinguishes itself from the mechanical eye of the camera, as the scenes cut back and forth between the jumbled cuts portraying the group of unsuspecting campers and the calm, focused persistence of the track shot that follows the car from the rear as it approaches the cabin.

The incantation Ash and Scotty find in the basement is the trigger—the ancient spirit of evil arises from the recording, endowing the lurking gaze of Evil with a sense of directionality and agency. That which has been merely tracking and feeling out with its probing gaze now turns into a thrashing haptic interface by enlisting the objects it has been visually caressing up until then in the following scene with Cheryl's brutalization. As in the case of the affective measure of Evil, it must be noted that the demonic possessor remains detached as a presence of its own even after its force begins to inhabit the seeing and acting bodies of the human victims, heightening the stakes of its bodily occupation by moving on from trees and non-living beings. The crackling sounds of bones crunching between the gnarling teeth of the possessed, their convulsing, distorted faces, and the guttery growls and screams escaping their mouths are more valuable objects for the gaze to relish, because of the emotional and agential involvement the mechanism of control entails. The pulsating, feeling, revolting body is all the more to be prized, precisely because of the axiological nature of its connoisseur—the evil. And with each jump and start, the spectators are fused even tighter with the gazing and feeling presence, as the performer of the evil will; while Evil, the affective experience of this possession, brings the convulsing and tormented body of the possessed to the fore, overshadowing the malice that propels its pain. The finale tells viewers that, now deprived of all its possessed apparatus and returned to its original state of immateriality, evil turns head on to devour the last constituent of the narrative in a self-annihilating fashion (namely, concluding the narrative), crashing down upon the horror-struck face of Ash. And the spectators, thus released from the parasitic grips of the hellish gaze, are left to wade in the ripples that stretch out from its presence to the unseen body of unfortunate Ash being torn apart behind the flowing credits, basking in Evil.

By establishing the affect of Evil through its focus on the sheer materiality of perspective, perception, and action that the spectators perform by proxy in the signature tracking/POV shots, *The Evil Dead* cues us in to the real horror and terror beneath the repulsive faces of the possessed on the screen—what one might call a twisted version of Hegel's insight Slavoj Žižek refers to in his commentary on our indulgence in violence and excess. The reflexive nature of Evil, Žižek asserts, "resides in the innocent gaze itself which perceives Evil all around" (56),[3] as it not only foregoes but also extends beyond the positional value the audience's gazes assign to the object. Transcribed on to the medium of the film, whereby viewers are drawn to inhabit, perform, and *be* the gaze that possesses, viewers *are* the evil—at once the possessed, and the possessor.[4]

NOTES

    1. See: Benjamin, Walter. "The Work of Art in the Age of Mechanical Reproduction."
    2. See: McLuhan, Marshall. *Understanding Media: The Extensions of Man*.
    3. Uppercase E in the original text.
    4. Special thanks to my brilliant student William Sak, who helped me brainstorm about this essay during our last session for an independent study on William Gibson's Sprawl Trilogy. Thinking about voodoo gods and cybernetic possessions shed an interesting, comparative light on the film!

WORKS CITED

Benjamin, Walter. "The Work of Art in the Age of Mechanical Reproduction." 1936, *Marxists.org*, translated by Harry Zohn, marxists.org/reference/subject/philosophy/works/ge/benjamin.htm.
King, Stephen. *Stephen King's Danse Macabre*. New York: Everest House, 1981.
Massumi, Brian. "Notes on the Translation and Acknowledgments." *A Thousand Plateaus: Capitalism and Schizophrenia*, by Gilles Deleuze and Félix Guattari, translated by Brian Massumi. University of Minnesota Press, 1987, pp. xvi-xix.
McLuhan, Marshall. *Understanding Media: The Extensions of Man*. McGraw-Hill, 1964.
Radcliffe, Ann. "On the Supernatural in Poetry." *Fantastic Literature: A Critical Reader*, edited by David Sandner. Praeger, 2004.
Raimi, Sam, director. *The Evil Dead*. Renaissance Pictures, 1981.
Žižek, Slavoj. *Welcome to the Desert of the Real! Five Essays on 11 September and Related Dates*. Verso, 2002.

The Evil Dead and Punk Rock Cinema

ALEX PITOFSKY

"It wouldn't stop. It was over the top, it was like a thunderstorm in a bottle, just relentless."
—Stephen King

Critics, film historians, and horror fanatics have often labeled *The Evil Dead* as punk rock cinema. Ian Buckwalter, for example, writes that "[Sam] Raimi's 1981 debut is a masterpiece of punk filmmaking, a bunch of young enthusiasts who barely knew what they were doing ... stumbling blindly into the creation of a ragged landmark." Jordan Richardson observes that the film was made by "punk kids looking to create something on the cheap." Similarly, *Empire Online* points out that "[p]unk kids with no formal training (and more ambition than money) have always been drawn towards low-budget horror movies ... [but] *The Evil Dead* reigns supreme, the knock-off drive-thru cheapie that became an iconic, oft-imitated classic." These and other commentators suggest that *The Evil Dead* is punk mainly for reasons relating to business and logistics: the budget was low; the director, producers, actors, and crew were inexperienced; and the principal set—a cabin in the woods near Morristown, Tennessee—was an uncomfortable, and sometimes dangerous, place to work. All of that is true, but I suspect that the most important links between *The Evil Dead* and the 1970s punk scene have to do with the creative instincts of Raimi and his collaborators.

First of all, *The Evil Dead* resembles the songs on genre-defining punk albums like *The Ramones* (1976) and *Never Mind the Bollocks, Here's the Sex Pistols* (1977) because it combines overwhelming force with rigorous minimalism. How did the group of five college students get to know one another? How did they decide to spend some time vacationing together in the woods?

Are they all close friends, or are there tensions within the group? The screenplay spends very little time addressing these questions. Punk musicians insist on taking rock and roll back to basics, shunning long songs, instrumental intros that last for more than a few seconds, self-indulgent solos, and every other feature of mainstream rock they can possibly get rid of. As Greil Marcus points out, playing punk rock in the '70s meant "stripping the music down to essentials of speed, noise, fury, and manic glee no one had been able to touch before" (452). Similarly, Raimi gets to the point right away and refuses to digress. The students arrive in the woods. They find the ancient *Book of the Dead*. Then the fury released from its pages torments the characters and shocks the audience until the last frame of the movie. Like punk rock's pioneers, Raimi and company had little experience and technical sophistication, but they turned those apparent liabilities into *The Evil Dead*'s greatest strengths. They were proud, it seems, that their work has what Stephen King describes as "simple, stupid power" (quoted in Warren 90). They implied that lavish budgets and refined craftsmanship are not all they are cracked up to be. On the contrary, those advantages frequently give rise to bland, predictable finished products. Raimi has said in interviews that he thought most of the horror films of the late '70s "didn't deliver enough" ("Sam Raimi Director"). *The Evil Dead* shows how much visceral impact can be delivered with scant funding, a cast and crew of first timers, and a primitive screenplay. Raimi's stripped down, DIY aesthetic pervades nearly every aspect of the film. The opening credits are minimal, and so is the soundtrack. Only one carpenter was hired to work on the set and props. The dialogue is extremely limited, and most of the scenes were shot in and around only two locations— the cabin in Tennessee and the cellar of a farmhouse in Michigan. The characters are presented in a straightforward way and so is the demonic force that afflicts them.

Secondly, *The Evil Dead* is akin to '70s punk because it is a work in which nothing is wasted: every shot magnifies the film's intensity. Like the explosive songs on *The Clash* (1977), *The Evil Dead* takes the form of an onslaught that starts immediately and never lets up. Two minutes into the film, the students narrowly avoid being wiped out in a collision with a truck. One minute of screen time later, their Oldsmobile almost plunges through a ramshackle wooden bridge. After they open the *Book of the Dead* and hear the professor's tape recorded incantation of Sumerian funeral rites, *The Evil Dead* brings the expression "and then all hell broke loose" to life. The audience senses that Raimi and company are determined to cram every kind of fear and brutality into an 85-minute thrill ride. As the actor Bruce Campbell recalls, "we determined, whether our movie was good or bad, to go all-out, nonstop; if we were going to make a horror film, we were terribly concerned to make a horror film with a capital H" (quoted in Warren 36). The closing credits identify *The Evil Dead* as "the ultimate experience in grueling horror," but that tagline is not really necessary. As a reviewer in *Variety* has noted, to watch *The Evil Dead* is to know that you have seen "the *ne plus ultra* of low-budget gore and shock effect" (1).

A third link between Raimi's feature-film debut and '70s punk has to do with audience demographics. *The Evil Dead* is entertainment by and for young people. Raimi was 20 when he made the film. Co-producer Robert Tapert was 24. Their work feels like punk rock in part because it is an unmistakably adolescent burst of energy, a film that seems certain to make adults grimace and shake their heads. Take, for instance, Gene Siskel and Roger Ebert's 1981 thumbs-down review of the film on *At the Movies*. Ebert cannot help laughing while Siskel summarizes the plot; then Siskel chuckles while Ebert talks about Raimi's minimalist filmmaking techniques. (To his credit, Ebert's comments about the movie's structure are right on target: "This one distills everything right down to the very basic thing. Put the kids in the cabin, throw things at them for an hour and a half, and that's the movie.") These two middle-aged, mainstream critics conclude that "the kids" have gone too far this time. They notice *The Evil Dead*'s "eye-popping" imagery and inventive camerawork, but—like the rock journalists and radio programmers who looked down on punk music in the '70s—they seem offended by Raimi's blatant indifference to subtlety and traditional notions of good taste. The reason for that is no mystery: *The Evil Dead* was not made for Siskel, Ebert, and their contemporaries. It was made for what Raimi calls "the horror crowd," young aficionados who like horror movies "awash with blood, alive with violence, graphic, gruesome, and gleeful in [their] mayhem..." (Warren 8).

The critics' laughter brings to mind another way *The Evil Dead* is comparable to old-school punk music: a great deal of dark humor is built into its intense, lurid brand of storytelling. As Raimi pointed out in an interview not long after the film became a cult sensation, *The Evil Dead* is "a comedy *and* a horror movie" ("Sam Raimi Director"). Because '70s punk was widely viewed as a brutal, threatening subversion of rock's traditions, its comic elements often went unnoticed. From Johnny Rotten babbling frantically about the Berlin Wall in "Holidays in the Sun" to the mock-misery expressed in Ramones anthems like "Pinhead" and "I Wanna Be Well," punk songs routinely mixed violence, revulsion, and humor. That combination also dominates *The Evil Dead*. A gruesome stab wound is inflicted by a character wielding a pencil. It is hard not to laugh at the buckets of multi-colored, multi-textured gore displayed in the "battles with demons" scenes. And the cheerful, Charleston-era dance music that plays in the cellar and over the final credits is ridiculously mismatched with the movie's setting, atmosphere, and subject matter. Like Vince Gilligan, the creator of *Breaking Bad*, Raimi shows a darkly amusing knack for including familiar, normally harmless objects in scenes of maximum anxiety and violence. Gilligan manages to horrify his audience with things like large plastic tubs purchased at Home Depot, a brass service bell, and a Roomba vacuuming device. Similarly, Raimi uses everyday items like that infamous pencil, an old-fashioned record player, a sketchbook, and a light bulb to make viewers' blood run cold.

Stephen King's description of *The Evil Dead*—"over the top ... like a thunderstorm in a bottle, just relentless" (20)—could serve equally well as a description of '70s punk rock. Because the movie and the musical genre have so much in common, it should come as no surprise that *The Evil Dead* is very popular in the punk underworld. Two bands, Aces & Eights and Zeke, have recorded songs titled "Evil Dead." In 1988, punk icon Iggy Pop hired Sam Raimi to direct the music video for "Cold Metal." (The video highlights the director's penchant for humor and unconventional camera movement, but some may find it surprisingly tame. Pop and Raimi seem more determined to get airplay on MTV than to convey the outrageousness and intensity their fans expected.) And in his autobiography *Commando*, the guitarist Johnny Ramone included *The Evil Dead* in a list of his ten favorite horror movies, a few places ahead of such legendary films as *Freaks* (1932) and *Psycho* (1960). If Johnny Ramone—a lifelong horror-movie fan and arguably the most influential musician punk rock has ever produced—considered Raimi's debut one of the all-time classics, we can rest assured that *The Evil Dead* has earned its reputation as a key work in punk cinema.

Works Cited

Buckwalter, Ian. "Gruesome 'Evil Dead' Does Right by its Namesake." *NPR*, 4 April 2013, npr.org/2013/04/04/176173343/gruesome-evil-dead-does-right-by-its-namesake.
Ebert, Roger, and Gene Siskel. "*Twilight Zone: The Movie/The Grey Fox/The Ruling Class.*" 25 June 1983, *At the Movies*, siskelandebert.org/video/1RWABSN2MY9B/Twilight-Zone-The-Evil-Dead-The-Grey-Fox-1983.
King, Stephen. "Evil Dead." *Rod Serling's The Twilight Zone Magazine* 2, no. 8 (1982), p. 20.
Marcus, Greil. "Anarchy in the U.K." *The Rolling Stone Illustrated History of Rock & Roll*, edited by Jim Miller. Random House/Rolling Stone Press, 1980.
Raimi, Sam, director. *The Evil Dead*. Renaissance Pictures, 1981.
Ramone, Johnny. *Commando: The Autobiography of Johnny Ramone*. Harry N. Abrams, 2012.
"Review: 'The Evil Dead.'" *Variety*, 31 December 1982, variety.com/1982/film/reviews/the-evil-dead-1200425402.
Richardson, Jordan. "*The Evil Dead* (1981)." *Canadian Cinephile*, 20 October 2013, canadiancinephile.com/2013/10/20/the-evil-dead-1981/.
"Sam Raimi Director 1982 Evil Dead Part 1." *YouTube*, interview with Sam Raimi, uploaded 6 November 2007, youtube.com/watch?v=1rDT7SwheMo.
Thomas, William. Review of *The Evil Dead*. *Empire Online*, 28 October 2015, empireonline.com/movies/evil-dead/review/.
Warren, Bill. *The Evil Dead Companion*. St. Martin's Griffin, 2000.

Horrid Addictions and Curious Cravings

EMILY D. EDWARDS

More than thirty years after *The Evil Dead* (1981) appeared in drive-ins and movie theaters, the 2013 reboot, *Evil Dead*, related a similar story about five college-aged friends in a remote mountain cabin where they find a particularly evil Sumerian grimoire with instructions for summoning supernatural entities. *Evil Dead* is a contemporary mirror of the original film with some significant changes. The five characters in the reboot correspond to those in the original, but the protagonist in the newer movie is Mia (Jane Levy), the counterpart to Ash's sister, Cheryl, in the original film. Instead of the heroic brother, Mia will be the character to confront demonic possession and death, yet remain the only member of her party to outlive the ordeal in what Carol Clover describes as the horror movie's "final girl" (35–41). Another significant change from the original film is the reason for the friends to visit the mountain cabin. Unlike the Boomers in the original, who are on a festive holiday, these Millennials gather to help Mia, a heroin addict, kick her drug dependence in a weekend devoted to detox. The dedicated friends on Mia's journey to get sober include her brother David (counterpart of Ash), his girlfriend Natalie (counterpart of Linda), Eric (counterpart of Scotty), and Olivia (counterpart of Shelly). Also along to provide comfort and companionship is the family dog, Grandpa, who has no counterpart in the original. This weekend is not meant to be a boisterous school break, but is planned as a serious gathering with serious work to do.

In the 1970s and 1980s, spring and fall breaks from college were notorious in the popular culture as alcohol and drug binges. While the original film does not emphasize the anticipated partying, it hints at the intention for some heavy drinking and drug use. On the long journey to their remote rental cabin, Scotty drives while drinking clear liquid from a Mason jar, a visual code for moonshine and recklessness. Dinner will involve toasts and decanters on the table suggesting liquor and the partying to come. Out-of-control benders were still a cliché for college breaks in 2013; however, at the beginning of the reboot, it is clear there will be no partying in this film. Mia ceremonially dumps all her drugs down a well as her friends and her brother soberly watch. "I promise never to touch this shit again," Mia declares. "Okay, let's play Cold Turkey."

To have the central character of this horror also be a drug addict is a noteworthy addition to the reboot, evoking the occult connection between drugs and mysticism as well as providing a logical but false explanation for supernatural events. Several online critics have recognized Mia's addictions as a "competent subtext" for the horror (James, Lammers, Marks, Outlaw) but have also criticized the movie for not taking advantage of the potential story elements drug addiction offers or making more use of this real-life demon once the action and gore kick into high gear (James, Marks).

Like all movies in the *Evil Dead* franchise, the 2013 film belongs to the gothic subgenre of horror, which relies on supernatural or occult elements of myth, folklore, or urban legend for its gruesome story. The narrative in *Evil Dead* depends on the abandoned belief that ancient gods, demons, or spirits inhabit the world in its mysterious, unseen dimensions and that with occult or hidden knowledge these entities can be awakened with terrible consequences. Psychological horrors depend on the murderous insanity of deranged characters, which (like Ted Bundy) can exist in the social world. Science-fiction horrors concern the madness of scientists and their devastating discoveries or destructive tampering with futuristic technologies; however, gothic horrors involve the past and remnants of abandoned religious belief. Gothic horrors are cautionary tales about terrible things that will happen to those who scorn or tamper with ancient legends, suggesting that progressive explanations of logic and science have limitations, but the dark magic of folklore offers truthful answers to the human condition (Edwards 15).

While both occult beliefs and orthodox religions share the assumption that our physical reality is not the limit of our existence, mainstream culture will uphold or at least tolerate orthodox religions, yet occult beliefs are routinely ridiculed as superstition. Clover describes the occult movie as the "spectacle" of women in the snare of supernatural evil, but the "story" of a man in crisis, because ultimately the movie will not endorse "male" practices of logic, science, and reason, but will support the paranormal account (65). Typically, the gothic horror will suggest that folklore, urban legend, and so-called old wives' tales have more accurate explanations for the dreadful events characters experience, offering audiences this warning: reason, discipline, and knowledge have shaped a fragile masculine world that will quickly crumble in the grip of a cruel, ancient, and feminine reality. Ironically, the narrative's affirmation of the supernatural provides some of the comic response to gothic horror. A movie whose story illustrates the illogical, supposedly feminine position regarding the reality of the supernatural is inherently laughable. In addition, the emotional decisions characters make in these movies are so lacking in stereotypically male reason and good sense that they have become a well recognized comic cliché. For example, the Martin Agency poked fun at horror stereotypes in their 2014 Geico commercials, reminding potential insurance customers not to make obviously stupid decisions like characters do in horror movies (McClammy). The inability to think clearly is also a trait horror-movie characters share with the drug addicts that haunt our social lives.

Since the turn of the millennium, producers have combined chemical and supernatural possession in a fair number of horror films. Movies such as *The Addiction* (1995), *Cookers* (2001), *Goth* (2003), *Ginger Snaps 2: Unleashed* (2004), *The Jackhammer Massacre* (2004), *Dark Places* (2005), *The Tripper* (2006), *Rapturious* (2007), *The Garden* (2006), *Evil Bong* (2006), *Pop Skull* (2007), *Shrooms* (2007), *Mirrors* (2008), *The Despair* (2009), *Beyond the Black Rainbow* (2010), *Enter the Void* (2009), *Lovely Molly* (2011), *The Addicted* (2012), *The Cabin in the Woods* (2012), *Comedown* (2012), *Resolution* (2012), *Toad Road* (2012), and *Housebound* (2014) are among those featuring characters whose supernatural issues are initially diagnosed as drug induced. Drugs supply one of three logical explanations for the paranormal experience: the character is crazy, dreaming, or high. Sometimes drug-using characters are seekers, actively on a quest for an aesthetic or spiritual experience. For example, in the movie *Shrooms*, American students travel to a remote wooded area of Ireland in search of mushrooms that will open the "door to other perceptions," the boundless wisdom the psychedelic experience is supposed to provide. For other horror film characters drugs are an initial escape from an oppressive reality that ultimately open a gateway to horrors of addiction and paranormal cruelty. The film *Resolution* has a similar setting to the *Evil Dead* reboot with a character helping his addict friend through drug withdrawals in a remote cabin in the woods. In the preface to a collection of essays about addiction and culture, Marc Redfield and Janet Farrell Brodie maintain that the idea of addiction is a cultural concept (1–15). Addiction exists in the structure of a human spirit that is never sufficiently free and choices that are never purely voluntary. Many different substances and behaviors are labeled addictive: shopping, work, fast food, exercise, sex, alcohol, gambling, chocolate and, of course, drugs, and the watching of violent media.

Mia's Addictions

In the 2013 reboot, a bird's-eye shot follows David's red jeep as it makes the long, winding way toward his family's beloved vacation cabin, where it seems Mia and her friends have been waiting most of the morning for David and Natalie to arrive with the keys. Olivia (a nurse) and Eric (a teacher) are David and Mia's childhood friends, not the lovers of their 1981 counterparts. Both are annoyed with David for being late now and absent from their lives in recent years. David finds his sister Mia sketching a picture of the family cabin; she is an artist just as Cheryl was in the earlier film. Filled with nostalgia, Mia reminds David, "We always loved this place." David gives his sister a necklace made from a Buckthorn tree, which is supposed to have mystical properties that will make her resolve stronger for enduring the rigors of her approaching heroin withdrawals.[1] This scene reveals that David does not believe in "superstitious stuff" but Mia does. She will wear David's gift but will later tear it from her neck during a fit of annoyance, leaving her fully vulnerable to demonic possession. However, at the end of the movie, she will find the necklace and put it on again, reclaiming resolve through restorative superstition.

After the brother and sister reunite, David realizes someone has broken the lock on the family cabin and trashed the place. Mia tells David, "Mom would have hated seeing the cabin like this." Though this cabin or one very similar to it had been a gruesome spiritual battleground in 1981, it appears the cabin has since been the home of happier memories. Not worried by the mess David declares, "Let's make this place livable." Mia immediately objects to odors in the cabin, which the others cannot smell. Olivia suggests that because Mia is at the beginning stages of her heroin withdrawal, she is extra sensitive now.

The character of Olivia is not the ride-along girlfriend that Shelly was in the original, but a recent graduate from nursing school. Because of her medical training, Olivia is the voice of authority on Mia's addictions, cautioning David that Mia has attempted the same dramatic cold turkey cure in the past, only to surrender to her addiction once withdrawal symptoms became unbearable, "in less than eight hours." This is a clue to Mia's low tolerance for the discomforts of withdrawal, which would scarcely be within the beginning stages after eight hours and normally would not peak for another 40 to 72 hours.[2] Olivia and Eric warn David that his sister must get clean because she will not survive another heroin overdose. Olivia tells David, "When she breaks, and believe me she will, we don't want to let her leave." At her last overdose, Mia died and had to be revived with defibrillation, an explanation that telegraphs what will happen to Mia in the third act.

Once inside the cabin, brother and sister wander into a bedroom, which has family photos and childhood pictures of the five friends. Mia tries to remember a lullaby their mother used to sing. David warns her not to dwell on sad memories. Mia argues that memories of their mother are not sad, yet she goes on to tell David about the emotional pain she endured during their mother's mental illness. Mia lays a guilt trip on her brother for not sharing the burden, telling David that he was lucky not to see their mother that way. Mia's grief over their mother's death also provides an explanation for her drug dependency. The heroin experience is not typically the psychedelic event users seek from drugs such as LSD, mescaline, psilocybin or cannabis, but a drug that addicts will use to self-medicate for treatment of depression, emotional abuse, or other trauma. Citing addiction studies with large sample populations, medical doctor and ex-addict Marc Lewis believes self-medication is "the essence" of addiction. The reboot presents Mia as a character trying to survive sadness and loss, not a character seeking ecstatic experience. In this way, the film abides by the popular media rhetoric that depicts white addicts as suffering from very personal trauma, which is different from the typical media depiction of black addicts suffering from systemic poverty and institutionalized racism (Pierce 168). The drugs will take Mia to the horror, but tragedy took Mia to her drugs.

Mia continues to complain about smells, but when Grandpa also notices the nasty odors and scratches at a rug, David uncovers the trapdoor to the basement and discovers blood smeared around it. It appears that whoever trashed the cabin also messed around in the cellar. David and Eric investigate and encounter rotting animal corpses hanging from the ceiling. In a basement room they also discover the *Naturom Demonto*, wrapped in garbage bags and barbed wire. Eric seems compelled to bring the book out of the cellar for closer inspection. Later he clips the barbed wire that holds the black plastic around the book and ignores warnings to "leave this book alone" and "don't say it, write it, or hear it." Eric studies the book, makes rubbings, and reads aloud the passages that will beckon evil. Through Olivia and Eric, the reboot presents different versions of the horror movie's scholar-character trope, those intellectuals whose education will not allow them to see the "paranormal truth" that is the foundation of the movie's action.

Meanwhile, Mia's withdrawal is in full progress: abdominal cramps, nausea, anxiety, and irritability. She paces around in the rain, vomiting and ripe for possession. As Clover puts it, she is now "open" enough to be the "devil's portal" (70). Mia perceives the demons and tells her brother and friends that she needs to leave the cabin now. They believe this is her withdrawal talking. When they refuse to leave, Mia decides to leave on her own, taking Eric's car and driving off, only to wreck the car as she swerves to avoid an apparition in the road. Leaving the wreckage, she encounters possessed trees and vines. The possessed vegetation entrap and rape Mia, just as they raped Cheryl in 1981, allowing the demons to take control of her body. The demons seem to need direct contact, physically invading the body in order to possess it. Convinced she is deep in withdrawal, David finds Mia and brings her back to the cabin. After his possessed sister kills the family dog and scalds herself in the shower, David does try to take Mia to a hospital, but flooded roads prevent it. They return to the cabin, where Mia shoots and wounds David, then predicts that everyone will die. She proceeds to vomit in Olivia's mouth, spreading possession like a disease. After this point, Mia's heroin withdrawal is no longer an active part of the film's discourse.

Mia bites Natalie, infecting her and forcing the men to battle three demon-polluted women. In the end, Mia will be "purified" through processes of fire, death and burial. David revives her with a homemade version of defibrillation, but she survives only to watch as her brother and a possessed Eric die, while flames engulf the family cabin. As a bloody rain falls, Mia engages a demon in one last battle, where she loses her hand, but manages to dismember the demon before wandering alone into the woods. The moral of the story: like demonic possession, drug addiction will put your friends and family through hell.

The demons of *Evil Dead* are themselves addicts with irresistible cravings for human misery. Some media theorists argue that audiences may have similar cravings. Audiences seek to become engrossed in the ecstasy of a media "high" (Roberts 340) but horror violence provides an additional kick for some (Barbiero, Johnston). In the documentary *The Killing Screens* (1997) the famous media violence researcher, George Gerbner, compares violent media contents to an addictive drug, claiming that American entertainment is so flooded with violent representation that producers must increase subsequent "dosages" of mayhem in order to achieve desired effects. According to Gerbner's research, it may not be Mia as much as her audiences who are addicted.

Millennials and Addictive Pleasures of the Torture Chamber

The target audience for the original film, *The Evil Dead*, was Baby Boomers, people born in the two decades after World War II and coming of age in the era of the drive-in, a favorite place for teens and young adults to gather, party, and meat-market. The filmmakers intentionally kept the pace fast and the bloodletting furious to appease this young audience. The horror genre has always had an appeal for young viewers, with the largest number of viewers in the 18–34 age range. However, this popularity for horror tells us very little about viewer approval of the ideologies or values the film presents (Renner 111) nor does it reveal how Millennials found gratification in the remake of a film more than 30 years old. Apparently they did. Grossing out its audience allowed the movie to gross US$26 million in its opening weekend, leading competitors and easily returning its US$17 million investment (Smith).

There is considerable speculation about what drives audiences to any horror movie. Rutgers University professor of anthropology, Lionel Tiger, suggests that as descendants of hunter-gatherers who were also the prey of other hunting carnivores, human beings are hard-wired to pay attention to violence, though this may not explain the enduring popularity of stories about human misery and why a young, hard-core fan base seeks it out while others actively avoid it. Dolf Zillman and his colleagues put forward a "snuggle theory," suggesting that horror movies function as heterosexual gender socialization. Males enjoyed a horror film more when their female companions were upset, while females enjoyed watching horror more when their male companions displayed bravery (586–594). Several factors may combine to provide audience gratification: tension (created through suspense, gore and shock), relevance (which can be universal, cultural, or personal) and the knowledge that the events on screen are not real (Walters). The same audiences that could not stomach violent documentary footage showing cows at the slaughterhouse would be happy to watch a horror movie and maybe laugh as characters are disemboweled in an orgy of blood (Haidt, McCauley, and Rozin). Fear may be conceived as a positive emotion when explored in a horror movie and may also desensitize the viewer to violent content (Bantinaki 383–392). In a seminar on morbid curiosity, Jack Haskins and his colleagues suggested that morbidly curious audiences could be sensation seeking, looking for an escape from boredom. Audience motivations may exist at an "unconscious level of needs, drives, instincts and urges" (28).

In order to better understand the gratifications audiences found in the *Evil Dead* reboot, I interviewed fourteen Millennials who self-identified as fans of both *Evil Dead* films (8 men, 6 women). Six additionally claimed to be fans of the entire movie franchise. All of the subjects were college students. Although this is not a random sample and their responses cannot be generalized to the larger population of horror movie fans, their responses and interpretations of the film's text suggest that some of the ideas regarding audience attraction/addiction to horror may have validity.[3]

Thirteen of the interviewed fans said they went to see the reboot because they were fans of the original film. Only one respondent saw the reboot first, which inspired him to search out and watch the original movie. One respondent saw the film with his family, mentioning that his father was an avid horror enthusiast. Most respondents saw the film with a group of friends or at least one other person. As one female respondent suggested, "Horror movies are the most fun when they are watched with other people at the theater or on somebody's big flat screen … like riding a rollercoaster, it's just more fun when you're with other people so you can all scream together." Another male respondent added that, "Horror works best in a theater atmosphere because of the good sound and other people around you make you more connected to the film." Another respondent explained that part of the fun of horror movies is the tension of knowing jump scares are coming but getting caught off guard when they happen and hearing the reactions of others who were also caught off guard. There was nothing in the responses to support a heterosexual "snuggle theory" in their attraction to the film. One female spectator said *Evil Dead* was a fun group activity but she would not consider it the best date movie.

Respondents seemed to like the changes in the reboot, saying these variations kept the movie "cringe-worthy." Respondents did not consider the reboot more violent than the original but thought the production values were better, though several respondents added that they liked the rugged aesthetics of the original. Most appreciated Mia as the protagonist and thought her drug problem was interesting. One male respondent said addiction provided "a reason for the remake," but added, "I missed Ash. Ash was bad-ass." A female respondent said, "I didn't identify with Mia but I did have concern for her. I had seen the original and knew she was going to die, so her survival was a nice surprise. I fully expected that David would be the one to survive. The rain of blood at the end reminded me of *Carrie* but Mia is nothing like Carrie.... Mia's violence is not her fault. She isn't looking for revenge. She loves her brother and her friends. She can't help her addiction or her possession." A male respondent said drug addiction "…showed Mia's inner evil. It didn't take much for her to be corrupted." A female respondent added, "Horror movies always show a lot of pot and beer. It's an excuse to torture corrupt characters…. We [Millennials] had to go through DARE programs, and drugs are more serious these days, especially the heavy drugs like heroin. Today you have to worry about dirty drugs, AIDS, and crime, so no more Age of Aquarius." Another woman added, "Mia wasn't a weak character. She survives. I guess heroin addiction makes you tough … but her heroin problem made this a dark movie from the beginning." Another female respondent disagreed, "Mia was weak, turning to drugs because of her emotional pain … but, she was trying to fix her problems, so she was the excuse for the movie to happen." Five of the male respondents said Mia's addictions gave the movie a purpose or provided an interesting metaphor. Another male respondent added that the drug element, "…made this film more serious than any of the others [in the franchise]."

The two elements respondents disliked the most about the reboot were Mia's rape in the woods and Grandpa's death. Said one man, "I didn't like that [rape] scene in the original and hated it equally in the reboot." Another connected Mia's rape to her drug use, saying the scene made more sense in the reboot than in the original because of the drugs, but he still did not like it. Grandpa's death was perhaps the most disliked element. Even though respondents knew that the dog was not really hurt, they did not like the idea of killing his character. "It was unnecessary to kill Grandpa or even to have a dog. Mia smelled the odor; she could have just pulled back the rug." Other respondents added that animals are innocent and should not be killed for a plot point. Said one man, "It's just lousy to watch a dog get bludgeoned to death." A woman agreed, "That made me hate Mia, even though demons had replaced the drugs in her system and I knew she couldn't help it." Another male respondent said, "It's not so upsetting when human characters die, but you don't enjoy seeing animals hurt." These responses suggest that audiences may not be reacting to documentary versus fictional violence, but to the idea of violence against animals. Americans, Millennials in particular, may see dogs as substitute children that must be protected (Ferdman).

Respondents objected to the idea that watching horror was addictive. One man explained, "I don't *have* to watch horror movies. I *like* to watch horror movies. I can go for months without watching any horror at all." Another man offered this, "You put yourself out there when you go to watch a horror movie. A good jump scare gets your heart pumping. The characters on the screen may be dead, but you know you're alive." A woman suggested that exploring worst case and impossible scenarios in horror movies made real problems seems less serious, "If you can watch Mia cut off her own hand, normal shit like a midterm isn't so bad, but I don't think there's anything addictive about watching it." One man added, "I thought the second movie was a tornado of energy and insanity. This is what you go to horror movies to see." One fan admitted that he knew he was not as likely to be bored watching horror films. "I'm not hooked on horror movies, but they are exciting." If horror cinema, like drug use, is a form of escape and source of visions, it also creates a social bond that differentiates users from the average person. The respondents suggested that there was a "cool factor" to watching horror movies; it means that the viewer is also "bad-ass."

The representation of Mia's withdrawal in *Evil Dead* clearly contributes to what Maurizio Viano calls the "schizophrenic" film history of drug-addicted characters following the escalation of the War on Drugs in the 1980s. The vision of drug withdrawal in the reboot is even more over-the-top than the frenzied, drug-induced tragedies of the famous anti-drug propaganda film, *Reefer Madness* (1936). In "Cinema of Intoxication and Addiction," the movie representation of drugs and addicts creates a context for "Zero Tolerance" (Viano 135). Given the conservative nature of most horror films, wherein guilty characters are punished for their social transgressions, Mia suffers plenty. She literally becomes the nonhuman "malignant essence" of Henry Cole's description of the opium eater. This message is not lost on the film's young fans. In the end, Mia must be brought back to her miserable life, for there is no continued suffering or contrition in the grave and limited possibilities for sequels.

Notes

1. Like its botanical relative the Hawthorn, the Buckthorn is associated with several superstitious beliefs. These are not detailed in the movie but broadly suggested. For example, ancient Greeks believed chewing the bark of the Buckthorn would banish evil spirits of the dead. See Mona A. and Edwin Radford, *Encyclopedia of Superstitions* (54). Also, fastening the branches to doors and windows was also supposed to keep out witches, so it follows that wearing a necklace made of Buckthorn bark would hinder possession (145).

2. There are several documentaries dealing with the symptoms of heroin addiction and withdrawal. Two readily available ones are Discovery Channel's *Heroin Nation*, which has segments streaming on YouTube and HBO's *Dope Sick Love*. Although Mia complains to her brother about how bad she looks, Mia is nothing like the gaunt, toothless addicts portrayed in these documentaries.

3. The subjects included in these informal interviews were recruited from three undergraduate media courses and constitute a convenience sample. These subjects were not offered any compensation for their participation. These subjects signed up for the interviews, which were held on campus in a faculty office during specific time slots between February 27 and March 27, 2015. Four of the subjects were not students in these classes but fans who had heard about the study and either accompanied friends who had signed up for an interview or just dropped by the office inquiring about the study and volunteering participation. Not all students who had signed up to interview actually arrived for their time slot, so the sample includes these unrecruited volunteers. All the subjects were Millennials (born between 1982 and 2004). Core questions in the interview dealt with: how the subjects came to see the movie and the viewing context, their strongest memory from the reboot, their responses to Mia as protagonist and Mia's addictions, their thoughts while watching the film's "high gore" moments, their least favorite moment from the reboot, and their general ideas about why people can be drawn to horror as a genre.

Works Cited

Álvarez, Fede, director. *Evil Dead*. TriStar Pictures, 2013.
Bantinaki, Katerina. "The Paradox of Horror: Fear as a Positive Emotion." *Journal of Aesthetics and Art Criticism* 70, no. 4 (2012), pp. 383–392.
Barbiero, Elena. "Addiction and Type-T Personality: Addicted to Horror." *HealthGuidance.org*, healthguidance.org/entry/16460/1/Addiction-and-Type-T-Personality-Addicted-to-Horror.html.
Benson, Justin, and Aaron Moorhead, directors. *Resolution*. Tribeca Film, 2012.
Breathnach, Patty, director. *Shrooms*. Potboiler Productions, 2007.
Brodie, Janet Farrell, and Marc Redfield, editors. *High Anxieties: Cultural Studies in Addiction*. University of California Press, 2002.
Clover, Carol. *Men, Women and Chainsaws: Gender in the Modern Horror Film*. Princeton University Press, 1992.
Cole, Henry. *Confessions of an American Opium Eater*. Boston, 1895, gutenberg.org/ebooks/2040.
Conte, Felice, director. *Dope Sick Love*. HBO, 2005.
Edwards, Emily. *Metaphysical Media: The Occult Experience in Popular Culture*. Southern Illinois University Press, 2005.
Ferdman, Roberto A. "Americans Are Having Dogs Instead of Babies." *Quartz*, 10 Apr. 2014, qz.com/197416/americans-are-having-dogs-instead-of-babies/.
Gerbner, George, et al. "Cultural Indicators: Violence Profile No. 9." *Journal of Communication* 28, no. 3 (Sept. 1978), pp. 176–207.
Haidt, Jonathan, et al. "Individual Differences in Sensitivity to Disgust: A Scale Sampling Seven Domains of Disgust Elicitors." *Personality and Individual Differences* 16, no. 5 (1994), pp. 701–713.
Haskins, Jack, et al. *Morbid Curiosity and the Mass Media: Proceedings*. Gannett Foundation, School of Journalism, University of Tennessee-Knoxville, 1984.
Heroin Nation. Discovery Channel, 2009, topdocumentaryfilms.com/heroin-nation/.

James, Jonathan. "Review: *Evil Dead.*" *Daily Dead: Horror and Scifi Magazine*, 24 Mar. 2013, dailydead.com/review-evil-dead/.
Jhally, Sut, director. *The Killing Screens*. Media Education Foundation, 1997.
Johnston, Deirdre D. "Adolescents' Motivations for Viewing Graphic Horror." *Human Communication Research* 21, no. 4 (1995), pp. 522–552.
Lammers, Tim. "Review: New *Evil Dead* Bloody Good Time." *Bring Me the News*, 5 Apr. 2013.
Lewis, Marc. "Addiction as Self-Medication: Brain Patterns Formed by Trauma Sometimes Need Fixing—At Any Price." *Psychology Today*, 22 Aug. 2012.
Marks, David. "*Evil Dead* (2013)—Big on Blood, Short on Creep." *Blog of the Living Dead*, 7 Apr. 2013.
McClammy, Wayne, director. "It's What You Do." Geico Commercial, The Martin Agency, 2014.
Outlaw, Kofi. "*Evil Dead* Review: Remakes Don't Get Much Better Than This—In Terms of Revitalizing the Franchise and Servicing both Veteran and Newcomer Viewers." *Screen Rant*, 15 Nov. 2014, screenrant.com/evil-dead-reviews-2013/.
Pierce, Todd G. "Gen-X Junkie: Ethnographic Research with Young White Heroin Users in Washington, D.C." *Cocktails & Dreams: Perspectives on Drug and Alcohol Use*, edited by Wilson R. Palacios. Pearson Prentice Hall, 2005.
Radford, Mona A., and Edwin Radford. *Encyclopedia of Superstitions*. Philosophical Library, 1949.
Raimi, Sam, director. *The Evil Dead*. Renaissance Pictures, 1981.
Renner, Karen J. "Generational Conflict, Twenty-First-Century Horror Films and the Cabin in the Woods." *The Millennials on Film and Television: Essays on the Politics of Popular Culture*, edited by Betty Kaklamanidou and Margaret Tally. McFarland, 2014.
Roberts, Mark. "Addicts without Drugs: The Media Addiction." *High Culture: Reflections on Addiction and Modernity*, edited by Anna Alexander and Mark S. Roberts. State University of New York Press, 2003.
Smith, Grady. "Box Office Report: *Evil Dead* Brings Life to Industry with $26 Million Debut." *Entertainment Weekly*, 7 Apr. 2013, ew.com/article/2013/04/07/box-office-report-evil-dead/.
Tiger, Lionel. "The Danger Vitamin." *Morbid Curiosity and the Mass Media: Symposium Proceedings*, Gannett Foundation, School of Journalism, University of Tennessee–Knoxville, 1984, pp. 182–206.
Viano, Maurizio. "An Intoxicated Screen: Reflections on Film and Drugs." *High Anxieties: Cultural Studies in Addiction*, edited by Janet Farrell Brodie and Marc Redfield. University of California Press, 2002.
Walters, Glenn D. "Understanding the Popular Appeal of Horror Cinema: An Integrated Model." *Journal of Media Psychology* 9, no. 2 (May 2004).
Zillmann, Dolf, James B. Weaver, Norbert Mundorf, and Charles F. Aust. "Effects of an Opposite-Gender Companion's Affect to Horror on Distress, Delight and Attraction." *Journal of Personality and Social Psychology* 51, no. 3 (Sept. 1986), pp. 586–594.

Dismembering, Repeating and Working-Through

Queer Disability and Neoliberal Crises of Deracination in Sam Raimi's Evil Dead *Trilogy*

CLAYTON J. PLAKE

With characteristic bravado, an aging Ash Williams (Bruce Campbell), proffers sexual services in lieu of payment to a young truck-stop server named Nancy (Rachel Blampied) midway through the first season of *Ash vs. Evil Dead* (2015–2018), adding, as proof of his sexual acumen, that the loss of his right hand has made the other "extra sensitive." While Nancy quite understandably has no interest in the proposition, this scene ought to be of immense interest to us. In it, Ash, in insisting that he literally embodies the ableist notion that the disabled body may develop miraculous sensory capabilities to compensate for its perceived deficiency, seeks to mask the financial insecurity that would undermine his white masculinity. Here, Ash actually re-asserts his claim to it through his disability by deeming it proof of his virility. We see something very similar in the films that inspired the series. I hold that Sam Raimi's manipulation of persistently reoccurring representations of disability in the *Evil Dead* trilogy transform monstrously queer and disabled bodies into sites along which white male fears regarding a destabilization of subjectivity are represented and negotiated. Ultimately, watching Ash overcome the somatic traumas of demonic possession and other bodily injuries renders these films an extended fantasy in which the traumas associated with the destructive neoliberal turn of the latter twentieth century are replaced with the promise of a recuperated white masculinity.

Hell to Pay: Reaganite Assaults, Neoliberal Nightmares and the Body Disabled

Disability's presence in modern horror remains largely unconsidered. Theorizing disability therein begins with exploring the socially contingent ways in which disabled bodies have been literally and figuratively viewed. In a visual context where able-bodiedness is the unspoken norm (Galusca 141–3; Murphy 140–2), the disabled body is at once a problem body and a queer body. Its existence equals interruption and inversion.[1] "Disability," contends Lennard J. Davis, constitutes "a disruption in the visual, auditory, or perceptual field as it relates the power of the gaze" (129). Disability's stubborn tenacity within a discourse constantly seeking its erasure "disrupts narrative equilibrium," setting "in motion a questioning of the status quo and even" as Harry M. Benshoff famously theorizes the queer, "the nature of reality itself" (5). As a result, the "rebellion of the visual" the disabled body signifies, like any queer body, "must be regulated, rationalized, [and] contained" (Davis 129). Like the photographs of disabled bodies that provide "an opportunity for viewers to witness spectacles of bodily difference without fear of recrimination" (Snyder & Mitchell 180–1), disability's filmic representation proffers a form of containment through transforming it into a trope. Robbed of any opportunity for counter-expression, the disabled body thusly becomes a screen for able-bodied fantasies, or what Rosemarie Garland-Thomson calls "a repository for social anxieties about such troubling concerns as vulnerability, control, and identity" (6). Raimi's films use disability to negotiate anxieties stemming from the neoliberal turn that gained momentum during the Reagan years.

As more than one critic has noted, white masculinity is discursively associated with dominance, success in competition, and interrelated forms of independence (Kimmel *Manhood* 26–7; Roediger 19–20). Such traits are also contingent upon what one critic has called a "compulsory able-bodiedness" (McRuer 3). The drive for market deregulation under Reagan decimated gains made by redistributive social movements during earlier decades that had allowed many working white men to maintain the self-sufficiency integral to preserving their identities. The interlocking oppressions so essential to capitalism guaranteed that the neoliberal assault most severely impacted communities who were already suffering. But neoliberalism's destructive momentum was so great that even some white men experienced economic and other hardships at levels that were unprecedented in the period following World War 2 (Wacquant 41–8).[2] Unemployment rates spiked dramatically as jobs were taken from workers in the U.S. and shipped overseas where poor populations in economically depressed regions would perform the same tasks for a lower wage and at greater physical risk (Fletcher

89). The development and proliferation of new forms of technology in certain sectors also displaced workers as production was further rationalized and global circuits of capital accumulation expanded due to technical "innovation" (Moody 26–36). These changes coincided domestically with a dramatic decrease in wages for both union and non-union workers (Western & Rosenfeld 513–14). Additionally, diminished external oversight of workplace conditions led to a steady increase in work-related injuries, including fatalities, in roughly the same period (Wood 72–5). In a cultural context where white masculinity is equated with autonomy, economic stability and able-bodied virility, neoliberalism imperiled white male subjectivity through attacking the security the positionality guaranteed, rendering perceptions of self and future equally uncertain.

Raimi's trilogy takes as its primary vehicle for ableist fantasy the once able body diminished by injury or accident as an expression of these subjective uncertainties. As Paul Darke notes, this body-become-disabled is uniquely positioned in cinematic representation. "The body that becomes disabled in films," Darke holds, "is routinely devalued and degraded by the creation, intimation, or presentation of a glorious past or alternative normality seen in parallel with an abject present" (98). On one level, this is precisely the dichotomy on which much of Raimi's trilogy relies for its capacity to frighten and engage viewers: watching the young Ash and his companions experience fates ranging from possession and dismemberment to death in *The Evil Dead* (1981) and *Evil Dead 2* (1987) terrifies us through proffering the parallel view of which Darke speaks.[3] But, in Raimi's first two films, the body disabled also becomes a representation of neoliberalism's destructive effects, with the body's sudden, violent transformation emblematic of the manifold sudden and violent changes neoliberal restructuring incited.

Animated Monsters: The Bodily Economy of Possession in The Evil Dead *and* Evil Dead 2

In the *Evil Dead* trilogy, demonic possession is the first form in which the abuses of the neoliberalized market materialize. Though it has been totally overlooked in considerations of possession in modern horror, disability has historically been equated with infernal infestation of the body. In the *Psychosocial Aspects of Disability*, George Henderson and Willie Bryan inform us that "mental illness and physical afflictions were generally viewed as the work of evil ... spirits" that were punishing the afflicted individual (quoted in Norden 4–5). Throughout Raimi's trilogy, possession is similarly associated with physical incapacity. In the first instance of human possession we see, when the Force inhabits Cheryl's (Ellen Sandweiss) arm and forces her to draw a crude version of the *Necronomicon*, Cheryl's movements evoke the rigidity medically associated with certain orthopedic disabilities. John Kenneth Muir actually refers to Cheryl's initial possession as a "seizure," oddly evoking antiquated associations of epilepsy and similar physical differences with otherworldly contact (31). The monstrous physical deformities and loss of bodily control that accompany Scotty (Hal Delrich), Linda (Betsy Baker), and Cheryl's possession in *The Evil Dead*, and that of Ash and others in *Evil Dead 2*, clearly equate possession with physical disability. Representing possession even induced temporary physical impairments in the cast: Ellen Sandweiss recalls that the contact lenses their characters wore made them nearly blind (quoted in Muir 44). More than simply reiterating the equation of disability with monstrosity, possession also carries an economic dimension. Marx famously holds that work robs the laboring body of its autonomy, making it "subservient to and led by an alien will and an alien intelligence" that commands it in a clear evocation of demonic possession (*Grundrisse* 470). Given that neoliberalism is an intensification of earlier forms of capitalist exploitation (Smith 261–2), the possessed bodies in Raimi's films represent the neoliberal market's foul possession of working bodies to which Marx draws our attention.[4]

Although Ash presents a unique exception, the recurring tropes of physical injury and dismemberment likewise mirror neoliberal violence. Interestingly, Marx evokes images of dismemberment as well as possession in describing capitalist exploitation. "The 'free' laborer," so Marx maintains, "sells his very self, and that by fractions" (*Labor* 20). Though Marx is talking about hours of the worker's life, and not her or his physical body, Marx is also calling our attention to what David McNally terms "the corporeal realities" of economic exploitation. "In dividing labor processes into ever-smaller motions that can be repeated with ever-greater speed," says McNally, "capitalist manufacture anatomizes the laboring body," cutting it into more manageable portions (139). In the *Evil Dead* films, the multiple scenes of dismemberment and injury, and the repeated emphases upon the unnatural, autonomous movement of severed hands and limbs, evoke how capital routinely fragments the exploited body through equating the process with disability and death. Raimi's reliance upon intercut extreme close-ups to register the violence intensifies this fragmentation, visually reducing whole bodies to individual pieces. The frenetic pace of this excessive violence reveals that neoliberalism's intensification of prevailing forms of exploitation is the source of the films' deeper anxieties.

Demonic possession, dismemberment, and other bodily injuries serve as the primary source of horror in the trilogy's first two films because of the way the queered bodies thusly produced disrupt white, able-bodied masculine subjectivity. As Barbara Creed notes, in films "depicting invasion by the devil, the victim is almost always a young girl, the invader the male devil" (32). The same gender dynamic initially prevails in *The Evil Dead*. The deeply disturbing scene in which the Evil Force brutally rapes Cheryl prior to her possession preserves its phallic and penetrative connotations. Yet, in what becomes its equal appetite for both male and female bodies, a polymorphous desire animates the Force that queers the gender binary that Creed mentions. The Force's disabling possession of Cheryl's body creates a triangulation in which a lethally queer desire is visually positioned against the normative identities of two white, able-bodied, heterosexual couples and the reproductive potential they represent as the possessed Cheryl hovers before Ash, Linda, Scotty, and Shelly. In Raimi's films, the Force's hunger is all the more terrifying because, like the neoliberal market's rapacious appetite, its indiscriminate bloodlust inverts white manhood and challenges the social relations that have traditionally upheld it. It is possessed women whose subsequent attacks emasculate Ash and Scotty, who will each be placed in positions that parallel Cheryl's violation early on in the film to signal their emasculation. When the Force finally reanimates Linda's corpse, and Ash decapitates her with a shovel, Linda falls upon him in what Campbell himself calls a simulated sex act, replete with convulsive thrusts and a dreadful, blood-soaked climax. Ash's screaming, prone body combines with the fast-cutting and predominantly high-angle shots here to recall Cheryl's rape. Ash is violated in a direct affront to his masculinity. Later on, a horribly injured Scotty will return near death after a failed escape attempt. Unable to walk, Scotty, who once cruelly mocked Cheryl, is now the object of the possessed Cheryl's derision. His gory dishabille (his bloodied trousers are torn in back, invoking the possibility of sodomy, and recall that the possessed Shelly called him "pretty" earlier) suggests that the Force has also violated, disabled, and feminized him in a distorted representation of the neoliberalized market's assaults upon white male subjectivity.

The Force continues its destabilizing rampage in *Evil Dead 2*. The second Linda's (Denise Bixler) possession early on once again establishes demonic possession's traditional gender hierarchy only to subvert it. In Raimi's sequel, it is Ash who the Force then violates to satisfy its rapacious hunger. At *The Evil Dead*'s close, a wide-angle POV shot sends the Force barreling through the rear of the cabin and into Ash's open mouth, suggesting that the Force has violated him orally. This scene is revisited and extended in *Evil Dead 2*, where the Force not only orally penetrates Ash, but also levitates, spins, and slams his prostrate body onto the forest floor. When Ash regains consciousness, a close-up of his monstrously transformed face reveals that he is now possessed. Although the dawn's light saves him, the scene's framing suggests that the Force has entered Ash from behind in an act of emasculating penetration.

In *Evil Dead 2*, the Force is equated again with an insatiable queer desire that upends white masculine subjectivity and the social relations supporting it. This expresses itself most forcefully in the scene when a terrified Ash, who just moments before had been playing an upright piano and watching while a semi-nude Linda performed an impromptu ballet routine, watches as the Force compels her reanimated corpse to dance in the moonlight. Where once Ash effectively controlled Linda's body through the music he played, the Force has now robbed Ash of the masculine sway he once held over Linda's feminine form. Later, the Force will literally consume the hyper-masculine Jake (Dan Hicks) in a graphically visual depiction of neoliberal capital's metaphoric consumption of the white male body, but not before Annie (Sarah Berry) accidentally penetrates him with the vulgarly phallic Kandarian dagger, reducing him to a state of helplessness reminiscent of Scotty's in *The Evil Dead*. The Force also transforms Annie's deceased mother Henrietta (Lou Hancock) into a disabled terror. As if to underscore the Force's queering effect, Raimi's brother Ted replaces Hancock as the possessed Henrietta, hobbling about encased in a polyurethane/foam-rubber suit replicating her bloated body in a move that also emphasizes the fungibility of able-bodied gendered identity (Warren 123). Throughout *Evil Dead 2*, the Force again queers and upsets the social relations that once supported white, able-bodied masculinity, evoking anxieties that neoliberalism's ever-encroaching effects produced.[5]

"Hail to the King, Baby": Rescuing White Manhood in Evil Dead 2 *and* Army of Darkness

Though not immune to the vile Force, Ash's relation to it merits special consideration. Because Raimi's trilogy only challenges neoliberalism insofar as it challenges white masculinity, Raimi grants Ash what, borrowing from Robert McRuer, I call a "flexibility" that is denied other characters. Flexibility is not to be confused with transgressive queer fluidity or postmodernism's infatuation with fragmented subjectivities. "Under neoliberalism," McRuer maintains, "individuals who are indeed 'flexible and innovative' make it through moments of subjective crisis. They *manage* the crisis, or at least show … management potential; ultimately, they adapt and perform as if the crisis had never happened" (17). Neoliberal attacks on white masculinity thusly become means of recuperating and proving that very subjectivity in a fanciful reimagining that insures conformity and consent. In the *Evil Dead* trilogy, Raimi fashions out of Ash's struggle for bodily mastery a fantasy of recovering a modified, more flexible masculinity that has adapted to, rather than rebelled against, neoliberalism's demands. Attaining this modified subjectivity, however, also entails preserving, as opposed to overturning, the neoliberal order.

Along with the queer, disabled bodies that endanger it, Ash's struggle to save his white masculine subjectivity is another key source of horror in the *Evil Dead* trilogy. Whereas modern horror's terrorized protagonist is frequently female, Bruce Campbell reveals that Raimi's decision to cast him in this stereotypically "female" role was intended to make the initial films "even more terrifying." Raimi's logic was that "if you could reduce a man to scrambling and screaming and yelling ... it would be even more horrifying than a woman doing that" (quoted in Warren 36–7). Raimi effectively "feminizes" Ash only to dramatize his attainment of the manhood that he initially lacked in what Campbell characterizes as Ash's journey from "'cowardly wimp' to 'leader of men'" (173). Ash's struggle to regain his embattled white male subjectivity animates the mirror scenes that materialize in all three of Raimi's films. In *The Evil Dead*, a newly solitary Ash stands before a mirror on the cabin wall. He touches his bruised face and then reaches out to touch his reflection, only to have his hand pass through the mirror's surface like water. Ash's terrified screams register his fear upon confronting the instability of his own subjectivity due to the Force's queering effects. In *Evil Dead 2*, Ash again stands before a mirror, but with a crucial difference: this time, his crazed reflection leaps out of the mirror and attempts to choke him to death. The camera tracks back and up out of what first appeared to be a first-person subjective shot aligning us with Ash's sinister twin only to reveal that Ash is literally struggling with himself. Where once Ash is passive against the Force, here Ash is actively battling it. In *Army of Darkness*, Ash must fight miniature doppelgängers that spring from shards of a broken full-length mirror. In the ensuing melee, one jumps down Ash's throat and develops into a full-grown personage—"bad Ash"—from whom "good Ash" separates and who, as necrotized leader of the Deadite horde, "good Ash" will battle at the film's end. The trilogy's final installment makes clear what was implicit all along: to recover his endangered white, able-bodied manhood, Ash must be flexible. He must be willing to sever and destroy that part of himself that is "weak," "feminine," and susceptible to the Force's disabling violation.

Ash's uncannily Freudian struggle follows an earlier, more gruesome separation of the self: willful self-dismemberment. After a penetrative bite from the possessed Linda's severed head in *Evil Dead 2*, the Force infests Ash's right hand, endowing it with murderous intentions. Initially, Ash appears distraught to the point of tears ("You bastards," he half-demands-half-begs, "give me back my hand!"). Eventually, Ash shoves a kitchen knife through the demonic appendage, pinning it to the cabin floor before using a chainsaw to sever his hand at the wrist. Raimi again offers us a graphic moment of masculinizing transformation. In a vulgarly phallic power reversal, where once the Force penetrated Ash, Ash has now penetrated it. In this moment, Ash transitions from an emasculated object in the Force's possession to asserting masculine dominance over it. But Ash's assertion carries a price; he must literally relinquish a part of himself and, along with that, his extant self-concept. He must adapt. True, Ash's self-mutilation is a moment of pure horror. "Who's laughing now?" Ash exclaims, his face in extreme close-up as it becomes drenched in his own blood and his amplified screams echo over the chainsaw's motor. Yet the humorous events surrounding the scene obviate its impact. Prior to, and after Ash's doing of the grisly deed, he and his possessed hand engage in physical battles evoking *Tom and Jerry* and *The Three Stooges* (Muir 115). Ash's war against his Lilliputian twins in *Army of Darkness* has likewise been called a "dark Warner Brothers cartoon" (quoted in Warren 153). McRuer's observations allow us to understand the comedy: "Attention must be drawn to the crisis in order for the resolution to be visible," he argues, "but to draw too much attention to the subjective crisis" is to undermine the same embattled subjectivity (17). In Raimi's films, the comedy mitigating the horror of these scenes distracts us. Ash's interlocking somatic and ontological crises become more acceptable to the viewer as they shift from expressions of neoliberal horrors into the crucible that proves Ash's newly minted manhood.[6]

In its odd assertion of masculine agency, Ash's self-inflicted disability becomes, not a debilitating limitation, but a conduit to new forms of embodied white masculine power that disavow neoliberalism's destructive impact. Most immediately, Ash's modified body allows for a reimagined relationship to technologies of mechanization. Raimi's brother Ivan reveals that the pair had always been fascinated with the idea of "technology vs. the supernatural," and so they "wanted to make a movie idolizing technology, saying it can defeat the supernatural" (quoted in Warren 142–3). In *Evil Dead 2* and *Army of Darkness*, the "high technology" that threatened able-bodied white manhood because it "exacerbated the de-skilling process, led to greater unemployment, and to the intensification of the exploitation of labor" becomes another mode of reinvigorated masculine self-expression for Ash (Berberoglu 41). An iconic series of fast cuts in *Evil Dead 2* show us that Ash (with Annie's help) has used his technical acumen to affix the famous chainsaw where his hand formerly was. Ash's fragmented, disabled body is transformed into a seamless combination of man and machine, a visual metaphor for the harmonious synthesis of humanity and technology that belies neoliberal mechanization's exploitative effects. Raimi further develops this metaphor in *Army of Darkness*. In preparing for his quest to attain the *Necronomicon*, Ash, with help from an anonymous blacksmith (Timothy Patrick Quills), transforms a steel gauntlet into a fully functional prosthesis in another series of fast cuts. We soon learn that Ash's robotic hand allows him superhuman strength: a rack shot in extreme close-up shows the robo-hand effortlessly crushing a metal goblet. The camera zooms forward to focus upon both Sheila (Embeth

Davidtz) and the blacksmith's awestruck faces. The two-shot showing us Sheila and the blacksmith does more than emphasize their shared surprise. It suggests that Ash is an object of desire for both; the blacksmith's feminized position alongside Sheila communicates that Ash, in essence, is a more of a man than he is. Throughout *Army of Darkness*, Ash uses his superior mechanical proficiency to mock and terrorize the medievalites, referring to them as "savages," "primates," and "primitive screw-heads." The technological innovation that effectively "unmanned" Ash in the modern world allows him access to an unparalleled power in Arthurian England. Ultimately, it is Ash's knowledge of basic chemistry that allows him to lead the medievalites to victory over the Deadites in battle, at one point even charging onto the field behind the wheel of a weaponized 1973 Oldsmobile Delta 88 Royale, in the film's single greatest equation of technological progress with a reclaimed white masculinity. It is high technology that enables Ash's violent expressions of his new manhood.

The virile and aggressive Ash in *Evil Dead 2* and *Army of Darkness* is vastly different from the terrified youth in *The Evil Dead*. In *Evil Dead 2*, Ash's relationship with Linda has lost the virginal innocence that his coy gift-giving game evokes in Raimi's first film. Instead, a lustful Ash intermittently gazes at Linda's half-nude twirling body as she dances before, insinuating that he is sexually starved and very much in the mood. In *Army of Darkness*, Ash is finally allowed the overt sexual conquest that the Force prevents in the two prior films, indulging in it with an even more forceful assertion of reformulated masculinity, effectively forcing himself onto Sheila. Ash is also more physically aggressive in *Evil Dead 2* and *Army of Darkness*, transitioning from reluctantly dismembering his former friends to dispatching scores of anonymous Deadites with a level of satisfaction that is, at times, oddly sexual. When Ash exterminates a Deadite hag in Arthur's castle, his body quivers as he slowly exhales with orgasmic satisfaction before delivering the explosive *coup de grâce*. Ash's relish in sexualized aggression is yet another sign of the enhanced masculine subjectivity he rescued from the Force's queer effects. Ash's narrative transformation required that Campbell undertake a physical one, involving a grueling weight-training regimen and strict diet to develop "a sturdy physique that would work ... with the hero-in-a-torn-shirt concept" (173). Ash's adventures in *Army of Darkness* required that the actor endure even more physical training. Choreographing the film's final battle scenes used a front-screen projection process requiring Campbell to perform a series of complex, controlled movements, with some scenes involving nearly forty takes (Muir 157). Ash's voluntary corporeal diminishment coincides with the cultivation of his masculine form, once more equating adaptation to the neoliberal market's demands with recovering a modified—even enhanced— white masculinity, all the while obscuring the market's ill effects. Indeed,

Ash's access to this fictive masculine identity is still contingent upon Campbell's real self-denial and forms of corporeal regimentation that are uncomfortably reminiscent of neoliberal capital's anatomization and control of laboring bodies.

While I agree with Tison Pugh's observation that the medieval world in *Army of Darkness* operates as a fantasy-scape for the newly re-masculinized Ash (123), we ought not to overlook the manifold ways in which Raimi's entire trilogy operates as a fantasy-scape in which a modified masculinity is attained and proven. More significantly, we ought not to overlook the ways in which this fantasy attempts to negotiate the neoliberal traumas that are its object-cause.[7] "Sure, I could've stayed in the past. Could've even been king," Ash informs us after vanquishing one last Deadite as *Army of Darkness* ends, "But in my own way," he reasons, "I am king." The trilogy ends with Ash's candid admission that he accepts his position as a low-level retail clerk while remaining a king in his own mind; Ash's royal fantasy insulates him from the baleful monotony of de-skilled drudgery to which he has been reduced. The fantasy intended to rescue Ash in fact insures that he remains trapped in a subject position that leaves the interlocking regimes of neoliberal exploitation unchallenged. Still, I hold that the final film in Raimi's trilogy forces us to more carefully consider the danger in indulging in our own solipsistic fantasies. For, while insular fantasies may provide an escape from harsh political realities, it is only through our collective confrontation with these realities that we may endeavor to change them.

NOTES

    1. Social constructionist theories of disability inform my treatment of it. See especially Susan Wendell's *The Rejected Body* or Rosemarie Garland Thomson's *Extraordinary Bodies*.

    2. For a concise economic description of this shift's racial and class dynamics, see Kimmel (*Angry Men* 8–9).

    3. Raimi has identified Ash and his initial band of friends as college students (quoted in Muir 20). Given the neoliberal context that the trilogy reflects, Ash's proletarianization in *Army of Darkness* suggests that he was either forced to drop out, or was incapable of finding work with his degree, and was thusly unable to become part of the managerial class, in yet another critique of neoliberalism's assault on white manhood.

    4. The routine presentation of the Force as an ancient evil in Raimi's trilogy may seem to contradict my equation of it with modern market forces. Marx observes in *The Grundrisse* that a historically specific mode of production and its effects are often "encased in eternal laws independent of history" or otherwise presented as "inviolable natural laws" incapable of changing as part of a process of bourgeois mystification (87). Raimi's trilogy takes this mystifying principle and subverts it; in Raimi's films, an ideological move intended to normalize and stabilize social relations defamiliarizes and destabilizes them.

    5. The same gender fluidity is also visible in *Army of Darkness*. See Warren's insights in *The Evil Dead Companion* (151–2).

    6. For an alternative view of humor's role in Raimi's trilogy, see Michael Arnzen's treatment of the splatter film and postmodernity.

    7. For additional insights, see D. Harlan Wilson's "Schizosophy of the Medieval Dead."

Works Cited

Arnzen, Michael. "Who's Laughing Now? … The Postmodern Splatter Film." *Journal of Popular Film and Television* 21, no. 4 (1994), pp. 176–84.
Benshoff, Harry M. *Monsters in the Closet: Homosexuality and the Horror Film*. Manchester University Press, 1997.
Berberoglu, Berch. "The Dynamics of the Labor Process in the Age of Neoliberal Capitalist Globalization: A Class Analysis." *International Review of Modern Sociology* 38, no. 2 (2011), pp. 31–50.
Campbell, Bruce. *If Chins Could Kill: Confessions of a B Movie Actor*. L.A. Weekly Books, 2002.
Chivers, Sally, and Nicole Marcotić, editors. *The Problem Body: Projecting Disability on Film*. Ohio State University Press, 2010.
Creed, Barbara. *The Monstrous-Feminine: Film, Feminism, and Psychoanalysis*. Routledge, 1993.
Darke, Paul. "No Life Anyway: Pathologizing Disability on Film." *The Problem Body: Projecting Disability on Film*, edited by Sally Chivers and Nicole Marcotić. Ohio State University Press, 2010, pp. 97–108.
Davis, Lennard J. *Enforcing Normalcy: Disability, Deafness, and the Body*. Verso, 1995.
Fletcher, Bill, and Fernando Gapasin. *Solidarity Divided: The Crisis in Organized Labor and a New Path Toward Social Justice*. University of California Press, 2004.
Galusca, Roxana. "From Fictive Ability to National Identity: Disability, Medical Inspection, and Public Health Regulations on Ellis Island." *Cultural Critique* 72 (2009), pp. 137–63.
"The Killer of Killers." *Ash vs. Evil Dead*, season 1, episode 6, Starz, 5 Dec. 2015.
Kimmel, Michael S. *Angry White Men: American Masculinity at the End of an Era*. Nation Books, 2013.
_____. *Manhood in America: A Cultural History*. The Free Press, 1997.
Marx. Karl. *The Grundrisse*. Penguin, 1993.
_____. *Wage-Labor and Capital*. International Publishers, 1976.
McNally, David. *Monsters of the Market: Zombies, Vampires, and Global Capitalism*. Haymarket Books, 2012.
McRuer, Robert. *Crip Theory: Cultural Signs of Queerness and Disability*. New York University Press, 2006.
Moody, Kim. *US Labor in Trouble and Transition*. Verso, 2007.
Muir, John Kenneth. *The Unseen Force: The Films of Sam Raimi*. Applause, 2004.
Murphy, Robert. "Encounters: The Body Silent in America." *Disability and Culture*, edited by Benedict Ingstad and Susan Reynolds White. University of California Press, 1995, pp. 140–58.
Norden, Martin F. *The Cinema of Isolation: A History of Physical Disability in the Movies*. Rutgers University Press, 1994.
Pugh, Tison. "Queering the Medieval Dead: History, Horror, and Masculinity in Sam Raimi's *Evil Dead* Trilogy." *Race, Class, and Gender in "Medieval" Cinema*, edited by Lynn Tarte Ramey and Tison Pugh. Palgrave, 2007, pp. 123–136.
Raimi, Sam, director. *Army of Darkness*. Renaissance Pictures, 1992.
_____. *The Evil Dead*. Renaissance Pictures, 1981.
_____. *Evil Dead 2*. Renaissance Pictures, 1987.
Roediger, David R. *Working toward Whiteness: How America's Immigrants Became White*. Basic Books, 2005.
Smith, Neil. *Uneven Development: Nature, Capital, and the Production of Space*. University of Georgia Press, 1990.
Snyder, Sharon L., and David T. Mitchell. "Body Genres: An Anatomy of Disability in Film." *The Problem Body*, edited by Sally Chivers and Nicole Marcotić. Ohio State University Press, 2010, pp. 179–206.
Thomson, Rosemarie Garland. *Extraordinary Bodies: Figuring Physical Disability in American Culture and Literature*. Columbia University Press, 1996.
Warren, Bill. *The Evil Dead Companion*. St. Martin's Griffin, 2000.

Wendell, Susan. *The Rejected Body: Feminist Philosophical Reflections on Disability.* Routledge, 1996.
Western, Bruce, and Jake Rosenfeld. "Unions, Norms, and the Rise in US Wage Inequality." *American Sociological Review* 76, no. 4 (2011), pp. 513–37.
Wilson, Harlan D. "Schizosophy of the Medieval Dead: Sam Raimi's *Army of Darkness*." *The Journal of Popular Culture* 41, no. 3 (2008), pp. 509–35.
Wood, Phillip J. "The Politics of Industrial Injury Rates in the United States." *Review of Radical Political Economics* 27, no. 1 (1995), pp. 71–96.

The First Horror Film Shot in Michigan

RON RIEKKI

Chapter 1, "Birth of a Genre," in Scott Von Doviak's *Stephen King Films FAQ* opens with:

> It always seems to start with Georges Méliès. The French stage magician turned silent film pioneer directed what is generally regarded as the first science fiction film, 1902's *A Trip to the Moon*. But six years before that groundbreaking piece of cinema, Méliès made a three-minute short called *Le manoir du diable* [1896], literally translated as "Manor of the Devil" but also known by the English titled *The Haunted Castle*. With its ghosts in sheets, creepy skeletons, and bat that transforms into a demonic figure (played by Méliès himself), it's certainly no stretch to call *Le manoir du diable* the first horror film [1].

For Michigan, as far as the first true Michigander horror film, it seems to start with Sam Raimi, the Russian-Hungarian-Jewish cinematic magician and horror film pioneer. Michigan's *Le manoir du diable* equivalent is *The Evil Dead* (1981) (a sort of *Le cabine du diable*), the first horror film to be shot in the state with an actual Michigan cast and crew.

A misnomer is that *The Evil Dead* was shot completely in Tennessee.[1] It was not. On January 23, 1980, the Tennessee "filming was declared 'kind of finished'" (Campbell, *Chins* 117), but the reality was that filming would continue throughout the remainder of that year in south-central and southeastern Michigan, the area where Raimi grew up. Although often rarely credited in the mainstream, *The Evil Dead* and *Evil Dead 2* (1987) filming, reshooting, looping, etc., also occurred in the Michigan towns of Ferndale (*The Evil Dead* looping/voice recording), Franklin (*The Evil Dead* car sequence), Gladwin (*The Evil Dead* bridge sequence), Marshall (basement sequences), and Dearborn (*Evil Dead 2* reshoots), as just a few examples.[2] Some of the most iconic moments in the films were shot in Michigan, e.g., the decomposition special effects of *The Evil Dead* climax and the infamous shot of Linda mistakenly almost chainsawing her own headless body in half in *Evil Dead 2*.

Bruce Campbell, in his HeyUGuys interview with Ezequiel Gutierrez, explained "the first *Evil Dead* we stopped and started four and five times over a four-year period to make the movie." Based in Michigan, the low-budget film's crew would never have been able to keep returning to Tennessee, so several aspects of the film, including "close-ups ... all of the basement sequences, a lot of inserts in Sam's garage, and also some scenes out in rural Michigan" were shot in the state (Muir 46). Makeup/visual effects man Tom Sullivan explained that the "final effects and several other FX shots were done in a final three-and-a-half-month shoot in Bart Pierce's basement" in Michigan (Muir 48) and "this sequence dragged on into the frigid months of Michigan in winter" (Campbell, *Chins* 128). For Campbell, the 1980 summer filming in Michigan "ran the gamut from shots of blood splattering on a wall to an entire sequence where a character gets raped, literally, by vines" (*Chins* 128). All of this is not to mention the "stills, a foreign textless, an M&E [music and effects], a dialogue continuity, an inter-positive," etc. (*Chins* 138) and even the film's iconic poster that was staged in a Ferndale warehouse that were all done post–Tennessee.

Beyond the Michigan cast, Michigan director, Michigan film crew, shooting in Michigan, and the financing in Michigan (private investors, as well as loans from the National Bank of Detroit and mid–Michigan bank in Gladwin [Campbell, Chins 127, 133]), another critical aspect of the film's Michigan-ness was the original audience itself. The film seems made for Michigan horror fans, as the ideal target audience was considered to be Michiganders. In *If Chins Could Kill*, Bruce Campbell discussed the test-screening process, saying, "We had to try *Evil Dead* in front of a pure audience and see if it still played. The decision was an immediate one—take it to Michigan State University" (136). That pure Michigan audience—I am reminded of the Pure Michigan ad campaign launched in 2006—was an extension of the pure Michigan combination of producer-director-actor Tapert-Raimi-Campbell. Throughout *If Chins Could Kill*, Campbell refers to the three of them as "the three Midwesterners" (141) and states, "We're from Detroit!" (109) with continual references to his "Midwest roots" (48).

In a June 2015 phone conversation I had with actress Betsy Baker, she explained that the vine scene, which Campbell stated was shot in Michigan, happens to be the most talked about scene in the history of the franchise whenever she attends conferences. When Campbell talks about his "Michigan roots," it has a double entendre when one thinks about that scene in particular. One might take a Gilles Deleuze/Felix Guattari rhizomatic approach, but here I will emphasize a place-focused biographical-sociological-historical-gender literary theory where the scene needs to be read in what I will term as a combined Michigan Literary Theory. The film is best understood in terms of the tropes, metaphors, obsessions, and interests of 1980s Michigan.

Speaking of his childhood in *If Chins Could Kill*, Campbell said, "Michigan is all about trees" (8). The very name of Ash is etymologically linked to the Old English *aexe*, with connotations of the wooden-handled weapon; the name also reminds one of the common Michigan tree[3] of the same name, a tree that would have been plentiful in the woods-focused Michigan childhood that Campbell describes so nostalgically in his memoir, and a tree that, coincidentally, is often found by swamps,[4] reminding one of the significance of *The Evil Dead*'s opening shot. In that filmic swamp, literally in Michigan, the extreme horror of the vine-rape scene of the forest plays out against the backdrop of what was happening in Michigan from 1961 to 1980 and beyond. (The scene was filmed in the summer of 1980.) Examine the following forcible rape statistics for the state and notice the statistical tendencies:

Michigan Forcible Rape Statistics[5]

1961	1,092	1969	2,832	1977	3,555	1985	6,140
1962	1,133	1970	2,402	1978	3,636	1986	6,167
1963	1,220	1971	2,404	1979	4,100	1987	6,184
1964	1,603	1972	2,657	1980	4,304	1988	6,462
1965	1,970	1973	3,173	1981	4,366	1989	6,624
1966	2,358	1974	3,377	1982	4,246	1990	7,209
1967	2,282	1975	3,488	1983	5,085	1991	7,372
1968	2,732	1976	3,287	1984	5,880	1992	7,550[6]

From 1961 to 1981, the forcible rapes in Michigan almost exactly quadruple. The murders are more than two-and-a-half times as many in that same timespan. Robberies and aggravated assault increase by about three-and-a-half times the number. Michigan's population in 1960 is slowly moving downwards from the sixth largest state in the country down to its current rank as the tenth largest, the opposite direction of the aforementioned Michigan Forcible Rape Statistics. The horror on the screen is reflecting the horror of the state, especially in terms of violent crimes directed at women.

My argument is that the forest in the film is representative of Michigan. The literal Michigan filming in those specific places represents a metaphorical Michigan, an onscreen representation of the actualizing of the horrors happening off-screen. Growing up in Michigan, Raimi and Campbell took in *The Ghoul Show* (1971–2004) horror movie showings on TV, but they also took in the horrors shown routinely on Detroit's news broadcasts. The most horrific scenes in *The Evil Dead* are the ones shot in Michigan, i.e., as mentioned, the vine scene, the basement scenes, and all of the intricate special effects sequences. Horror films, like the influential *The Hills Have Eyes* (1977),[7] typically fall into the cliché of outsiders being attacked when they stumble upon a new place. That new place, à la *Deliverance* (1972), is the place to be feared. But with *The Evil Dead*, the true reading is the reverse of this. There is a wish to escape, similar to Spring Break teens, to go to a place warmer and distant and Other. Tennessee, unlike the fictional Cahulawassee River in *Deliverance*, is not the place to fear. The place to fear in *The Evil Dead* is Michigan. The cabin is representative of the wish to transcend away from hometown. Tennessee was the one place that welcomed Sam, Rob, and Bruce's dreams of filming. Campbell explained, "We contacted the Michigan Travel Bureau, but nothing came of it"; whereas, "The Tennessee Film Commission, much to their credit, made the best case for shooting there.[8] In fact, they were the *only* state that seemed to give a rat's ass" (Campbell, *Chins* 96). Tennessee is the escape from Michigan to accomplish the dream. But in that escape, they become haunted *by* Michigan, by all of the sequences that were later shot in Michigan, by the horrors imagined in their youth, the horrors of the current state, the horrors of the handcuffs of Midwest life ... the true horror being trapped *in* Michigan. Leaving the Tennessee cabin in any form in the film—e.g. going into the woods or going into the basement—meant literally returning to Michigan (in terms of the editing); the deepest horrors come from the post–Tennessee Michigan cinematic images.

Campbell would explain in *Chins*, "an old adage I'd heard as a Detroit actor—'If you want to work in Detroit, you have to leave.' The idea behind it was simple: If you lived in Michigan, you weren't considered a *serious* actor" (184). The basement floor door rattling to be opened was Michigan warning of its inescapable presence. Michigan surrounds them in all of its aspects of childhood—woods, basement—the places where kids go when they have no idea where else to go, but the same places that they then fear at night. These are the places where they got lost in their imaginations in their youth in the day and avoid for their horrors at night. The basement and the woods were for creating horrors of the mind to get through the boredoms of Michigan winters.

Remember, as Sam Raimi explains in *The Evil Dead* commentary, "There was no cellar in this cabin. We cut a hole in the floorboards." The basement scenes were shot in a combination of a basement, a garage, and a barn in Marshall, Michigan.[9] Readers of this article who spent their childhoods in Michigan will see the connection. The overall complete Michigan-ness of the film makes a Michigan Literary Theory reading commonsensical. Obviously place influences metaphors, tropes, angles, worldviews; along those lines, *The Evil Dead* is a thoroughly Michigan film.

Keep in mind that Raimi, Tapert, and Campbell were all born in Royal Oak (in 1959, 1955, and 1958 respectively).[10] Raimi and Tapert went to Michigan State University, Campbell briefly to Western Michigan University. Director of Photography Tim Philo had to return to teaching at Wayne State

University in Detroit after working on *The Evil Dead* (Campbell, *Chins* 111). Other crew included Michiganders David "Goody" Goodman and Josh Becker, Wayne State University teacher John Mason, Bruce's brother Don Campbell, and Tom Sullivan of Marshall. Actors included Betsy Baker from Michigan State (who grew up in St. Joseph), Teresa Seyferth and Ellen Sandweiss (both born in Detroit), and Richard de Manincor (who grew up in Michigan's Redford Township).[11]

The significance of place, especially Detroit to their background, is that the film should be appreciated specifically as a part of Michigan cinema. *The Evil Dead* is working-class Detroit moviemaking from opening rural Michigan swamp shot to final climactic Michigan basement Bart Pierce animation. In fact, the opening shot exemplifies a DIY Detroit attitude. In the film's commentary, Campbell explained, "The opening shot of *Evil Dead* consisted of me pushing Sam in a rubber raft across a [Michigan] swamp while he leaned out, skimming the camera across the water and swooping over decaying branches."

Keeping with the Michigan-specific horror metaphors, what is intriguing to me is what ends up happening to the state of Michigan as a whole—its relentlessly increasing crime throughout Raimi's youth. I remember writing an article on contemporary crime and alcohol/drug addiction in Michigan and having an editor at the magazine ask me if the crime was not due to the "boredom of Michigan." I laughed at the time, but I understand her point. Raimi's positive use of the arts is a critical (and very positive) counter to criminal alternatives in real life. I think here of the infamous 1984 Devil's Night antics in Detroit with arson and worse taking place. Raimi's Devil's Night is captured on film, contained to film, where no one ultimately gets actually hurt, beyond the occasional bruise or scrape while filming.[12] Almost magically—fitting for the actual magician aspirations of his youth—Raimi's cinematic vision transforms this economically depressed area that is not encouraging to filmmakers into a subsequent post-*The Evil Dead* series explosion of horror filming in Michigan. It is like the trapdoor for horror has burst open in the state and it cannot be contained anymore. The number of horror films in the state starts gradually, but it does take off, thanks in part to Raimi's commitment to Michigan filmmaking.[13]

Ironically, the indifference of the Michigan Travel Bureau did not stop what has become a revolutionary transformation in filmmaking in Michigan. Six months of editing of *Piranha 3D* (2010) was done in Ann Arbor ("Metro"). *Scream 4* (2011) filmed all over Michigan, including a month at a family home in Ann Arbor (Halpert), and the instant horror classic *It Follows* (2014) filmed in Berkley, Clawson, Detroit, Northville, Sterling Heights, and Troy.

The timeline of horror films by year below shows how there has been a steady increase in horror shot in the state.

Full-Length Horror Films Shot in Michigan ("Films")[14]

2017: 5th Kind, Crepitus, Dead Rising, Eloise, Hearse Life, Inside Ben, Locked Away, Monsters Among Men, Needlestick, Pay to Play, R–Naught 15, Ruin Me, Strain 100, Thaw of the Dead, They Were Lost, Wolf

2016: 60 Seconds to Die, 8989 Redstone, Accidental Exorcist, The Alchemist Cookbook, And Hell Awaits, Beautiful Prison, Dead End, Don't Breathe, Elder Island, The Factory on 5th, Hectic Knife, Lake Eerie, Moonwick Circle, Pitchfork, Return of the Dead, The Visitors

2015: Animus: The Tell-Tale Heart; Autumn's End; Black Paper; Bye, Felicia; Cabin of Horror; Fangboner; A Haunting in Cawdor; The Fly; Fractured; The Horror; Intent; Meshes of Dusk; My Soul to Keep; Revolution 666; Shadow World: The Haunting of Mysti Delane

2014: Amerikan Violence, Awaken the Devil, Axe Giant: The Wrath of Paul Bunyan, Beyond the Dark, Buzzard, The Cabining, Chubbies, Dogman 2: The Wrath of the Litter, A Haunting on Washington Avenue: The Temple Theatre, It Follows, Jinn, Lost River, Monsters: Dark Continent, Night of the Living Dead, The Werewolf of Glenslake

2013: Devils in the Darkness; A Haunting in Saginaw, Michigan; Last Girl; The Last Vampyre on Earth; Only Lovers Left Alive; Resident Evil: Red Falls; The Wicked [note: Evil Dead is not listed as it was filmed in New Zealand]

2012: The 6th Extinction, Blood Angel, Blood Orgy at Beaver Lake, Crave, Creep Van, Detention of the Dead, Dogman, Garden Island: A Paranormal Documentary, Little Creeps, Locked in a Room, Playback, Silver Clutch, Vamps, Waterfront Nightmare

2011: 13th Sign, Bite Me: The Movie, Deadheads, Deadrise (Fitful), Exit 33, Ghost of New Orleans, Hostel: Part III, The Melonheads, Mimesis, Scream 4, Zombie Apocalypse: Redemption, The Zombie Factor

2010: American Scream King, Cyrus: Mind of a Serial Killer, Grey Skies, Piranha 3D, Secrets in the Walls, Vanishing on 7th Street, Zombie Abomination: The Italian Zombie Movie—Part I, Zombie Apocalypse

2009: Blood Siblings, Blood Ties, The City That Never Sleeps, Dog, Evil Offspring, The Final Curtain, Heavy Mental, Jingles the Clown, Offspring, The Steam Experiment

2008: th3 bas3m3nt, Born of Earth, The Day the Earth Stood Still, Little Red Devil, The Tower

2007: The Dread, The Final Curtain, Nevermore, Sigma Die!, Weenie Roast Massacre

2006: *Conjure, Mr. Jingles, The Remake, Return of the Curse, Sickness House, They Must Eat, The Woodland Haunting 2 (Tomb of Terrors)*
2005: *From Venus, Silent Scream*
2004: *Dead End Road, The Eternal Present*
2003: *13 Seconds, Beaver Lake Zombies, Invitation, Next Victim, An Ordinary Killer, Terror at Baxter U*
2002: *Below, Dark Heaven, Dark Tomorrow, Dead/Undead, Hatred of a Minute, Lurking Terror, Rachel's Attic, WitcHunter*
2001: *Biker Zombies from Detroit, Knight Chills*
2000: *Chasing Sleep*
1999: *In the Woods*
1998: *The Cabin*
1997: *Lost Souls*
1995: *Legend of the Night, Frostbiter (Wendigo)*
1994: *Mosquito*
1993: *Back from Hell, The Nostril Picker*
1992: *Hellmaster, Mindwarp* [*Army of Darkness* is not listed with the Michigan Film Board as shot in Michigan at all; it was filmed in California][15]
1991: *Children of the Night*[16]
1989: *Blind Faith, Moontrap*
1988: *The Carrier, The Hackers*
1987: *Evil Dead 2: Dead by Dawn, The Rosary Murders*
1985: *Crimewave*
1981: *The Evil Dead* [the first successful full-length horror film shot in Michigan by Michiganders][17]
1977: *Death Bed: The Bed That Eats,*[18] *Demon Lover*
1970: *Night of the Bloody Transplant*
1946: *The Spiral Staircase*[19]

With the sole exception of 1996, at least one horror film has been shot in Michigan every single year since 1991 (the year when filming for *Army of Darkness* began); this is due in very large part to Raimi leading the way. Considering that only a very few horror films were shot in Michigan before 1981—just four full-length films by my count[20]—Michigan's film economy owes a lot to the groundbreaking *The Evil Dead*. With its $350,000 budget and $30 million box office, the film proved the potential for low-budget horror to have big-time payoffs. Incredibly, the effect has been more than a hundred horror films shot in the state in the last decade (from 2008 up until October 31, 2017).

The problem I have is that each of the *Evil Dead* franchise movies has gotten farther and farther away from Michigan with each filming. *The Evil*

Dead, as I have argued, is more of a Michigan film than people have recognized. *Evil Dead 2: Dead by Dawn* was shot in North and South Carolina[21] with "reshoots that were actually done in Dearborn, Michigan," but with much less of a Michigan presence. With *Army of Darkness*, Michigan falls off the map completely and the film becomes stereotypically Californian. For the *Evil Dead* remake and the current television show *Ash vs. Evil Dead* (2015–2018), all of the filming has been done, so far, according to reports, solely in New Zealand. Outsourced. Each time, Michigan seems to become more and more of a ghost. The ramifications, economically, are hinted at in *If Chins Could Kill*, where Campbell writes in his "*Hercules: The Legendary Journeys* / Fun Facts" that "More than $150,000,000 / (NZ) spent locally / shooting the series." I can only imagine the help for Michigan's economy if *Evil Dead* and *Ash vs. Evil Dead* were shot in the state.

But one can't complain.

The forefathers of Michigan horror have paved the way and paid the way for others to step in place and create the next great Michigan horror film, to only try to escape themselves beyond the haze of Hollywood to get to the other side of the Earth, as far away from home as possible. With New Zealand, Raimi, Campbell, and Tapert have done just that. They escaped.

I think of the roaming of the Frankenstein monster in Mary Shelley's book, the distance you have to go to escape your past. Perth is considered the farthest city from Detroit, almost 18,000 kilometers from the Motor City. With *Army of Darkness*'s California, the only way of getting farther away from Michigan would be ocean. That happened. With the next projects, the Midwest threesome left Michigan's horrors behind in what seems like will be forever.

If I can add a happy ending to the story: Bruce Campbell did find his home away from home, the place that he has finally settled down happily; in fact, Campbell "spoke so highly of where I live" (Campbell, *Chins* 337) that Josh Becker from Sam Raimi's early short films ended up moving there as well; the place, Oregon, where—similar to the post–*Army of Darkness* move to filming in New Zealand—you can't get any further away without heading into ocean.

And the happy ending for Michigan is that Raimi did come back for filming. I will insert here, in case you didn't know, but *The Evil Dead*, *Evil Dead 2*, and *Army of Darkness* are the three films to make the least amount of money for Raimi as a director (as long as you ignore the clunker *Crimewave*) in terms of lifetime gross in theaters ("Sam"). And along with the billion-dollar lifetime gross for Raimi's *Spider-Man* films, his biggest monetary success has been *Oz the Great and Powerful*, a project he brought to Michigan for filming. With its half-billion dollar total lifetime gross, *Oz* is the type of movie that can have big economic impact for a state with a city that has been considered the poorest in America, Detroit (Kennedy). Michigan needs more of its people who go on to big-time success to come back and help the state to thrive.

Ash vs. Evil Dead's filming in New Zealand does not have much economic benefit for Michigan, but the show's complete dedication to the state in terms of fictional setting and references does help the horror mystique of the region. Upcoming directors and actors wanting to become new versions of Raimi and Campbell keep emerging in the state. And when those up-and-comers have strong voices and true artistic talent, they allow their horror films to speak of the atrocities of contemporary living that so often go ignored in other genres.

That mix of reportage and horror is true to the entire history of film. Georges Méliès's *Le manoir du diable* 1896 might seem like eons away from a Michigan film timeline, but that is far from the truth; just three years later, in 1899, film emerges in Michigan with the release of several silent documentary-style short films given titles such as "Michigan Naval Reserves and the Detroit Light Guards" and "Police Drill." The feel of Orwellian panopticon and military-industrial complex appears to be immediate with Michigan film, where horror is interlaced in the very first images caught cinematographically—notably "Male Prisoners Marching to Dinner" (1899) and "Female Prisoners: Detroit House of Correction" (1899). Sam Raimi's Morristown cabin might most accurately be read as a "Detroit House," equally horrific.

NOTES

1. In Morristown and Knoxville.
2. In the last five minutes of *The Evil Dead*, in the commentary, Bruce Campbell explains that even the cockroaches used in the filming were from Michigan: "Those were some delightful cockroaches. Some of them were Madagascar cockroaches that when you picked them up, they would hiss at you. They're about three inches long. We picked those up courtesy of Michigan State University in the science lab."
3. Likewise, the character raped by the forest is named Cheryl, which is etymologically linked to *cherry*, another common Michigan tree (and, also, a strong sexual innuendo). Cheryl is, coincidentally, Ash's brother. There is a familial and etymological link between the characters' names, both of them so tied to the woods by name and by the horrors that play out in the woods in the film.
4. Furthermore, Bruce Campbell's full character name is Ashley; the -ley suffix is linked to the Old English *lēah/leigh*, which means forest clearing or meadow, so the name means a clearing among ash trees, furthering the symbolism of forest in the film and in the name.
5. "Michigan Crime Rates 1960–2013," http://www.disastercenter.com/crime/micrime.htm.
6. Worth mentioning, the forcible rape statistics go in decline starting in 1992 to now, reaching a low of 4,344 in 2011, the lowest number since 1980.
7. The homage of the torn *Hills* poster is also homage to the history of Midwest horror cinema—director Wes Craven being born on just the other side of Lake Erie (eerie) from Detroit, in Cleveland, Ohio.
8. The sad part of the Michigan indifference to filming was that the intent originally was to film in "northern Michigan" (*Chins* 88), which has been traditionally even more eco-

nomically depressed than many areas of southern Michigan. The lack of encouragement of Michigan filming was compounded with the oncoming winter at the time.

9. Bruce Campbell explained in *If Chins Could Kill* that "personal loans, corporate loans, temporary loans, emergency loans ... [and] National Bank of Detroit ... loans, in all of the forms, allowed us to shoot the last third of our film in fits and starts. The first spring after our return, we filmed for two additional weeks in the Tapert Farmhouse in Marshall, Michigan" (Campbell 127).

10. With the love interest of the film wearing a Michigan State sweater in both *The Evil Dead* and *Evil Dead 2*, immediately the tone is set about where the main characters are from (the narrative seems to be that innocent Michigan goes to horror-filled Tennessee, but the subtext is really innocent Tennessee is plagued by horror-filled Michigan; the cabin was peaceful until the insane Michigan film crew arrived).

11. Robert Tapert, at the opening of the commentary to *The Evil Dead*, says, "all the cast people that are in the car all came from Detroit" (Raimi). Raimi, Campbell, and Tapert continuously point out the Michigan-ness of the filming in interviews, commentaries, and articles.

12. I should add as part of the Spooky Empire 30th Anniversary *Evil Dead* Reunion, Campbell said, "It is interesting that we are having a pain discussion. I think the moral of the story is *The Evil Dead* movies were basically beat-the-crap out of anybody who came near them, including even the audience. So I think it's safe to say that everybody here in some form or another witnessed shame, indignation, pain, psychological" turmoil ("'Evil Dead' 30th").

13. Raimi is part of the holy troublemaker duo of Raimi and Michael Moore for amount of projects that have been Michigan connected.

14. I have never seen a full (or nearly full) list of horror films shot in Michigan, so I am glad to include one here. To be included, films must have been more than an hour in length.

15. The number of horror films shot in the state goes on a slow, steady incline after that original *The Evil Dead* filming, especially after the further successes of *Evil Dead 2* and *Army of Darkness*. The result is more money spent and more of a creation of a film industry that creates an explosion of other genre films triggered from that original Michigan success of *The Evil Dead*. Examples of these post-*The Evil Dead* Michigan-connected films include *Detroit* (2017), *Deadpool* (2016), *A Most Violent Year* (2014), *Transformers: Age of Extinction* (2014), *The Ides of March* (2011), *A Very Harold & Kumar Christmas* (2010), *Transformers: Dark of the Moon* (2010), *Red Dawn* (2009), *Up in the Air* (2009), *Gran Torino* (2008), *Dreamgirls* (2006), *Transformers* (2006), *Bowling for Columbine* (2002), *8 Mile* (2001), *American Pie 2* (2001), *Road to Perdition* (2001), *Escanaba in da Moonlight* (2000), *Detroit Rock City* (1999), *Out of Sight* (1998), *Grosse Pointe Blank* (1997), *True Romance* (1993), *Hoffa* (1992), *Zebrahead* (1991), *Die Hard II* (1990), *Presumed Innocent* (1989), *Roger and Me* (1989), *Beverly Hills Cop II* (1987), *Midnight Run* (1987), *Beverly Hills Cop* (1984), *Doctor Detroit* (1983), and, of course, *Oz: The Great and Powerful* (2011), to name just a few. Thank you, Sam Raimi! It is also important to consider that before those original "'scream tests' at Sam [Raimi's] house" (Campbell, *Chins* 92) in October 1979, only a small handful of films had *ever* been shot in the state. Other early non-horror Michigan films include the Oscar-nominated *T-Men* (1947), *This Time for Keeps* (1947), *Anatomy of a Murder* (1959), *Where the Boys Are* (1960), *Scarecrow* (1973), and *Detroit 9000* (1973), but not exactly a long proven history of films shooting in the area to inspire a Michigan film economy ... until Raimi comes along.

16. As far as I can tell, this is the first horror film shot in the Upper Peninsula of Michigan, unless *Anatomy of a Murder* is argued to be a horror film, which, of course, I would insist it is not.

17. The first horror film shot in Michigan was actually 1946's *The Spiral Staircase*, shot in Detroit, but the film was directed by Robert Siodmak of Germany, adapted by Mel Dinelli of New Mexico, and starred Dorothy McGuire of Nebraska and co-starred the Oscar-nominated Ethel Barrymore of Pennsylvania. There was a hit-and-run aspect to the filming where outsiders came-and-went. The film, though, did usher in the Michigan film industry but an *outsider* industry, setting up the filming for 1947's *This Time for Keeps* and *T-Men* and

predating 1959's seven-time Oscar-nominated *Anatomy of a Murder*, three films that were also hardly Michigander in their cast and crew. The *Evil Dead*'s grand significance was showing that those living in Michigan could also make *successful* films. This is why the frequency of Michigan-made films explodes after the cost-versus-box-office successes of *The Evil Dead* and *Evil Dead 2* and only minimally after the Oscar-nominated *The Spiral Staircase*.

18. Writer/director George Barry was born in Royal Oak, Michigan. (Note: I do not include 1976's *The Northville Cemetery Massacre* on this list as the title implies more horror than the actual film, which is much more in the crime/action genre.)

19. The sole Michigan connection with this film—other than the Detroit filming location—was special effects by Vernon L. Walker, born in Detroit. (Some might question the inclusion of this film as horror, but the serial killer plot, effectively whispered line of "Anything can happen in the dark," hide-under-the-bed advice, and countless other horror tropes make it undeniably a part of the genre.)

20. From my research, there were also only four pre-1981 short films in the history of the shot-in-Michigan horror genre: *Inspector Klutz Saves the Day* (1969), *Imp of the Perverse* (1973), *Within the Woods* (1978), and *Clockwork* (1978), but half of those films—the latter—are from Raimi as well.

21. The move to the Carolinas for filming seemed to be predicted with the end credits of *The Evil Dead*, which plays the jazz composition "The Charleston" (as in South Carolina).

Works Cited

"Bruce Campbell Interview–Evil Dead." HeyUGuys YouTube Channel, 16 April 2015, youtube.com/watch?v=W_iBEUY1pic.

Campbell, Bruce. *If Chins Could Kill: Confessions of a B Movie Actor*. L.A. Weekly Books, 2002.

_____. "DVD Audio Commentary." *The Evil Dead*, 1981, directed by Sam Raimi. Anchor Bay Entertainment, 1999.

"Films Made in Michigan." *Pure Michigan Film Office*. MFO Michigan Film Office, michiganbusiness.org/mifilmanddigital/.

Halpert, Julie. "'Scream 4' Turns Local Family's House into Movie Set for a Month." *The Ann Arbor News*, 26 Aug. 2010, annarbor.com/entertainment/scream-4tesars/.

Kennedy, Bruce. "America's 11 Poorest Cities." CBSNewswww, 18 Feb. 2015, cbsnews.com/media/americas-11-poorest-cities/12/.

"Metro Detroit Firms Grow Thanks to Film Post Production Work." *MetroMode: Metro Detroit*, 7 Sept. 2010, secondwavemedia.com/metromode/oaklandcounty/inthenews/metrodetroitfilmpostprodu tion0176.aspx.

"Michigan Crime Rates 1960–2013." DisasterCenterwww, disastercenter.com/crime/micrime.htm.

Muir, John Kenneth. *The Unseen Force: The Films of Sam Raimi*. Applause Theatre & Cinema, 2004.

Panels on Pages. "'Evil Dead's 30th Anniversary Reunion from Spooky Empire's MAY-HEM! PanelsOnPages.com!" Panels on Pages YouTube Channel, 12 June 2011, youtube.com/watch?v=LZGe3Og_GJY.

Raimi, Sam, and Robert Tapert. "DVD Audio Commentary." *The Evil Dead*, 1981, directed by Sam Raimi. Anchor Bay Entertainment, 1999.

"Sam Raimi." *Boxofficemojo*. boxofficemojo.com/people/chart/?view=Director&id=samraimi.htm&sort=gross&order=DESC&p=.htm.

Von Doviak, Scott. *Stephen King Films FAQ: All That's Left to Know about the King of Horror on Film*. Applause Theatre & Cinema, 2014.

Part II
The Franchise and Adaptations

"Don't call me Ash!"
Success, the Bruce Campbell Way
MICHAEL FUCHS *and* MICHAEL PHILLIPS

If you are reading this book, you no doubt have at least a passing familiarity with the legendary origin story of the *Evil Dead* franchise.[1] Three fearless young filmmakers armed with a Super-8 video camera set off into the woods to make a horror movie on a shoestring budget: Sam Raimi, the visionary, would-be auteur; Bruce Campbell, the aspiring actor; and Rob Tapert, the man "doing anything that nobody else was doing" (Campbell, *Chins* 95). The resulting short film, *Within the Woods* (1978), set off a chain of events that would determine the courses of their lives. The ensuing *Evil Dead* movies served as a springboard for Tapert's career as a producer of campy entertainment products and launched Raimi on a directing career trajectory that would lead him to mainstream success with the *Spider-Man* trilogy (2002, 2004, and 2007). However, of those three intrepid filmmakers, we would suggest that the *Evil Dead* franchise has had the most lasting impact on the life of its lantern-jawed frontman and unofficial official standard bearer, Bruce Campbell.

In this chapter, we will explore the manifold ways in which Campbell has leveraged the "subcultural capital" (Jancovich) garnered from his signature role into a transmedia B-movie superstar persona. Drawing on critical discourses dating back to Richard Dyer, we will examine this persona as an "intertextual construct produced across a range of media and cultural practices," which "demand[s] analysis as a text in its own right" (Gledhill xii). Accordingly, our examination will highlight some of the key values that inform the cult sensibility and how these values are constructed and maintained across media and in interactions between the producers and consumers of these texts. As Matt Hills has pointed out, whereas industrial forces tend to define mainstream stardom, cult stardom attempts to integrate discourses of stardom with audience agency. That is to say, the processes associated with a star becoming cult are often strongly linked to subcultural audience discernment, recognition and valorization rather than marketing-led or industry/PR-related constructions of stardom ["Cult Movies" 22].

We will show how Campbell has used his keen awareness of this special characteristic of cult stardom to tap into these processes and transform his public persona into "a full-fledged cult industry unto himself" (Felsher 3).

A (Cult) Star Is Born

Bruce Campbell burst onto the cult movie scene (if that is possible) with the release of *The Evil Dead* in 1981. Although Campbell had the athletic build, wavy hair, and signature square jawbone of a typical Hollywood star, his performance undermined the leading man aura. While Kate Egan has claimed that "Campbell's understated and rather amateur performance is frequently valued for making Ash appear to be a normal person rather than a Hollywood hero, allowing fans to believe in his predicament and thus the film's horror to seem more realistic" (*Evil Dead* 41), we suggest that Campbell's acting ability resonates beyond the storyworld. Rather than transforming Ash from "a Hollywood hero to a normal person," the amateurish acting turns Campbell from a Hollywood star into a "normal person." Instead of sustaining the film's realism and thereby generating horror, Campbell's acting appeals to the alternative ethos of cult horror. The cult community embraces this deviation from mainstream cinema and "celebrate[s it] as unique, courageous and ultimately subversive cinematic experiences" (Sconce 385).

Although J. P. Telotte has argued that it is "difficult to *design* a film for cult status," since "trying to dictate desire seems almost inimical to the cult spirit" (15; italics in original), this is precisely what Raimi, Campbell, and company set out to do with *Evil Dead 2* (1987), which was "designed to please a cult audience, ignoring the Milquetoasts who would never enjoy or understand it anyway" (18). While *Evil Dead 2* maintained the parodic elements of the first film, the target of parody shifted. Where the first movie subverts the conventions of horror, the second movie takes on the Hollywood practices behind the overblown action movies of the 1980s. Where *The Evil Dead*'s Ash had been an exaggerated horror movie victim, harassed and mocked by evil undead throughout the film, *Evil Dead 2*'s Ash fights back. The character takes on the typical swagger of the wisecracking 1980s action hero. Ash's famous trash-talking catchphrases (e.g., "Let's carve ourselves a witch" and "You're going down") lampoon the iconic action hero utterances of the era, when stars such as Sylvester Stallone and Arnold Schwarzenegger were vying for masculine dominance.

To subvert this macho image, Raimi and Campbell doubled down on the (perhaps unintentional) slapstick elements of the first movie. These elements played an important role in shaping the evolving Bruce/Ash persona. Unlike in the first movie, *Evil Dead 2*'s exaggerated absurdism highlights the conscious intent behind the film, lending the production an air of authenticity by suggesting it was produced by people who understand and share the values of the B-movie audience. In this context, the scene most often singled out by fans and critics alike is when Ash fights his possessed hand, which includes Ash smashing plates over his own head and flipping himself by the back of the neck. These absurd scenes are what motivates fans to write, "Even though you're in some of the cheesiest movies I have ever seen, you are great at what you do" (quoted in *Fanalysis*). As evidenced by this quotation, the fans appreciate these subversive practices, which become a kind of secret handshake between the fan community and the films' creators and function as a tool for uniting them.

When contemplating this budding cult fan/actor romance, it is important to briefly mention the role of technology. In the early years, the emergence of VCRs strongly affected the development of the Bruce/Ash persona in two main ways. First, videotapes expanded the potential size of a cult following: "*The Evil Dead*'s theatrical release … was a success but hardly a blockbuster," before it became "a rental smash," Michael Felsher notes in the booklet accompanying the Book of the Dead edition (6). Through the VCR, existing cult members could simply loan their videotapes to potential new recruits or perhaps encourage them to pick up the film at the local video store. Second, by bringing the viewing experience into the more intimate setting of the viewers' living rooms and enabling repeat viewings, technology helped deepen the relationship between fans and character.[2]

Establishing the bond between fan and character was the first step, but the next step was to transfer this bond to the actor himself. In the late 1980s, Campbell benefited from the emergence of another cultural practice: the fan convention. Watching videos of Campbell's convention appearances from the late 1980s/early 1990s (faithfully posted on *YouTube* by his devoted followers), one can see Campbell developing his "cult star" persona. At that time, Campbell's convention performances were closely linked to the creation myth of *The Evil Dead*. Campbell's "act" was answering questions pertaining to the mythology of *The Evil Dead*, which seems to have been made "to foster cult interest in the film" by "emphasizing its marginal status" while also "valorizing its achievement in the face of adversity" (Barratt 27). Indeed, if one sat down to write a script about the making of a cult movie, it would be difficult to top the "actual" history (as propagated by Campbell, Raimi, and Tapert) of the making of *The Evil Dead*.

Balancing out the irreverent humor that informed the original movies, one main theme that emerged from the origin myth was nothing more than the celebrated Protestant work ethic dressed up in fake blood and flying eyeballs. When asked at a 1989 convention to name the favorite movie he had been in, Campbell, for example, responded, "Probably *Evil Dead 2* because ... it was the most demanding.... So, I think everyone should work hard" (*Bruce Campbell at Convention 1989*). After fifteen years of polishing this line at conventions and in interviews, it would come out more elegantly in an interview with Salonwww: "It's the old cliché about grabbing the bull by the horns.... There is no mystery to it, just an incredible amount of elbow grease, and most people just aren't built for that" (quoted in Thill). The interviewer contributes to the propagation of these blue-collar values by describing Campbell and Raimi as "the two do-it-yourselfers [who] first decided to produce and shoot their own films instead of waiting for a billionaire studio to discover them" (Thill). Campbell and Raimi emerge as self-made outsiders, who rejected the mainstream and earned their success by sticking to their own oddball artistic ethos and putting in the hard work.

A Farewell to Ash

The third installment of the "Ash trilogy," *Army of Darkness* (1992), takes this concept of hard work, resisting the lure of hollow mainstream consumerist society, and projects it onto the big screen. Reading the film as a socioeconomic parable, one could say that the depiction of Ash is a critique of the conspicuous consumption of the leisure class in capitalist society. First, the movie calls into question the meritocratic claim that material success comes from hard work, since Ash's self-proclaimed "superiority" in medieval society is based on nothing more than pure chance (the possession of a twentieth-century firearm and having a chemistry book in his trunk). And second, the depiction of Ash implies that the leisure class are not only worthless, but an actual burden to society. Ash has become a tragic hero whose hubris has destroyed his respect for the values of equality and hard work.

Only when Ash is inspired to take on the demons and rescue the damsel in distress (i.e., get back to work and accept his stereotypical active male role) can he be reformed and once again become the workingman's hero. When Ash joins up with the "simple" townsfolk, it shows that "we are all in this together," and that even (or especially) the hero needs his supporters. And just in case that message was delivered too subtly, Ash sums it up at the end, when he decides to return to the future present and his job at S-mart: "Sure, I could have stayed in the past. Could've even been king. But, in my own way, I am king." In other words, it is better to be a regular person with a "real" job than a member of the bourgeois aristocracy.

Allegorically, the film develops the emerging Bruce/Ash persona. On this level, the arrogance and boorishness Ash displays upon first meeting the medievalites parodies Hollywood stars who buy into their own cults and consider themselves superior to their fans. Just as Ash needs the villagers to accomplish his goals, Campbell is nothing without the community of fans who support him. In the end, when Ash chooses to go back to his own time and his low-wage job (because "[his] place is [t]here") rather than stay in medieval England and be king, it carries an off-screen resonance for the Bruce Campbell persona: It is better to be a cult star than a Hollywood superstar. The film encourages this melding of the Ash and Bruce narratives by offering a genre hybrid that only loyal *Evil Dead* fans could comprehend and appreciate. If the second movie was consciously made for B-movie fans, *Army of Darkness* was even more narrowly targeted toward Deadites. The tongue-in-cheek slapstick elements of the previous film take over completely, resulting in full-on Three Stooges routines that would be ridiculous for anyone unfamiliar with the previous movies and their backstories. This higher level of intra-group self-awareness cements the relationship between Campbell and his anti-establishment cult fans, as if Campbell was saying, "This may be the end of Ash, but Bruce will live on."

Cultifying Bruce

In the wake of *Army*, Campbell's work in such small-screen cult favorites as *The Adventures of Brisco County, Jr.* (1993–1994), *Hercules: The Legendary Journeys* (1995–1999), and *Xena: Warrior Princess* (1995–2001), as well as his continued presence on the convention scene helped further establish his Bruce/Ash persona. The release of the first DVD versions of *The Evil Dead* in 1999 presented a new opportunity for Campbell to deepen his relationship with existing fans and expand the reach of his constructed persona beyond the hard-core convention-going audience.

One DVD special feature that offers a useful insight into the process of technology-enabled star/fan interaction is *Fanalysis*, Campbell's documentary about cult fans and conventions. In this twenty-six-minute film, Campbell illuminates the values that bind the cult community together and simultaneously reinforces his position as an esteemed member of this community. Accordingly, Campbell demonstrates his community spirit by inviting fans onto the screen to speak for themselves. The image emerging from the documentary refutes the popular perception of cult fans as slightly unhinged, anti-social weirdos, as perpetuated by mainstream entertainment products such as *The Big Bang Theory* (2007–). First, *Fanalysis* contests this alleged anti-social attitude by depicting convention participation as a temporary escape from an inherently uninteresting normalcy and a quest for freedom from the roles allotted by mainstream society. The film shows a man dressed as a Stormtrooper Squad Leader who says, "I work for the county. I am an electrician.... But they don't know ... the man behind the mask." Another man dressed as Boba Fett reports, "I work as a paramedic every day, and this is kind of a stress relief. I get away from that situation entirely ... and I enjoy doing that."

While the mainstream perception is that the guy in the Boba Fett costume either thinks he is Boba Fett or wishes he could be, Campbell shows that these fans are just people who want to play with their identities and have a bit of fun. For example, one convention attendee explains, "I like all the fun people and the different atmosphere than [in] my boring little hometown." These "fun people" make up the community that is so crucial for cult fans. As J. P. Telotte has argued, cult fandom presents a manifestation of a "subcultural desire, a desire not simply for difference, but for an identifiable and even *common* difference, in effect, for a *safe* difference" (11; italics in original). Mary Hazelwood, identified as a "Convention Queen," alludes to this safety when she describes the goal of the convention organizers:

> We try to make people realize that they can come here. It's a safe environment.... There's a place where they can go where they aren't chastised for what they like or they aren't teased for being weird, or any of that.... It gives them a safe outlet for their creative energy.

Another convention attendee takes this statement a step further when he describes the democratic ideal of the cult community: "When you come to a convention, no one cares what your race is, what's your religion, your education, how much money you make. It's like we're all here because we're fans of *Star Trek*, *Star Wars*, *B[abylon] 5*, and so we can all be friends together." The documentary shifts the image of cult fans from "abnormal" to "exceptional." The film replaces the idea of passive victims of social excommunication with a concept of active, self-aware fans who *choose* to belong to a different, less "conventional" community of equals.

However, in *Fanalysis*, Campbell does more than just show his appreciation for his fans. Unlike the mainstream star, whom Violette Morin characterizes by "the art of ascending" to the ranks of the gods (118), Campbell has no desire to join what Morin calls the "Olympians." Campbell uses his film to reinforce his cult credibility by suggesting that he is a part of the grassroots cult community. To accomplish this, the documentary constantly blurs the lines that separate Campbell and the fans *depicted in* and, by extension, the fans *watching* the documentary. This is evident from the opening scene, in which Campbell is at an airport, clad in an uber-geek outfit of khaki trousers and a Hawaiian shirt. The camera angle and picture quality imply a simple video camera placed on a chair opposite Campbell. As he looks through his Filofax, Campbell's voice launches into a monologue in mock horror style about his existential crisis: "Airports are my life. I am a gypsy trapped in an actor's body. I go from place to place. So we transfer, we switch off, we take carry-on bags, we check our luggage, we tip people, we travel, 'cause that's what we do. Help me. Help me."

The speech captures the kind of alienation felt by people who do not "fit in," and the production techniques enhance the effect. Throughout the monologue, the camera angle remains unchanged, but the scene alternates between two kinds of shots. In one, Campbell is pacing back and forth, accompanied by a voice-over, and in the other, Campbell is sitting in the chair next to the camera and leans in to speak directly into the camera. Already in this opening scene, there is a sense of ambiguity. Is Campbell making the documentary, or is he the subject of the documentary? This disorientation continues in the next scene, in which a woman interviews Campbell about the making of *Fanalysis*. Suddenly, viewers are watching a documentary about a documentary about the making of the original documentary.

By twisting perspectives and subject positions throughout the documentary, Campbell weaves himself into the fan community, conveying the impression that he is one of them. Later in the film, the same young filmmaker asks Campbell, "What's probably the most surreal moment that's ever happened to you?" She probably expects some story related to Campbell's cult status, but instead, Campbell cites the costume show he had attended the night before with the other fans. The film then shows Campbell interviewing the costume contestants, thereby, reversing the fan/star relationship, as the star puts the fan on display.

All of these cinematographic strategies diminish the distance between Campbell and the fans.[3] While it is a given for convention-goers and viewers of the documentary that Campbell is a "subcultural celebrity" (Hills, "Subcultural Celebrity") and thus in some way extraordinary, the film emphasizes that Bruce is also an ordinary part of the community in that he shares their values and lifestyle. That is, like most of them, he, too, in some way has a "regular" job. He, too, values "difference" from the mainstream. The documentary functions as a reaffirmation of shared values and a portrayal of the symbiotic relationship between star and fan within the community.

In the film, Campbell describes the fan/star relationship as the "yin and yang" that complete each other. To reinforce this idea, the film others the "mainstream" during the closing credits when Campbell interviews a theater employee who is labeled "not a fan." As Bruce goads her on, she says that cult fans are "un-intellectual college guys." Bruce concludes, "So we have a bunch of dumbbells here tonight." When she clarifies that they "don't necessarily have to be *that* dumb," Bruce closes the film with the line, "You have to be *sort of* dumb to buy it." This last scene illustrates the boundaries between "us" (the *sort of* dumb cult people) and "them" (the mainstream theater employee who does not get the humor and does not understand that Campbell is poking fun at her), while handily inverting the normal power relationship between these two groups.

Beyond the mini-documentary, the re-release of the *Evil Dead* films on DVD opened up yet another avenue for Campbell to connect with his fan base—the commentary track. Campbell's commentary track for *The Evil Dead* has been repeatedly singled out as "the best feature on the disc" (Pierce).[4] Just as the VHS tape brought Ash into viewers' living rooms, DVD capabilities now brought Bruce "himself" into his fans' homes, thereby grafting the sense of intimacy with the character onto the actor. Campbell reinforces this effect by frequently addressing the viewers as if he were in the room with them. In a particularly revealing example, Campbell remarks at one point, "Obviously, the story is about to heat up now. Some bad things are about to happen. I don't wanna spoil it for ya; you know, for those of you who've seen the movie forty-seven times." With this quip, Campbell evokes the common practice of ritually rewatching cult movies with other fans and symbolically positions himself as a fellow fan of the original text.

Of course, Campbell is no ordinary member of the cult, but rather a highly privileged one with particular status. While this inevitably increases the distance between actor and regular fan, Campbell uses his trademark self-deprecating humor to counteract this distancing effect. Examples of this self-deprecation are legion. Before one of Ash's particularly wooden lines, Bruce quips, "Let's sit back and watch some fine acting." And subsequent comments include such utterances as, "Yeah, I was twenty-one years old, so you can't really blame me," and "These are just early acting experiments." The emphasis on the amateurishness of his performance continues throughout the commentary and allows Bruce to position himself as an ordinary man viewers can identify with.

Campbell fosters the illusion that he is just "one of the guys" by frequently interjecting personal stories that emphasize the humble beginnings of his film career. For example, when the tape recorder appears on-screen to play the voice recordings of Professor Knowby, Campbell says, "That cheeseball Panasonic recorder was one that my father used to use in advertising for years, and we decided to use it to put sound to a lot of our Super 8 millimeter films." Such background information helps create specialist knowledge about both the production and the star and aids in establishing a more intimate relationship between fan and star, or at least between fan and the Bruce/Ash persona Campbell is constructing.

A few years after the release of the first DVD edition, Campbell crossed into a new medium to further this process of establishing the core characteristics of his Bruce/Ash star persona and strengthening the bond with his fans with the publication of his first book, *If Chins Could Kill: Confessions of a B Movie Actor* (2001). One part autobiography, one part behind-the-scenes look at the making of the *Evil Dead* films, this book cements the core values behind the persona that he had been propagating for years in his convention appearances. By blending his personal background with the origin myth of the *Evil Dead* films, Bruce highlights two key values that are typically seen as mutually exclusive: play and work. On the play side, he mentions seeing his father in a stage performance at the age of eight and realizing, "[I]f I was an actor like Dad, I could skip that adult responsibility thing and just stick to the silly stuff" (20), and then backs this up with stories of their adolescent filmmaking hijinks. On the other hand, the book is replete with passages about the "working class" actor/filmmaker. In the blurb, Bruce implores potential readers to take a "ride with [him] through the choppy waters of blue-collar Hollywood." He then delivers, with plentiful stories of the less-than-glamorous life of a non-star actor, even going so far as to break down the numbers to show that second-rate actors are not as rich as people sometime assume, closing the section on a sarcastic, "You, too, can become a rich movie star" (218). Ultimately, he captures the essence of the Bruce Campbell persona when remarking, "Once you look past the hype, actors are nothing more than fugitives from reality who specialize in contradiction: we are both children and hardened adults—wide-eyed pupils and jaded working stiffs" (298).

To see the effectiveness of this exercise in persona-building, one need look no further than the reader reviews on Goodreads.com. One enthusiastic reviewer sums up his response to the book as follows:

> Great directors & actors don't spring out of the earth, but work their tails off & are gambling the whole way. It gives me a new respect for them. Self-employment is scary enough. To do it in the face of the whimsical executives of Hollywood is down right [sic] terrifying. To have a sense of humor about it is just fantastic. Campbell has both my thanks for all the entertainment he's provided me & my respect for having the courage to make a decent living in this weird industry [Jim].

Other reviews are littered with descriptions of Campbell as "a friendly and considerate man" (Richard), "a common man whos [sic] done common things in a [sic] uncommon way" (Marcus), and "a genuinely Nice Guy trying to make a living simply by honest hard work in an industry that doesn't exactly encourage niceness or honesty" (Bjorn). Referring to Campbell's anecdotes about the tough side of the business, one reader even points out the link these passages establish between Bruce and Ash (and Campbell's other characters): "These are the details that make you feel such a strong connection with Campbell—it also helps the reader connect the person with the 'every day [sic] persona' he displays on the screen" (Clausen). These sentiments, which echo throughout the over one thousand reviews of the book on Goodreads and Amazon, testify to the semantic power of the Bruce/Ash persona, particularly among his cult fans.

Meta-Cult: The Bruce Campbell Way

Having created this half-real/half-fictional persona, the next logical career move for Bruce Campbell was to put it "on stage." The Bruce/Ash persona entered the world of fiction most explicitly in two key works from the Campbell oeuvre: the "autobiographical novel" *Make Love!: The Bruce Campbell Way* (2005) and the meta-film *My Name is Bruce* (2007). In *Make Love!*, Campbell tells the story of his getting an important role in an "A-list romantic comedy starring Richard Gere, Renée Zellweger, produced by Robert Evans, directed by Mike Nichols" (7). Of course, there never was such a movie, and in one interview, Campbell called the book, "a pseudo-attempt to convince readers that I'm actually going through everything that's in it" (Thill). As with his earlier movies, the book is clearly targeted toward his established cult fan base. This is evident from the Bruce-penned blurb, in which he states:

> You picked up the book already, so you either:
> A. Know who I am
> B. Liked the cool smoking jacket I'm wearing on the cover
> C. Have just discovered that the bookstore restroom is out of toilet paper

In general, the book takes fans on a behind-the-scenes tour of a glamorous Hollywood production, all the while highlighting how superficial and self-absorbed the various A-list stars are and how completely detached they are from the reality of the common people who go to see their movies. Although the Campbell character is portrayed as a bit starstruck, he highlights the value of the "working-class" actor when he shows the Bruce persona lending a certain hard earned, B-movie "real world" wisdom to the otherworldly reality of the A-list stars. For example, in one scene, "Bruce" walks in on a fitting session for Zellweger. To the horror of the costume designer, who refers to him disdainfully as "the B movie expert" (205), "Bruce" proceeds to make a case for making Zellweger sexier by accentuating her curves with padded bras. When the two women seem to get defensive, he proclaims, "Well, you can't expect paying customers not to treat you like a commodity. They cough up the dough, they want to see the goods" (204). "Campbell" ultimately wins the argument by inviting a random bicycle messenger in to give his opinion about the "enhanced" Zellweger's outfit, which he eloquently states as follows: "Well, it's tight, and she's awesome. She looks like that chick from *Tomb Raider*" (206), leaving "Bruce" wondering how "these A-list pro-

104 Part II: The Franchise and Adaptations

ductions" could "ever get along without [him]" (207). Here, Campbell contrasts his character's grasp of the commercial aspects of filmmaking with the delicate artistic and gender-political sensibilities of the A-list star. This contrast emphasizes the character's status as a liminal figure who can infiltrate the glamorous Hollywood realm as a B-list actor while reporting back to the "real-world" cult fans.

In a clever move, Campbell even brings these fans into the book in the form of fan email to the Bruce character, in which they express their suspicions that their beloved hero has succumbed to the lure of the commercial dark side. "Bruce" reports the following:

> To the average genre fan, working on an A-list Hollywood film meant that I had turned my back on the very people who shouldered me through years of struggle, only to walk away when the going got good. I could feel their pain, but as an actor, as a purist, my first responsibility was to the character.... I had a prime opportunity to enrich the lives of people all across the globe, not to mention myself through some serious residuals, and I wasn't about to let it slip away [34].

With the phrase "their pain," Campbell performs a clever bit of narrative sleight of hand. The third-person pronoun implies that "Bruce," the character-narrator, believes he is writing for an audience of mainstream fans, whom he has attracted due to his budding A-list movie career. Together, they can muse on the B-list sensibilities of his "old" fans. This artificial construction highlights the actual conversation between Campbell (i.e., the author of the book) and the actual reader, who in all likelihood is one of those B-list fans who would be inclined to write the emails the narrator describes. In the typical Bruce Campbell self-deprecating manner, the author shares a laugh with the reader at the character's unfounded hubris. Campbell's real "loyalty" emerges in the ensuing events of the book, as the fictional movie production and then the book itself eventually succumb to the "B movie virus" (350). In fact, the final pages could be lifted from the script of a lazy Hollywood writer (however, laced with self-deprecating and sarcastic undertones), employing every hackneyed cliché that (remotely) makes sense, including a breathtaking police chase. Ultimately, Campbell, the author, invites his cult fans to laugh at a caricature of himself as an aspiring A-list star, all the while casting a critical eye on the shallow, commercialized, and artificial world of Hollywood productions.

In the film *My Name is Bruce*, the loyal members of the Bruce/Ash cult get their day on the silver screen in the character of Bruce superfan Jeff. The film imagines a Bruce Campbell bitter and disillusioned about his failure to ever make it out of the B-movie world. It effectively plays out as a bromance between "Bruce" and Jeff. Jeff, who, despite his teenage angst, embraces his status as a cult outsider, ultimately helps "Bruce" embrace his inner Ash. The turning point is the scene where Bruce enters Jeff's room and discovers a wide array of Bruce Campbell memorabilia. When Bruce grasps the important role his Bruce/Ash persona plays for superfan Jeff, he locates a purpose in his B-movie career and starts to believe that he can be heroic, as Jeff expects him to be. In the long run, Bruce can only overcome the evil Guan-Di with the help of Jeff and the other "locals," a fact which symbolically reinforces the importance of the symbiotic relationship between Bruce, Ash, and the fans, as well as reaffirming the value of the cult community of outsiders.

Similar to *Chins*, Campbell (as director) and writer Mark Verheiden lace the movie with intertextual references that appeal to the members of the *Evil Dead*/Bruce Campbell community. The film shows Bruce on the set of his latest (fictional) B-movie *Cave Alien 2* (an allusion to the TV movie *Alien Apocalypse* [2005]) and also features numerous references to the (real) *Evil Dead* movies and other "seminal" Bruce Campbell "texts," including the rehashing of famous Campbell catchphrases. There are even references to *Make Love!*, such as when Bruce is shown reading *The Complete Dummies Guide to Acting*, a fictional book that is mentioned several times in *Make Love!*, and a poster in Jeff's room for *Death of the Dead*, a (fake) film which figures prominently in the book's plot. As Campbell points out in the DVD/Blu-ray commentary, most of the memorabilia in Jeff's room was real, including a spare Brisco County, Jr., costume that Campbell owned, while some items were created to fill up space (e.g. a poster for the fictional film, *The Stoogitive*). In a final absurdist twist, the film ends with a closing narrative frame, which highlights that everything has just been a movie, only for the monster to jump out of the screen to attack Bruce. All of these elements are included to draw in the "true" fans. As Kate Egan and Sarah Thomas have argued, "the ironic, the overtly performed" as well as "the playful juxtaposition between 'fact' and 'fiction' … may be seen to be as 'authentic'" by cult audiences (8). Campbell is, in effect, "keeping it real" for his fans. Ultimately, they are the only ones who can appreciate the ironic contrast between the on-screen Bruce, who struggles to escape the expectations imposed on him by his signature screen character, and the "real" Bruce Campbell, who has maintained a career-spanning relationship with Ash and his legions of fans.

The Return of Ash

While another *Evil Dead* renaissance started in 2013 with the release of the *Evil Dead* reboot directed by Fede Álvarez, in the context of this chapter, the film is best summarized with a line from an IMDb fan review, which suggests, "no Ash = no point" (Albatross). The real fans had to wait two more years for the return of Bruce Campbell *and* Ash in the television show *Ash vs. Evil Dead* (2015–2018). With this series, the Ash character returned to the screen in a version that bears remarkable similarity to the Bruce character in *My Name*: grumpy, out-of-shape, and disillusioned with his "normal guy" status in the "real" world. One could interpret the show as a television remake of *My Name*, with Ash playing the role of "Bruce." This intertextual overlap reinforces the Bruce/Ash persona, deepening the relationship with the original Deadites and, as a gateway text into the *Evil Dead* world, no doubt welcoming a new generation of fans.

While the show represents the return of Ash to the screen, the related promotional efforts have also featured the return of the Bruce/Ash hybrid persona. This time around, Campbell even made it to mainstream TV when he appeared on Stephen Colbert's *The Late Show* with costar and fellow B-list icon Lucy Lawless. In this appearance, Campbell took the opportunity to release his well-honed convention-circuit persona on the mainstream, once again blurring the lines between actor and character in a way only true fans could appreciate. During the interview, Lawless and Campbell segue effortlessly into a mock, in-character debate as Ash and Ruby argue over who was responsible for releasing the demons in the fictional universe. The contrast between this performance and the typical talk show interview, in which "serious" actors are careful to speak of their film characters in the third person, could not be stronger.

Even when Lawless and Campbell speak as "themselves," they refuse to take the whole concept of a late-night interview seriously. The performance rules of the late-night interview genre demand a show of spontaneity. Pre-interviews conducted by the staff or prepared topics of conversation have to be concealed behind a performance, which suggests that "real people" are having a friendly, impromptu conversation, but Lawless and Campbell do not play along. She first asks, "Have you got your glasses here, Bruce? Put 'em on." Bruce, with mock surprise that clearly signals that this is a pre-planned routine, answers, "Why would I put them on, Lucy?" The routine leads to Campbell taking over Colbert's chair, thereby inverting the normal power dynamic between guest and host, and, in this case, between mainstream A-list comedian and cult B-list actor. Colbert is relegated to the sidelines as the "straight man," while Campbell takes over the spotlight and wastes no time going straight into his B-movie "bumbling actor" shtick. His exaggerated imitation of Colbert's mannerisms soon gets the audience playing along, chanting "Stephen," as if his imitation were so good that he had them fooled. Pulling them in further, Campbell then interrupts the crowd cheers with the line, "Wait! I've got a line of dialogue I gotta say." This line turns out to be a snarky imitation of Colbert's signature line "Nation" from *The Colbert Report* (2005–2014), after which Campbell stops and says, with fake humility, "And that's it—it's a—it's a one-line imitation."

In essence, Campbell's appearance on Colbert is a condensed version of the theme he explored in *Make Love!*: B-list actor infiltrates A-list world, or as Campbell's website says, "Bruce is still living the dream as a 'B' movie king in an 'A' movie world" ("Book Release"). This word "king" embodies the mock swagger that Campbell brings into the situation. Just as the "Bruce" character in *Make Love!* ultimately "prevailed" by dragging the A-list production down into the B-list world, here Bruce essentially forces the A-list production to play by his rules. Starting with his unapologetic in-character description of his show's absurd plot, and culminating in his cheesy, overblown Colbert impression, Campbell's trademark overacting and slyly self-deprecating humor invites the audience (both in the studio and beyond) in on the fun. For five "glorious" minutes, Deadites saw their quirky cult sensibility hijack one of the mainstreamiest of mainstream shows. This is success—the Bruce Campbell way.

NOTES

1. We would like to express our gratitude to Kate Egan and Sarah Thomas for their comments on a much earlier version of this essay.
2. For more details on the cultification of *The Evil Dead*, see Kate Egan's book on the movie in Wallflower's Cultographies series (2011).
3. The documentary cleverly employs several other stylistic means to highlight that Bruce is part of the community, but due to spatial constraints, we cannot go into details here.
4. Remarkably, the overwhelmingly positive feedback the original commentary tracks received led to the recording of a new commentary track featuring Campbell, Raimi, and Tapert for the Blu-ray release. This track is less Campbell slapstick and more straightforward production history. For a more detailed discussion of *The Evil Dead*'s 1999 commentary tracks, see Egan's contribution to *B is for Bad Cinema: Aesthetics, Politics, and Cultural Value* (2014).

WORKS CITED

Albatross. "The Most Remaky Remake Ever Made." *Amazon.co.uk*, 22 Aug. 2013, amazon.co.uk/gp/aw/cr/rR328EI1Z2Z6SGX.
Barratt, Jim. *Bad Taste*. Wallflower Press, 2008.
Bjorn. "Review of *If Chins Could Kill: Confessions of a B Movie Actor*." *Goodreads*, 7 May 2013, goodreads.com/review/show/609561102.
"Bruce Campbell at Convention 1989." *YouTube*, 19 Aug. 2009, youtube.com/watch?v=iB27aQzocBQ.
Campbell, Bruce. "Book Release—*Hail to the Chin: Further Confessions of a B-Movie Actor*." BruceCampbellwww, 15 Aug. 2017, bruce-campbell.com/events.asp?specific=148.
_____. *If Chins Could Kill: Confessions of a B Movie Actor*. LA Weekly Books, 2002.
_____. *Make Love! The Bruce Campbell Way*. Thomas Dunne Books, 2005.
Campbell, Bruce, director. *My Name Is Bruce*. Dark Horse Entertainment, 2007.
Clausen, Daniel. "Review of *If Chins Could Kill: Confessions of a B Movie Actor*." *Goodreads*, 23 July 2011, goodreads.com/review/show/163260433.
Collis, Clark. "*Ash vs Evil Dead*: Bruce Campbell Teases Season 3." 12 Dec. 2016, *Entertainment Weekly Online*, ew.com/article/2016/12/12/ash-vs-evil-dead-season-3-bruce-campbell/.
Dyer, Richard. *Stars*. New ed. BFI, 1998.
Egan, Kate. *The Evil Dead*. Wallflower Press, 2011.
_____. "*The Evil Dead* DVD Commentaries: Amateurishness and Bad Film Discourse." *B Is for Bad Cinema: Aesthetics, Politics, and Cultural Value*, edited by Claire Perkins and Constantine Verevis. State University of New York Press, 2015, pp. 181–195.
_____, and Sarah Thomas. "Introduction: Star-Making, Cult-Making and Forms of Authen-

ticity." *Cult Film Stardom: Offbeat Attractions and Processes of Cultification*, edited Kate Egan and Sarah Thomas. Palgrave, 2013, pp. 1–17.
Fanalysis. Directed by Bruce Campbell. Campbell Entertainment, 2002.
"Fan Expo Canada 2009: Bruce Campbell Q and A Part 6." *YouTube*, 4 Sept. 2009, youtube.com/watch?v=di687H7XB6U.
Felsher, Michael. *Bringing the Dead Home for Dinner: A History of The Evil Dead in Your Home.* DVD Booklet, 2002.
Gledhill, Christine. "Introduction." *Stardom: Industry of Desire*, edited by Christine Gledhill. Routledge, 1991, pp. xi–xix.
Hills, Matt. "Cult Movies With and Without Cult Stars: Differentiating Discourses of Stardom." *Cult Film Stardom: Offbeat Attractions and Processes of Cultification*, edited by Kate Egan and Sarah Thomas. Palgrave, 2013, pp. 21–36.
_____. "'Subcultural Celebrity' and Cult TV Fan Cultures." *Mediactive* 2 (2002), pp. 59–73.
Jancovich, Mark. "Cult Fictions: Cult Movies, Subcultural Capital and the Production of Cultural Distinctions." *Cultural Studies* 16, no. 2 (2002), pp. 306–22.
The Late Show with Stephen Colbert, season 1, episode 41. CBS, 11 Nov. 2015.
Marcus, Joey. "Review of *If Chins Could Kill: Confessions of a B Movie Actor*." *Goodreads*, 15 Apr. 2008, goodreads.com/review/show/20186086.
Morin, Violette. "Les Olympiens." *Communications* 2, no. 2 (1963), pp. 105–121.
Pierce, Ken. "*The Evil Dead*: Special Edition." dvdfuturewww, 7 June 2011, dvdfuture.com/review.php?id=220.
Raimi, Sam, director. *Army of Darkness*. Renaissance Pictures, 1992.
_____. *The Evil Dead*. Renaissance Pictures, 1981.
_____. *Evil Dead 2*. Renaissance Pictures, 1987.
Richard. Review of *If Chins Could Kill: Confessions of a B Movie Actor*. *Goodreads*, 11 July 2008, goodreads.com/review/show/26961413.
Sconce, Jeffrey. "'Trashing' the Academy: Taste, Excess, and an Emerging Politics of Cinematic Style." *Screen* 36, no. 4 (1995), pp. 371–93.
Telotte, J. P. "Beyond All Reason: The Nature of the Cult." *The Cult Film Experience: Beyond All Reason*, edited by J. P. Telotte. University of Texas Press, 1991, pp. 5–17.
Thill, Scott. "Shut Up and Act." Salonwww, 14 July 2005, dir.salon.com/story/books/int/2005/07/14/campbell/print.html.

Ash vs. the Cult of Personality

ALEX LIDDELL

The *Evil Dead* franchise is a notorious example of canon and tone discontinuity in the horror genre, flipping from gory melodrama to "splatstick." As is the norm in similar franchises, it is the monsters that tie the chapters together; in this case, the Deadites summoned from the *Necronomicon* are the running villains headlining the movies, comics, video games, television series etc. What sets the *Evil Dead* franchise apart from its peers is one man: Ash. The iconic main character, Ashley J. Williams, is the protagonist that connects all media associated with *The Evil Dead*. Casts and context may change, but Ash always seems to be at the center of the action; he is the fan-favorite and a constant presence on *Evil Dead* merchandise, marketing and in pop culture references. Even in Fede Álvarez's *Evil Dead* (2013), a full reboot movie with seemingly no canonical connection to any previous or subsequent *Evil Dead* media, Ash makes an appearance after the end credits to send off the film with one last catchphrase, "groovy." It is as if the movie could not be considered a true continuation without linking to Ash, played once again by Bruce Campbell, another staple of the series. Whether you put it down to fan service or having deep significance, one thing is certain: There can be no *Evil Dead* without Ash.

The reason for this might seem obvious at first; Ash was the protagonist from the beginning and is a fan proclaimed badass ("Ashley"), both are valid explanations for why the *Evil Dead* keeps returning to him. However, unlike most slasher movie protagonists, he has enjoyed an unprecedented legacy of fame, pop cultural longevity and iconography that sets him apart. This is notable given that in the horror genre (particularly slasher films of the 1980s), protagonists like Ash are surprisingly rare. Despite his popularity, or perhaps because of his almost untouchable icon status, few horror franchises center sole survivor male heroes, preferring instead to foreground the monsters/villains or sole survivor females (aka "final girls"). Consequently, Ash subverts many of the tropes associated with mainstream horror, which not only makes him stand out but also grounds him as a compelling character. He remains instantly recognizable as a pop culture icon and opens new possibilities for plot development.

Ash vs. Character Progression

As with much of the creative process behind Renaissance Pictures' early productions, Ash's character construction was born far more from experimental and practical factors than from conscious narratives. Renaissance Pictures[1] chose indie horror as a medium not simply for the love of genre, but for the low-budget potential, it held for developing their burgeoning styles. The lack of narrative planning is evidenced by the original script for *The Evil Dead* (1981) being roughly fourteen pages in length, with actions and atmosphere taking priority over dialogue and complex character arcs to foreground visuals (Muir 34). This led to the focus of the film being Ash's losing battle with the supernatural, employing key strategies used to develop suspense in horror films of the 1970s and 1980s, much of which relies on Bruce Campbell's physicality as an actor rather than the witty lines. Because of the limited resources available (from casting to location), the team distilled a quintessential tale of terror without being bound by conventions of storytelling of the time. The filmmakers managed to create a visceral Lovecraftian story that lay the foundation for the *Evil Dead* franchise's most enduring theme: Tormenting Ash.[2]

His first incarnation is noticeably different from the Ash popularized in subsequent *Evil Dead* installments; he doesn't lose his hand, doesn't wield a chainsaw nor does he get to say any memorable one-liners, he's not even recognizable as the main character at first. The movie begins as a standard slasher: A group of young people enters a secluded cabin; one by one they are brutally tortured and killed leaving behind one character to defeat the monster or stay alive long enough to be rescued. But that is where the similarity ends.

Ash's defining feature is revealed to be cowardice, he is well meaning but shown to be useless when his friends are assaulted, he makes costly mistakes and is in a constant state of terror. Slasher cliché dictates that Ash, as a cowardly male character, would be outlived by the more developed, heroic characters. In fact, a new viewer might assume that Ash's friend, Scotty, as the bravest of the group, will be protagonist; but Scotty betrays his friends and runs away into the woods, only to be killed, leaving Ash to fend for himself alone. It is in this second half of the film where Ash gains his rite of passage from (as Bruce Campbell puts it) "sniveling college student" to "man," as he barely defends himself from the chaos surrounding him (Campbell, Audio). He derives his bravery purely from survival instinct, he is only the hero by default; but rather than making him an unlikable character, audiences warm to Ash.[3] He becomes relatable precisely because he is vulnerable, because he (like the viewer) is not good in a crisis like this and is in real peril, which makes it more satisfying when he wins and devastating when he loses.

The first Ash's legitimacy as an authentic version of the character is often debated among fans, just as the movie itself is contested as a better or lesser part of the trilogy because of the dramatic differences in tone, budget, and performances. The main shift in *Evil Dead 2* (1987), however, is rather than playing the straight man to the black comedy of the Deadites, Ash engages with the mischief of the supernatural forces screwing with him, and puts up more of a fight against it. When they taunt him, he fires one-liners back at them and directly challenges them when they threaten him or his friends. *Evil Dead 2* is the film where Ash makes a stark transition from cowardly, eternally tormented victim to iconic badass. Here, even without the context of the first film, he is instantly recognizable as the protagonist, given the most screen time and character development, conforming to a more conventional slasher film.

Again, there is a prolonged focus on the violence that Ash endures; the violations are more comedic than the previous film, but it is nonetheless gruesome watching a powerless Ash suffer and have everyone around him die horribly. That first characterization of vulnerability is still present, helping him to retain some relatability, but it is eventually overcome to make way for a survivalist power fantasy. *Evil Dead 2* also sees Ash showcase his ingenuity, demonstrated via his chainsaw hand that he creates, defying all logic and physics as one of Ash's main "Swiss army appendages."[4] Its construction also seems to be developed more out of the desire to survive than genuine bravery, genius, or even cosmic destiny; but it is nevertheless a facet of the cult power figure he becomes. Unlike his predecessor, this Ash clearly does survive the horror, but in escaping one hell, he is transported to another to fight the same enemies only in a medieval setting, further from home and safety than when he started. A prospect that makes Ash cry out in despair; even after triumphing and cheered as the savior of humanity, his ending is still bleak, he ultimately does not win.

In *Army of Darkness* (1992), Ash's flaws and the chaos he enters gets ramped up to a cartoonish degree. The cabin is replaced with a high fantasy setting, and he is now officially at the center of the story. Ash provides his own exposition via narration at the film's beginning (a motif that would be repeated in the subsequent comics and video games); he's recognized as the "chosen one." He is foregrounded as the hero but introduced, once again, as a disempowered fool, as a captive in chains. His transformation from weak coward to heroic warrior is much faster paced, not to mention more morally dubious. Ash flits from one extreme to another throughout the film, sometimes within a matter of minutes. A perfect example of this is when Ash's captor threatens to throw him in a pit to his death, Ash's first response is to pathetically beg his fellow captives to tell everyone that he is not with them and thus gain his freedom. When refused, Ash is reduced to a desperate mess, which just gets him booed by the crowed and thrown in the pit. Once more, Ash is faced with the choice of letting the pit's demon kill him or fight back, and it is only then that he makes the rapid switch from wuss to tactical fighter. Fright is replaced with aggressive overconfidence, turning him into a genuine force to be reckoned with, as if Ash has been possessed by a different personality.

Ash repeats this process many times after this moment; the catalyst is always Ash backed into a position where he cannot run away, either literally or emotionally. Still, Ash's obvious prime concern is his own wellbeing. It is his compulsion to survive that drives his moments of heroism rather than any sense of moral righteousness or aptitude. Granted, after the events of previous film, he is now practiced at killing the undead at this point, yet he still has a boneheaded nature, which paradoxically allows him to access his heroism and is his greatest obstacle. Through misremembering an incantation to complete his quest, he inadvertently unleashes an army of undead, yet his priority is still just getting himself home, even if it means dooming everyone else. Raimi's central ethos is foregrounded further: "Self-sacrifice is for ninnies" (Royal 39–51). It's only toward the end when he is called out on his cowardice and is therefore not guaranteed a trip back home, when he's essentially run out of easy options, Ash finally steps up and uses his skills to rally an army against the oncoming hordes. While his intentions are far from pure, Ash's last-minute, manic acts of resistance are undeniably effective, with the help of his allies; for once, Ash is finally victorious, at least for a while.

This characterization remains relatively consistent through all the subsequent continuities of the *Evil Dead* comics, video games and the current television series *Ash vs. Evil Dead* (2015–2018). The official personality of Ash, in terms of what is perceived in canon, is that of a buffoonish jerk who (vague prophecies and technical aptitude aside) only accidently becomes the hero, and whose cowardice and ignorance causes him to either make the situation worse or to make a mockery of an otherwise serious situation. He is a braggart who does not fight unless he cannot avoid it, despite being inexplicably good at fighting. His contradictory character and instability acts as a compliment to the unpredictability of the *Evil Dead* universe; the horror is heightened by the fact that nobody is guaranteed safety or retribution that slasher formula allows for, even Ash can be dangerously inconsistent to the point of loathsomeness. However, he is still relatable enough to be beloved despite his flaws, whether audiences love seeing him get tortured for his hubris or rooting for him to overcome evil, they can neither ignore Ash nor can they fail to be entertained. It is rare that a revered film character would ever be allowed to progress like this, let alone become beloved by foregrounding cowardly jackassery as his main motivation. However, looking a little closer at Raimi's iconography and popular tropes employed by the film industry at the time the trilogy was produced, it is hard to imagine Ash's conflicting personality evolving any other way.

Tropes vs. Ash

One of Raimi's talents is capitalizing on the zeitgeists of the medium and perfecting techniques from varied sources. The *Evil Dead* trilogy is no exception, wearing a lot of references to classics such as *The Texas Chainsaw Massacre* (1974) and *The Three Stooges* on its sleeve (Collura). But Raimi dovetailing elements from other stories into the *Evil Dead* saga also manifests in subtler ways, utilizing and subverting the tropes associated with them, which fundamentally affects the perception of Ash.

One prominent example is his subversion of the "final girl," first examined by Carol J. Clover's groundbreaking analysis deconstructing the trope. Initially the differences between Ash, the "final guy," and the common archetype of the final girl seem superficial, namely that the genders have been changed to misdirect expectations. However, gender takes on extra significance when placed within the context of a symbolically male fantasy, or rather nightmare. Unlike the scenarios final girls find themselves in, Ash is not a damsel in distress stalked by a monstrous male killer using appropriately phallic methods of murder and torture, the evil that follows him is distinctly supernatural and monstrously feminine. With the Deadites possessing primarily females to torment and trick their victims, they play upon societal expectations of the assumed innocent, weak and nurturing existence of women, only to horrifically dispel those notions by becoming deadly, demonic mockeries of womanhood. Initially, Ash's sentimentality is used against him in this way; his reluctance to dismember his beloved girlfriend after she is possessed, through seeing her in a beautiful, vulnerable state in contrast to her ugly demonic form, and through the demon sweetly begging Ash to not hurt her, has predictably terrible consequences for him. It is only through replacing his chivalry with cold, ferocious pragmatism that Ash survives and (if possible) saves the day, which is presented as the hypermasculine opposite of female manipulation: Stable and (mostly) honest as opposed to random and insidious, living male versus undead female.

The idea of weaponizing femininity is not a new idea in film, but it is rarely applied to a genre where male violence against female protagonists is the norm. This masculine presentation is highlighted by the choice of torture employed against Ash and the environments where they take place. Following Barbara Creed's analysis: "Whenever male bodies are represented as monstrous in the horror film they assume characteristics usually associated with the female body" (118). This is often the case with Ash's disempowerment, in which he is forced to "change shape, bleed, give birth, become penetrable" via supernatural forces possessing him, cutting him, attacking his genitals or other prized body parts, or infecting him with humanoid parasites. Because of the inhumane nature of these assaults, or the fact that these feminine concepts are applied to a man, the spectacle becomes unnatural and disturbing, but there is some enjoyment to be gained masochistically or through *schadenfreude*.

One explanation for this could be that the feminine torture provides a fitting punishment for Ash's macho hubris, in both providing a reflection for his violence and comedy by using an unconventional method of punishment. But equally, Ash's successful attempts to combat these assaults on his body and soul often take the form of adopting traditionally masculine affectations. His weapons, chainsaw hand and boomstick shotgun, are prime examples of this. Typical images of Ash in a position of power over evil or challenging it feature him posing, muscular and wielding the phallic weaponry, both in *Evil Dead* media and its advertising. In many depictions, he holds up his chainsaw in triumph or ready to take down a Deadite, swings his gun theatrically, and is sometimes accompanied by a gorgeous woman draped lovingly beside him, looking to him to protect her. The promotion for the second season of *Ash vs. Evil Dead* even involved imagery of the grandiose, male patriotism of Donald Trump's 2016 election campaign; posturing gun-in-hand with the tagline "make America groovy again," there's little doubt as to who Ash was parodying and what concepts he was associating with.

Even the same powerful magic used to control demons tends to backfire on Ash and his associates more than applying physical machismo does. This is evidenced not just by Ash getting magic wrong and having it rebound into something dangerous or characters dying to complete spells, it is those that are adept at magic that suffer more consequences for using it over hack and slash tactics. For instance, in *Ash vs. Evil Dead*, Ruby Knowby is revealed to be one of the Dark Ones responsible for creating the *Necronomicon*, but out of desperation recruits Ash to defeat her own demonic "children" who betray her after getting too powerful for her to control. Her magic, despite being powerful enough to "birth" the demons, is not enough to protect her or the world, if anything it makes the situation worse. At best, magic simply displaces problems by sending them into the past or other dimensions, leaving them to be summoned again or afflict someone else. In the "real world" of the *Evil Dead*, it is stabbing, immolation, dismemberment and shooting the evil that manages to truly destroy it, or at least it is required as part of the destruction. Once more, this is framed in a way that symbolically pits feminine against masculine; Ruby is (at first) on the side of "feminized evil," while Ash represents a "masculine good," Ruby eventually loses while Ash triumphs. Even Baal (Joel Tobeck), a main male villain, is a gender-nonconformist in appearance and behavior; he disguises himself frequently as women and relies on stereotypically feminine subterfuge of seduction and emotional manipulation rather than brute force. When he does get into a fistfight with Ash, Baal cheats with magic to win because he cannot defeat Ash with physical strength alone. It is ultimately a clash of male egos that defeats Baal, with Ash victorious at the end as the strongest ego, physically and tactically as the dominant man.

The domestic setting (usually the cabin in the woods where it all began) amid the untamed wilderness also reinforces masculine empowerment fantasies. The remote rural location plays on the "dichotomies between good and evil, wilderness and civilization, and order and chaos" (Murphy 30). The symbolism fits neatly with the central opposition of feminine and masculine, conjuring the idea of man versus nature. Tropes regarding taming the wilderness and the fear of succumbing to madness outside of civilization has long been masculinized, the anxiety of women that are under the protection of male protagonists being defiled by wild entities lies at the heart of this. So, in the context it is fitting that Ash's DIY melee weapon happens to be a tool used for felling trees, essentially imposing order on wildlife. Ash finds his salvation in a work shed, a stereotypical refuge for men, where he can engineer solutions to his problems. There is something ironic yet comforting about the idea of defeating inexplicable, all-powerful demons with something as simple and human as hitting it repeatedly with power tools. The viewer can find it easier to relate to the hands-on woodsman sensibilities like sucking evil out of your leg "like a snake bite" than by following an alien set of rules.

Furthermore, Ash's usually inconsequential role as an S-Mart department store employee is elevated as inexplicably useful when his knowledge is repositioned towards terrorizing a medieval mob with his "Shop Smart! Shop S-Mart" speech, which as well as being a clever gag further galvanizes the theme of meager facets of capitalist civilization overpowering the primitive. Equally, a rustic domestic setting, a place of safety and family, when infiltrated and turned into a torture chamber creates a "hearth of darkness" (Williams), which also plays on male fears of being usurped as the "head of the house." Indeed, the homes that Ash finds himself contained in often become an extension of the wild, whether it's the furniture coming alive or having an ordinary set of shelves completely immobilize him, Ash is constantly centered in hostile spaces as the one man bombarded by disorder. It is easy to cast this symbolism as misogynistic, or at least over-glorifying male pursuits, but that is never taken entirely seriously. The *Evil Dead* franchise is ultimately both comedy and horror, which somewhat neutralizes any potential propaganda that would result from a serious portrayal. The tongue-in-cheek tone can be attributed to Campbell's performance, but it also appears to be by Raimi's design. If he made Ash wholly serious throughout it is possible he would become insufferable to watch as a one-dimensional meathead; turning him into a self-aware parody, highlighting Ash as a loser, is oddly what makes him more bearable.

Undercutting patriarchal depictions with suffering or mockery was not popularized in the horror genre, but it was a common technique during the 1980s for another genre Raimi proved to be adept in, action cinema. I would argue that while Ash is comparable to a male equivalent of the final girl trope, he has more in common with action heroes like *Die Hard*'s (1988) John McClane (Bruce Willis) than he does with final girls like *Halloween*'s (1978) Laurie Strode (Jamie Lee Curtis). Most final girls are defined by their relative moral superiority over their friends who comprise the body count, their comparatively better resourcefulness and grounded natures, which is what ensures their survival. Ash is not morally superior to his peers, sometimes he is distinctly worse, his resourcefulness is hampered by his pigheadedness and goofy nature, but not only is he not killed by his flaws, being self-serving and crude ensures his survival and entertains. This can be taken as just a mirror image of the final girl trope, as a method of subverting the gender biases, but it can be read as placing a type of action hero in place of the final girl. The 1980s saw an increased marketability of the male body as spectacle, a throwback to the populist patriarchal heroes that emerged in the 1960s and 1970s. Due to progressing gender equality, 1980s culture had denaturalized these traditional male heroes to some extent, making their presence in modern cinema anachronistic at best and problematic at worst.

To combat this, two dominant strategies emerged: "Resorting either to images of physical torture and suffering or to comedy, the body of the hero, his excessive 'musculinity' ... subjected to humiliation and mockery at some level" (Tasker 237). Ash's portrayal uses both strategies, exploring his suffering through comedy horror rather than through action movie tropes. This "more wiseguy than tough guy" approach allows the viewer to enjoy the empowerment and spectacle of the male protagonist while avoiding over-glorifying antiquated gender roles or replicating the same cynical storylines. This effective combination echoes through most of Raimi's constructions of main characters, from *Darkman* (1990) to *Spider-Man* (2002), as his preferred approach to present the men as tortured characters with a sense of humor. It is easier to sympathize with the self-deprecating struggling hero, and thus celebrate the nostalgia of old cinema, without seeming reverent to its more problematic elements. Just as Ash manages to embody multiple roles as the jerkish party fool and admired role model, the representation can essentially have it both ways.

Supplanting the final girl for an action hero also proved to be a good stratagem for sustaining the franchise across media. The transition from film to television was easy specifically because it continued to mix these complimentary conventions; just as *Buffy the Vampire Slayer* (1997–2003) spun the final girl trope into a successful serial teen drama (Tincknell 251), *Ash vs. Evil Dead* took its format and applied the emerging trope of the aging action hero to it (Feasey 507–20). While preserving the quirks already established in the mythos, it has extended its longevity and multigenerational appeal by continuing the saga with a self-reflecting, aging Ash.

Ash vs. Himself

Knowingly or otherwise, the *Evil Dead* franchise became a case study of one man's journey fighting his demons throughout his life. It's true that Ash slays literal demons, but other than Deadites Ash's most consistent adversary is himself, which manifests either as the consequences of his own poor decisions or as the physical embodiment of his dark side. While under assault from feminized supernatural attacks, the evil's most effective antagonism against Ash is when it takes on his image or takes his worst traits to create a rival. This theme was first explored in *Evil Dead 2*, with Ash's reflection confronting him out of a mirror as a hallucination to unnerve him. The literal Evil Ash became fully actualized in *Army of Darkness*, where Ash is forced to give birth to an evil twin after being assaulted by multiple miniature versions of himself, this time born from a broken mirror. One might think the embodiment of Ash's inner darkness, created from a reflection, would be a mirror for Ash too, i.e., total opposites. Yet it becomes clear that they are both matched in goofiness and exuberance, and Ash is not quite the moral superior; evidenced by Ash responding to his doppelganger mocking him as a "goody two-shoes" with "I'm not that good" before shooting Evil Ash in the face.

While they do not easily fall into a dichotomy, there are interesting differences between the two (other than one being more evil and corpse-looking than the other). In opposition to Ash, in the *Army of Darkness* film, sequel comics and the video game *Evil Dead: Hail to the King* (2000), Evil Ash (aka The General) prefers using magic over science, he is physically stronger and, more significantly, he is far more organized and braver than Ash is. One interpretation of this could be that Ash's "goodness" is inexorably tied to his incompetence and cowardly self-preservation, implying the only thing separating him from evil is not his intent, but his inability to do evil effectively. This way Evil Ash not only presents a threat, but a living criticism of Ash's flighty nature.

Another incarnation of Evil Ash appears in the TV series, this time having grown from Ash's dismembered hand, who is indistinguishable from the real Ash. The twist that reveals the imposter is that the real Ash requests that his friends "shoot them both," which isn't a noble sacrifice but just another one of Ash's attempts to take the easy way out. A natural progression from encountering his doppelgangers would be for Ash to examine himself existentially, which is addressed directly in the episode "Brujo," where Ash goes on a drug-induced spiritual journey of the self. However, as a final punchline to Ash's self-examination, he does not find any deep meaning to his existence other than completing his current obligations and fighting yet another battle with demonic representations of himself. Despite being forced to deal with cosmic terror throughout his life, all he wants is to do is relax in a fantasy of Jacksonville, Florida, an idealized vacation spot he saw on a postcard. Neither does he desire any deeper meaning, he only wants an ordinary life, recognized as a good person, living happily with his friends, having casual relationships with women, and partying. The greatest tragedy for him is that he only ever partly achieves that dream, he is constantly interrupted by Lovecraftian enemies that he currently tends to find more frustrating than horrific.

Here lies the greatest irony of Ash's characterization: His existence and fictional reality is laden with subtext, which the viewer can interpret in a variety of ways, but none of it seems to amount to anything for Ash or in the grand scheme of things within his world. Under the circumstances, requiring only his basic needs of enjoyment and friendship be met, Ash's practical philosophy of "shoot first, think never" is not just applicable to dispatching Deadites, it is also good life advice. Because quests for deeper meaning are not only pointless but tedious for him, and it certainly does not save him or his loved ones. This creates another subversion of the hero's journey, instead of locating his purpose among the stars, Ash's preferred end game is acquiring earthly pleasures and avoiding the responsibility of being the chosen one. It is far from a romantic ideal of a hero, but incredibly relatable as it is humorous. It allows the viewer to laugh at the absurd story of a man fated to save the world from an apocalypse that he is partly responsible for. It dares the viewer to sympathize with Ash's simple and selfish wants, which are desires that the audience often shares with him. While providing a blood-soaked adventure and power fantasy, Ash's journey acknowledges that if an ordinary man was put into such a situation, it would most likely be a farce, undercutting pandering to male ego with biting commentary about the failings of imperfect men.

Notes

1. A coalition of Sam Raimi, Rob Tapert, Bruce Campbell and Ivan Shapiro.
2. Lovecraftian in that explorations of madness and world-building cosmic horror overtakes characterization.
3. For example, Mark Dutton, creator of fan-site "Within the Woods" notes that inexperienced acting and Ash's ineptitude helps put viewers "in his shoes" (Egan 41–42).
4. Ash develops a variety of attachments defined by this trope, including detachable weapons and fully operational false limbs ("Swiss").

Works Cited

"Ashley J. 'Ash' Williams." *Badass of the Week*, badassoftheweek.com/ash.
"Brujo." *Ash vs. Evil Dead*, season 1, episode 4, Starz, 21 Nov. 2015.
Campbell, Bruce. "Audio Commentary." *The Evil Dead*. Anchor Bay Entertainment, 2003.
Clover, Carol J. *Men, Women, and Chain Saws: Gender in the Modern Horror Film*. Princeton University Press, 2015.
Collura, Scott. "Sam Raimi Gives Us An Evil Dead History Lesson." IGNwww, 30 Oct. 2015, uk.ign.com/articles/2015/10/30/sam-raimi-gives-us-an-evil-dead-history-lesson.
Creed, Barbara. "Dark Desires: Male Masochism in the Horror Film." *Screening the Male: Exploring Masculinities in Hollywood Cinema*, edited by Steven Cohen and Ina Rae Hark, Routledge, 2002, pp. 118–133.
Egan, Kate. *The Evil Dead (Cultographies)*. Columbia University Press, 2012.
Feasey, Rebecca. "Mature Masculinity and the Ageing Action Hero." *Groniek* 190 (2011), pp. 507–20.
Muir, John Kenneth. *The Unseen Force: The Films of Sam Raimi*. Applause Theatre & Cinema, 2004.
Murphy, Bernice M. *The Rural Gothic in American Popular Culture: Backwoods Horror and Terror in the Wilderness*. Palgrave Macmillan, 2013.
Raimi, Sam, director. *Army of Darkness*. Renaissance Pictures, 1992.
_____. *The Evil Dead*. Renaissance Pictures, 1981.
_____. *Evil Dead 2*. Renaissance Pictures, 1987.
Royer, Carl, and Dianna Royer. "Horror, Humor, Poetry: Sam Raimi's Evil Dead Trilogy." *The Spectacle of Isolation in Horror Films: Dark Parades/* Haworth Press, 2005, pp. 39–51.
"Swiss Army Appendage." *TVTropes*, tvtropes.org/pmwiki/pmwiki.php/Main/SwissArmyAppendage.
Tasker, Yvonne. "Dumb Movies for Dumb People: Masculinity, the Body, and the Voice in Contemporary Action Cinema." *Screening the Male: Exploring Masculinities in Hollywood Cinema*, edited by Steven Cohen and Ina Rae Hark. Routledge, 2002, pp. 230–44.
Tincknell, Estella. "Feminine Boundaries: Adolescence, Witchcraft, and the Supernatural in New Gothic Cinema and Television." *Horror Zone: The Cultural Experience of Contemporary Horror Cinema*, edited by Ian Conrich. I.B. Tauris, 2010.
Williams, Tony. *Hearths of Darkness: The Family in the American Horror Film*. Fairleigh Dickinson University Press, 1996.

"For God's sake, how do you stop it?!"

The Powers and Limitations of the Deadites

MICHAEL P. JAROS *and* ROBERT I. LUBLIN

After more than three decades of continuing popular interest in the *Evil Dead* movies, Ash Williams (Bruce Campbell) holds a special place in the collective imagination, separate from the films, as a cinematic icon. The image he strikes inevitably includes a chainsaw and a shotgun. Thus armed, he manages, literally and figuratively, to carve a path through the Deadites that threaten humanity. Clearly, chainsaws and shotguns are essential weapons against the Evil Dead. But what powers do the Evil Dead actually have and what defenses do humans have with which to protect themselves?

These questions prove more difficult to answer than they might initially appear. Some characters are suddenly possessed without any sign that evil has struck. Also, Deadites are sometimes quickly dispatched, while at other times they can be extraordinarily resilient to attack. And sometimes the Evil Dead exhibit fantastical abilities to harm the living. A considered examination of the first three films (*The Evil Dead* [1981], *Evil Dead 2* [1987], and *Army of Darkness* [1992]) reveals that both the characters and the audience bear witness to a continual destabilization of each film's given circumstances. The defining characteristics and consonant limitations of the Evil Dead in one movie or even one scene fail to carry over to the next. The rules for the Deadites constantly change.

This is not by accident. Kate Egan has noted that confounding audience expectations was a deliberate strategy of the creators of *The Evil Dead* from the beginning of the franchise. Director Sam Raimi wanted to encourage audiences "to anticipate scares because of the film's previously established suspense patterns and then, suddenly, confound expectations by breaking these patterns" (64). This strategy elicits audience thrills, but it also threatens to undermine the movies' narrative integrity. By refusing to adhere to their own rules, the films run the risk of simply making no sense. The tendency of the movies to change their own rules and challenge their own internal logic can be found as early as the opening scene of the first film. As we learn from the tape Professor Knowby recorded, which we hear in both the first and second films, if one reads aloud the demon resurrection passages from *The Book of the Dead* (called *Naturom Demonto* in *The Evil Dead* and changed to *Necronomicon Ex-Mortis* in the two sequels), the evil in the woods will awaken and attack the living. This becomes one of the principal rules of the films.

But the power of the Evil Dead is felt by Ash and his friends before they ever reach the cabin where they will find the book. In the very first shots of the film, we are treated to what Raimi dubbed the "shaky cam," in which the camera is mounted on two-by-fours to simulate a Steadicam "demon-point-of-view (POV)" shot that would go on to be one of the filmic signatures of all three movies (Egan 14). We never get to see this evil force pursuing the living, but it flies low to the ground, over water and forest floor, in these opening shots. Additionally, as the characters drive along the road toward the cabin, their car is suddenly wrenched from the driver's control and almost crashes into an oncoming vehicle. Without ever reading *The Book of the Dead* or even reaching the cabin, how did the Evil Dead control the car? We can imagine that the evil in the woods remained awake after the professor's earlier reading of the book. And yet, if that is the case, then the decision by Ash and his group of friends to play the professor's recording is rendered inconsequential.

Scholars have noted inconsistencies that exist between the three films far beyond the brief summary presented here (Ndalianis, "The Rules of the Game" 512; Modleski 160; Egan 16; Pugh 134). Consequently, it is not our goal to track down all of the movies' discrepancies or contradictions. Rather, we are interested in establishing the meta-rules that maintain in a film trilogy that readily breaks its own internal rules. Considering the movies individually and collectively, we find that there are, indeed, rules according to which the movies hold together despite their ready willingness to exhibit inconsistencies.

The first rule governing the power of the Evil Dead is that they have always existed and always will; no method exists to defeat them utterly. *The Book of the Dead* has a role to play in each of the movies, but throughout all three films, it is of secondary importance to the ubiquity of the Evil Dead. At the end of the first film, *The Book of the Dead* has been incinerated and its power seemingly destroyed. Deadites smoke, decompose, and sprout demonic arms that tear their bodies apart in a lengthy, revolting sequence that seems conclusively to mark the end of the threat they pose to mankind.

Yet the film's final scene presents the triumphant Ash turning in horror to see the demon-POV camera racing directly towards his face (Modleski 160). The movie concludes with the certainty that the forces of darkness have, by no means, been eliminated. The internal rule that establishes the book as the means whereby evil is unleashed and then contained has been fundamentally undermined. The larger rule, the one that says that the Evil Dead will always threaten the living, is reified, and all three movies follow this larger rule. The reality of the unconquerable dead contributes to a fatalistic determinism with regard to the movies' human characters; the "possession and destruction of these characters is inevitable," argues Egan, and "any and all of the characters' actions and efforts are ultimately hopeless and futile" (71). Whatever resistance the living exert against the Deadites is for naught—eventually, they will swallow our souls. But the inescapable threat of the Evil Dead is not the only rule that maintains throughout the original series of films.

Equally true and utterly reliable is that Ash himself consistently offers a buffoonish hope to the otherwise futile human efforts to survive against the Evil Dead. Despite possessing few skills or personality traits whereby he might be expected to survive an attack by the Evil Dead, Ash proves literally undefeatable. Indeed, Ash is perhaps the character most singularly unqualified to be a hero or humankind's savior. His unsuitability to survive the first movie derives from his conspicuous lack of courage or even manliness. The other male character, Scott (Hal Delrich), offers a fearless potential hero, but he falls to the power of Deadites, becomes possessed, and must, himself, be defeated. On the other hand, Bruce Campbell describes his own character in *The Evil Dead* as a "cowardly wimp" (Campbell 173), and Tison Pugh convincingly argues, "from his very position as the protagonist of a horror film, Ash's character is effeminized.... Within the generic framework of the slasher/splatter film, the Final Girl [the horror movie's typical lone survivor] foregrounds a feminine gender as virtually a prerequisite of the horror genre" (124–125). The creators of *The Evil Dead* were aware of the convention that stipulated the female gender of the lone survivor and purposely chose to invert it. As Bruce Campbell has said, "Sam felt that could make it even more horrifying; if you could reduce a man to scrambling and screaming and yelling and being tormented, it would be even more horrifying than a woman doing that" (quoted in Warren 36–37). In *The Evil Dead* and throughout the trilogy, this scrambling, screaming, yelling, and tormented man is ultimately humankind's lone defense against the forces of evil.

Of course, Ash does not remain pathetic and sniveling throughout the three movies. He responds to the Deadite threat and adapts to deal with their myriad and ever-greater attacks. It is critical to note that Ash's response and adaptation to the Evil Dead is not rooted in the purposeful development of skills that might aid him in his efforts to survive. He does become more courageous and manly, to the point in *Army of Darkness* when he is a "loud-mouthed braggart," but his success against the threat of the Evil Dead lies in one of the simple rules governing the series: that he alone is unbeatable.

Considered together, then, the first two rules governing the *Evil Dead* trilogy pit an unstoppable force against an immovable object: the Evil Dead cannot be destroyed and Ash cannot be beaten. But these larger, unbreakable rules are unknown at the start of *The Evil Dead*. Consequently, the film's unclear rules and willingness to break those rules make for an unpredictable and thrilling horror movie. We can better understand the movie's particular brand of horror by noting that scholars have divided the genre into three categories: terror, horror, and revulsion. Kathryn Hume explains:

> Terror is the rarest and (according to Stephen King) the hardest to achieve. It consists of fear of what is about to happen and involves atmosphere, looming catastrophe, and nameless dread as much as any actual acts. Horror, more common, is our response to the ghastly sight of some brutality already perpetrated; horror involves a lot of fear, since we know that whatever happened to the tortured body could happen to ourselves. Revulsion is our disgust at what we see, in extreme examples an impulse to vomit rather than to scream [117].

By unsettling its own apparent rules, *The Evil Dead* manages to go beyond the limitations of most other horror films. The typical slasher film introduces terror by infusing the cinematic atmosphere with deadly potential. Film directors seek to extend this experience, and when they succeed, the hair on the audience's back stands on end in titillated anticipation. Next, horror strikes as the terror manifests in grisly murder and the surviving characters must face the tangible possibility of their own demise. And finally, revulsion follows as we witness the killer perpetrate gruesome acts.

The Evil Dead manages both to engage all three forms of horror as well as to circumvent the typical one-way progression from terror to horror to revulsion through its effective use of indeterminacy as a narrative device. The unique demon-POV provides an absolutely original source of terror. We do not know what it looks like or how it operates, but we know it wishes us harm. Moreover, that terror is linked to the woods, which means that evil surrounds the characters and provides no egress. In this manner, *The Evil Dead* provides the prototype for what Matthew Grant terms the "cabin horror" film, in which "the landscape is imbued with a malevolent agency that actively antagonizes the characters of the film" (9). This terror transforms to horror when Cheryl (Ellen Sandweiss) runs from the cabin, chased by the unseen, malevolent force. She cannot hope to escape and the movie amplifies her horror by employing the demon-POV to situate the audience in the role of the evil which pursues her. When she is caught, the very trees and vines in the woods rape her, as the movie engages revulsion to such a degree that even many fans of the film found this scene excessive (Egan 50).

What distinguishes *The Evil Dead* from other excellent genre films is how it succeeds in engaging terror again, even after it has seemingly shown its hand and moved on to horror and finally to revulsion. Such success is achieved through its continual deployment of indeterminacy. Cheryl is not killed in the woods. Rather, she returns to the cabin, bringing with her the truth that there are worse things than death. Although she has been horribly violated in full view of the audience, her friends refuse to believe her, and their activities proceed as if nothing has happened. But the audience knows otherwise, and the specter of true terror is invoked again. For fun, Shelly (Theresa Tilly) tests Linda for ESP by covering a playing card to see if her friend can guess it. Playfully, Shelly says that Linda keeps guessing the cards correctly when, in fact, she is not even close. In the background, quietly staring out the window into the woods where she was sexually abused, Cheryl guesses the card correctly. And the next one. Without even looking. In this moment, the audience realizes that the power of the Evil Dead is no longer confined to the woods outside the cabin: nowhere is safe. Terror looms large. With Cheryl's possession, we also learn that the Evil Dead's power is not limited to controlling the forest but can control people as well. The powers available to the Evil Dead have expanded but we have no notion of their limit or even if they have one.

Throughout the rest of the film and the trilogy, this process plays out again and again. We are introduced to a new, thrilling, and unexpected threat by the Evil Dead, then watch it wreak havoc among Ash and his friends as they strive to contain it. When they succeed, whether it be by locking Cheryl in the basement or dismembering Shelly, the possibility of calm descends, but it brings with it the terrifying certainty that further suffering and death await. Intrinsic to this certainty is the audience's dawning understanding, which grows scene by scene and movie by movie, that the next threat is likely to outdo the last one. As Michael Arnzen writes, "the only surety in the fragmented narrative comes from 'being ready for anything,' both visually and narratively. And the only viewer expectation that is guaranteed fulfillment is the anticipation of gory depictions of violence." *The Evil Dead* represents a radical threat with no certain limits.

Countering this threat requires Ash to make radical choices himself, ones that reveal his ability to adapt to the ever-changing powers of the Deadites. Ash achieves this growth as a protagonist through the course of the three films by engaging in his own set of inconsistencies that violate the movies' internal logic. Such rule breaking and subversion grows over the course of the three films and becomes so normalized that, by the time we arrive at *Army of Darkness*, audiences are prepared to suspend their disbelief surrounding Ash's increasingly ridiculous feats almost completely and indefinitely. As the films progress, we see these two forms of indeterminacy continually do battle against each other on an ever-expanding field of play. As the two meta-rules of the trilogy become more pronounced, the stakes surrounding their continual conflict are consequently raised.

The repetition and revision of *The Evil Dead*'s plot undertaken at the beginning of *Evil Dead 2* might initially seem like a haphazard attempt to remake the first film with a larger budget, but this is not the case. As Angela Ndalianis notes, "as extensions of both *The Evil Dead* and of the horror genre, *Evil Dead 2*'s refusal to repeat formulaically the prequel explores the generic process as a dynamic system" ("Rules of the Game" 512). The revised story works to reinforce the two meta-rules of the films, while offering additional chances for terror, horror, and revulsion to the audiences as the rules of the game are repeatedly broken, again. The playing field is cleared of a new wave of characters to reinforce the idea that Ash will continue somehow to survive, but at a continually greater cost to himself and with an incrementally higher body count; other characters become mere filler within the escalating battle between Ash and the Deadites.

In its repetition of the story of *The Evil Dead*, *Evil Dead 2* presents a streamlined plot and set of characters. Ash travels to the cabin alone with his girlfriend Linda, now played by Denise Bixler. Cheryl, Scott, and Shelly do not appear in the story. In the simplified version, several key events lay the foundation for Ash's own indeterminacy. There is no burning of the *Necronomicon*, reducing its centrality, and Linda is again possessed and dispatched after she attempts to kill Ash in the woods. The events of *The Evil Dead* conclude within the first seven minutes of the movie with the same ending: after he has apparently contained the Evil Dead, Ash turns in horror as an unseen demon rushes toward him. Now, however, we get to see what happens to Ash, and he is thrown an incredible distance through the air and slammed into a tree. He falls and lands, face down, in a puddle. When he stands, he is possessed by the Evil Dead. But a mere moment later, the sun rises, and its light banishes the evil inside Ash and drives the Evil Dead back into the ground altogether. Freed of possession and staring at the newly risen sun, Ash realizes that the power of the Evil Dead is not unlimited: it is confined to nighttime.

But this rule does not hold true beyond the moment. At no other point in the three movies does sunlight provide aid to the living in their battle against the dead. Additionally, and importantly, the three movies provide only one other significant instance in which a possessed character returns to the living.[1] Later in *Evil Dead 2*, after a host of new characters arrive at the cabin, Ash is again possessed but returns when he sees the necklace he gave to Linda. His love for her proves strong enough to win out against evil. But this rule also fails to hold any truth beyond the moment of its instantiation. In the same movie, Annie's possessed mother Henrietta attempts to trick and kill her own daughter. Trapped in the cellar, Henrietta, (played by Ted Raimi when possessed) assumes her human shape (played by Lou Hancock) and recalls touching details from the day of her daughter's birth. Despite their close bond, Henrietta's reversion to her human shape is merely a trick by the Deadites to lure Annie to her doom—Henrietta cannot be saved. Somehow we are expected to accept that Ash's love for his girlfriend is strong enough to pull him out of possession, but a mother's love for her own daughter is not.[2] And we do. We accept it, for we have been trained by this point in the second movie to understand that Ash is not confined by the same rules that limit everyone else. Naturally, other characters in the film do not understand Ash's unique role, and the newly recovered protagonist is almost immediately struck by the ax Annie swings at his head. Ash can only explain: "I'm alright now. That thing is gone." And it is.

Ash's hand provides another instance in which the rules change only for him and only once. Other characters in all three films are possessed with no instigating event, so there is no reason to believe that the Evil Dead require contact with a Deadite or the drawing of blood in order to possess the living. But when Linda's possessed, decapitated head bites Ash's hand, she infects it with evil, and Ash's own hand "goes bad" and attempts to kill him, ultimately beating him senseless and dragging him toward a cleaver with which it intends to finish the job. Ash responds to this new threat by stabbing his own hand with a knife. He then grabs a chainsaw and dismembers himself, insanely screaming "who's laughing now?" while his face is drenched with an impossible shower of blood (Arnzen).

This scene is not horror but comedy, and it continues. After his hand has been sawed off, it continues to try to harm Ash, and he pursues it through the cabin, blasting away with the shotgun in a scene redolent of both *The Three Stooges* and *Tom and Jerry*. *Evil Dead 2* makes a natural transition in genre, reacting to the Deadites' ever more creative attempts to kill the living and Ash's ever more outrageous, yet successful efforts to survive. And yet, for all of the comedy of this scene and others, *Evil Dead 2* never completely abandons the horror genre, using the ability to break its own rules to engage the conventions of both genres. The movie continues to invoke terror in an audience that knows something threatening lurks around every corner. And it embraces horror as Ash and his companions in the cabin seek to survive current threats in the face of certain new ones. And, of course, the movie famously relishes in opportunities to provoke revulsion (Ndalianis, "The Rules of the Game," 108; Warren 133). The movie achieves comedy by engaging the conventions of horror and pushing them far beyond their logical conclusions.

As a cinematic icon, Ash is defined by both comedy and horror. It is for this reason that Matt Dutton, creator of the *Within the Woods* website, has stated, "Ash didn't truly become 'Ash' until *Evil Dead 2*" (quoted in Egan 47).

We can even mark the moment "Ash" is born to when he goes to the shed to prepare for battle against the Evil Dead. Up to this point, he has merely reacted to the threat of the Deadites, but with the decision to arm himself, he emerges a new man. Quite naturally, the manner in which he accomplishes this is utterly ridiculous and thoroughly entertaining. Using the tools he finds in the shed, he fashions the chainsaw into a natural appendage, attaching it to where his hand used to be. Thus armed, he saws off the extended barrel to his shotgun, twirls it deftly, and confidently thrusts it into the holster that now appears on his back. The camera closes in on his face and he utters, for the first time, his now famous: "groovy."

Obeying the meta-rules established in *The Evil Dead*, the threat posed by the Deadites expands in *Evil Dead 2* and then further in *Army of Darkness*. At the end of the first film, the Evil Dead threaten the secluded cabin, at the end of the second, a medieval kingdom, and at the end of the third, they have unleashed themselves into our own postmodern world of the chain superstore. Ash develops right alongside the Evil Dead to counter the danger they represent. As Pugh notes, "From the beginning of [*The*] *Evil Dead* to the beginning of *Army of Darkness*, though a mere forty-eight hours of narrative time elapse, Ash's masculinity grows exponentially" (130). The third movie forefronts the metanarrative that Ash is unique, having the Wiseman state at the start of the film: "He is the one written of in the *Necronomicon*. He who is prophesied to fall from the heavens and deliver us from the terrors of the Deadites." It is essential that the audience, which may or may not have seen Ash's development over the course of the two previous movies, understand the unique nature of the protagonist.

Ash's first confrontation with the Deadites, at the Pit, confirms the Wiseman's words. Immediately before Ash, a nameless member of Henry the Red's army is thrown in. After a few moments of silent anticipation, an enormous geyser of blood erupts from the pit as the soldier is killed in the most spectacular (and outrageous) of ways.[3] Against an enemy that can annihilate a human so quickly and so decisively, what chance does humanity have? When Ash is thrown into the Pit, he proves that where others cannot hope to succeed, he can. Unarmed and missing a hand, he successfully fights off the Deadites in the Pit until the Wiseman throws him his chainsaw, which miraculously clicks into place as Ash leaps into the air to receive it, eliciting a "yes!" from a watching, sympathetic blacksmith (echoing the audience's own perceived reaction to this impossible prospect). Ash goes on to dispatch both pit-Deadites and emerge victorious.

Army of Darkness continues in such a fashion, pitting Ash, an unlikely and unwilling hero, against the Deadites that threaten medieval England and humankind. Continuing the escalation from the first two films, the third movie confronts Ash with unprecedented threats that offer a host of dangers to a character that lacks the intelligence, training, or weapons to confront them, yet always ultimately triumphs. In this third film, terror and horror, as they manifested in the first two, are not entirely left behind. Rather, they adapt to the film as they are pushed so far that they no longer inspire fear. Terror becomes "fascinated anticipation" for an audience that knows something unprecedented and outrageous awaits. Horror becomes adventure as our hero strives to survive against a supernatural enemy that does not evince any apparent limits. As the movie progresses, Ash manages to eke out victory after victory, rising to each new and unexpected challenge presented by the Evil Dead. The movie and the trilogy reach their logical denouement in the creation of Bad Ash. Since Ash is unbeatable, the Deadites' ultimate threat to the living resides in obtaining an Ash that can fight for their side.

The creation of Bad Ash represents one of the high points of *Army of Darkness*, referencing memorable moments from the earlier films to create new opportunities for the revised notions of terror and horror, while continuing to provide comedy. The scene begins with Ash being chased by the demon-POV-cam in a virtual recreation of the horror that infused *The Evil Dead*. He races into a windmill and locks himself inside, screaming and holding the door shut with his body just as Annie did in *Evil Dead 2* when possessed-Ash came for her. Locked in the windmill with the Evil Dead outside, Ash finds himself in a similar situation to the cabin of the first two movies. He then sees his reflection in the mirror move independently of him, referencing the hanging mirror of *The Evil Dead*, which responded like water when Ash reached out to touch it, as well as the mirror in *Evil Dead 2*, the reflection which reached out and strangled Ash.

Referentiality and self-referentiality are part of the horror genre. As Philip Brophy explains, "the contemporary Horror film *knows* that you've seen it before; it *knows* that you know what is about to happen; and it knows that you know it knows you know" (5). The *Evil Dead* movies revel in this aspect of the genre and offer continual revisions and surprises. Ash has faced threatening mirror reflections before, and he assumes that by shattering his reflection, he will "dismember" that threat. Yet he merely creates a host of Lilliputian Ashes who come forth from the mirror to attack him, eventually managing to tie him down like Gulliver and send one of their hosts diving into his mouth. Ash frees himself and gleefully pours a kettle of boiling water down his throat to cook the tiny Ash, again doing impossible harm to himself to avoid possession. While he does so, he repeats the line he spoke while sawing off his own hand, "who's laughing now?"

Ash's referential humor is cut short, however, when he exposes his shoulder and finds a large eyeball peering out from within his flesh as a Deadite Ash literally grows inside him. We subsequently witness Ash literally split in two. In this revision, Ash will go on to fight not merely his own hand, but a full-sized version of himself. The division of Ash into good and bad represents perhaps the most extreme shift of the rules in all three films and the pinnacle of indeterminacy. The Deadites have done more than possess Ash. Without precedent or explanation, they have made their own "Evil" version of their insuperable adversary. He is a separate entity that is still also Ash, and only comes to resemble a Deadite after Ash shoots him in the face with the shotgun and goes on to dismember him with the chainsaw. This scene redefines and refines the horror-inducing moments of earlier films, as Ash is not just dismembering a friend or a loved one, such as his girlfriend Linda, but himself. The uniquely personal nature of the moment of horror is foregrounded as we see an extreme close-up of his/Bad Ash's face as he literally saws himself apart.

In a movie and a trilogy famous for outdoing previous practices, including its own, these extraordinary measures undertaken by Ash to shoot, dismember, and bury his "bad" self are not enough to stop him. Bad Ash benefits from the meta-rule, which dictates that the Evil Dead cannot ultimately be destroyed as well as the one that acknowledges Ash cannot be beaten. Bad Ash also benefits from Good Ash's buffoonery: in forgetting the proper incantation to remove the *Necronomicon* from its resting place, Ash inadvertently resurrects his sawn-apart nemesis, along with the eponymous Army of Darkness. Just as Ash is the only person able to lead humanity to salvation, Bad Ash, alone, can lead the Deadites against mankind. Against a large and seemingly indestructible army of the dead, Ash galvanizes an ever more improbable series of weapons. With a chemistry book that apparently came back with him in time, he manufactures gunpowder. He transforms his car into a mobile killing machine, the Deathcoaster. And despite exhibiting no fighting skills in any of the movies, he trains a battalion of medieval polearm infantry to use martial arts against the dead. With no time to learn their new skills, the soldiers effectively line up and face off against the Deadites with a cry of "Ha-Hee-Ho-HA!" and successfully stave off the advancing army long enough for the inevitable meeting of Ash and Bad Ash in single combat.

The ultimate battle between the two primary antagonists pits Ash's determination and inconceivable resourcefulness against Bad Ash's equal determination and seeming invincibility. Ash is only finally able to destroy his evil doppelganger near the film's conclusion after burning him down to a skeleton, launching him midair on a catapult, and blowing him apart with gunpowder. Just as Ash endures various impossible levels of bodily harm, so does Bad Ash, until he becomes, via incineration and explosion, infinitely less *like* Ash and, therefore, capable of being destroyed.

The film concludes with a final twist that once more reifies the meta-rules while changing the game again. Ash successfully returns to his own time with the help of the *Necronomicon*, but we learn that, as he again fails to say the incantation correctly, he has brought the Deadites with him. After dispatching one in the middle of the S-mart superstore in which he works, he removes his employee uniform to reveal a western-style shirt and pants, complete with holster for his lever-action rifle. The indeterminate threat of the Deadites has been unleashed in our own world and Ash is already armed and ready to face it. The stage is set for the ongoing battle of the serialized plot of *Ash vs. Evil Dead* (2015–2018) twenty-five years later.

Notes

1. Technically, one additional character returns after being possessed. At the end of *Army of Darkness*, when Ash has defeated Bad Ash, Sheila (Embeth Davidtz) inexplicably returns to the living while other Deadites do not. Rather than comment upon the nature of the Evil Dead, this return serves merely to reward Ash for his victory and provide the movie with a happy ending.

2. Near the end of the movie, Annie does manage to distract Deadite-Henrietta by singing a lullaby from her childhood, but she cannot win her back to the living.

3. This scene recalls the one in *Evil Dead 2* in which Deadite-Henrietta grabs Jake, and as she drags him into the cellar to his death, an implausible amount of blood sprays forth.

Works Cited

Arnzen, Michael A. "Who's Laughing Now? The Postmodern Splatter Film." *Journal of Popular Film & Television* 21, no. 4 (1994), pp. 176–84.

Brophy, Philip. "Horrality—The Textuality of Contemporary Horror Films." *Screen* 27, no. 1/2 (1986), pp. 2–13.

Campbell, Bruce. *If Chins Could Kill: Confessions of a B Movie Actor*. St. Martin's Press, 2001.

Egan, Kate. *The Evil Dead*. Wallflower Press, 2011.

Grant, Matthew. "The Cabin on the Screen: Defining the 'Cabin Horror' Film." *Film Matters* 5 (2014), pp. 5–12.

Hume, Kathryn. *Aggressive Fictions: Reading the Contemporary American Novel*. Cornell University Press, 2012.

Modleski, Tania. "The Terror of Pleasure: The Contemporary Horror Film and Postmodern Theory." *Studies in Entertainment: Critical Approaches to Mass Culture*, edited by Tania Modleski. Indiana University Press, 1986, pp. 155–66.

Ndalianis, Angela. *The Horror Sensorium: Media and the Senses*. McFarland, 2012.

_____. "The Rules of the Game: Evil Dead II … Meet Thy Doom." *Hop on Pop: The Politics and Pleasures of Popular Culture*, edited by Henry Jenkins III, Tara McPherson, and Jane Shattuc. Duke University Press, 2003, pp. 503–516.

Pugh, Tison. "Queering the Medieval Dead: History, Horror, and Masculinity in Sam Raimi's Evil Dead Trilogy." *Race, Class, and Gender in "Medieval" Cinema*, edited by Lynn Tarte Ramey and Tison Pugh. Palgrave, 2007, pp. 123–136.

Raimi, Sam, director. *Army of Darkness*. Renaissance Pictures, 1992.

_____, director. *The Evil Dead*. Renaissance Pictures, 1981.

_____, director. *Evil Dead 2*. Renaissance Pictures, 1987.

Warren, Bill. *The Evil Dead Companion*. St. Martin's Griffin, 2001.

"Shoot first, think never"
Ash's Satire of Neoliberal Individualism
Jeffrey A. Sartain

The *Evil Dead* franchise, like most cultural productions, reflects and comments on the politics and ideology of the social and historical contexts surrounding it. Specifically, Ash's character has evolved into a complex satire of neoliberal ideological positions and their performance in popular culture. Ashley "Ash" Joanna Williams, played by Bruce Campbell, is the one constant in every iteration of the *Evil Dead* franchise.[1] In many ways, the character of Ash is a hyperbolic caricature of late 20th century American masculine individualism, embodying a wide range of stereotypes cobbled together into his unique persona. He is ruggedly individualist, racist, chauvinist, and anti-intellectual. An earnest reading of Ash sees his fight against the Deadites as a noble fight, one in which good must triumph over evil, no matter the sacrifice; however, the *Evil Dead* franchise has never been earnest in its tone, always satirizing the tropes of action and horror films in its larger narrative about Ash Williams's misadventures. Reading the satirical tone of the franchise reveals that Ash's character is an ironic commentary of the cultural dimensions of neoliberalism as they have evolved over almost forty years of the franchise's existence. John McWhorter, for *The Atlantic*, discusses the slippery evolution of neoliberalism in contemporary discourse: "Between *neoconservative* and *neoliberal*, then, the *neo* prefix means not 'new' but 'disingenuous.' The neocon cloaks right-wing barbarism to make it seem less threatening; the neoliberal poses as a liberal while actually being a right-winger." As McWhorter observes, there is little to differentiate the neoliberal from the neoconservative position in contemporary culture. In the *Evil Dead* franchise, the lines are often equally blurry, but the growth of Ash's prejudices as the franchise evolves demonstrates the creators' responsiveness to social events in popular culture. Symbolically, the character's particularly self-interested ethos and sense of masculinity coincides with the rise of populist neoliberal individualism that rose to prominence in the 1980s.[2] During this era of American culture, the rhetoric of rugged individualism and American exceptionalism became important touchstones of the political and popular discourse under Reagan, and these values were reflected in the way masculinity was exemplified by characters from popular film and television. Ash's downward spiral from fresh-faced college student in *The Evil Dead* (1981) to a bigoted Lothario in *Ash vs. Evil Dead* (2015–2018) reflects the cultural shift towards individualism associated with the rhetoric of contemporary neoliberalism as it evolved in the popular media.

While always ruggedly durable, Ash's masculinity is increasingly marked by anti-intellectualism, selfishness, cowardice, chauvinism, and racism. Particularly, Ash's racial views distinguish his guiding ideological framework as neoliberal, rather than neoconservative. For most of the franchise history, questions of race were conveniently elided. However, in the largest and most recent *Evil Dead* text of them all, *Ash vs. Evil Dead*, questions of race and racism appear numerous times, mostly centered on Ash's friend and sidekick, Pablo Simon Bolivar (Ray Santiago). Actor Ray Santiago succinctly outlines the background for his character, explaining how Pablo's heroism lends additional irony to the racial bigotry displayed by Ash: "[Pablo]'s got a history of being born in Honduras and his uncle was a shaman, a bru[j]o. And Pablo was supposed to become a bru[j]o, but he left his [father's] side to experience the American dream. And he's here as an illegal immigrant, in fact. And as our country is busy trying to deport him, he's trying to save the world from the evil dead, basically" (Ross). As the series matures, so does Pablo, becoming a critical member of Ash's Deadite-hunting team, "The Ghostbeaters," which also includes fellow Value Stop employee Kelly Maxwell (Dana DeLorenzo) and a rotating cast of support characters. Pablo eventually develops magical abilities, succeeding his uncle as *El Brujo Especial*, a powerful shaman with mystical powers to combat the Deadites. Pablo saves the world on several occasions, becoming a dear friend and compatriot, but Ash continues to find it necessary to deride him.

Ash's insults frequently take the form of stereotypes about Latinos and immigrants, objectifying and dehumanizing his best friend. For instance, Ash frequently refers to Pablo's heritage as Mexican, despite Pablo's protests to the contrary. In an effort to appear less racist, Ash attempts to distinguish his view on race and stereotypes to Pablo in "Books from Beyond" when he suggests they might have time to stop for churros, saying, "'That's not racist, Pablo, that's just a great dessert.'" Pablo corrects Ash, saying, "You know I'm not Mexican, right?" To which Ash replies with an even more insulting stereotype, saying, "That's the spirit" (Bassett, "Books from Beyond"). Ash even corrects Pablo for parroting one of Ash's own stereotypes about Latinos, observing, "That's a little racist, don't you think?" (Jacobson, "Home"). Ash's prejudices get added distinction when he ideologically distances himself from his friend, Lem (Peter Feeney), who belongs to a Michigan militia. When talking to Lem, Ash attempts to show regret at using a racial epithet in the past. Ash says that it was "before I knew it was racist" (Hurst, "Fire in the Hole"). Lem and his friends in the militia signify an extreme, conspiracy-oriented, right wing political ideology, expressed in their slogan, "always be stockpiling," that Ash regards as "a dumb motto" (Hurst, "Killer of Killers"). Ash's disavowal of the militia members and his periodic denial of racism are precise moments that help viewers mark Ash as representative of neoliberal cultural discourse, where neoliberalism "…also carries a whiff of *racist*, in that both neoliberals and neoconservatives dissent from the liberal consensus on race issues, with neither in line with the idea that whites are stained by 'privilege'" (McWhorter). Ash's apparent rejection of far right-wing ideology and the occasional self-policing of his racialized language demonstrates the characters' desire to be perceived as a liberally minded individual and hails the contemporary rhetoric of neoliberalism, specifically. Despite his efforts, Ash's racial biases continue to show through the thin veneer of progress that he adopts.

Ash's regressive belief in masculine strength and dominance also parallels ideology arising from contemporary neoliberal rhetoric. Ash's faith in violence and individualism is exemplified in *Army of Darkness* (1992) when Ash says, "Good. Bad. I'm the guy with the gun." As David Harvey explains in *A Brief History of Neoliberalism*, neoliberal ideological formations argue for a similar kind of might-makes-right morality that leads to "the anarchy of the market, of competition, of unbridled individualism … that becomes increasingly ungovernable. It may even lead to a breakdown of all bonds of solidarity and a condition verging on social anarchy and nihilism" (82). The nihilistic narrative world surrounding the *Evil Dead* franchise certainly appears to have suffered such a breakdown of solidarity and social identity. Within this neoliberal landscape, though, Ash makes a remarkable social and economic climb from a stock boy living in a trailer to a celebrated hometown hardware store owner with a house and a kind of makeshift domesticity. In "Family," Ash reopens the hardware store that he inherited from his father, Brock Williams (Lee Majors), reunites with his estranged wife, a former stripper named Candace "Candy" Barr (Katrina Hobbs), and meets his long-lost daughter, Brandy (Arielle Carver-O'Neill). Of course, ironic satire taints Ash's socioeconomic mobility because he had to inherit the store from his father after Brock's death in season 2. As season 3 opens, Ash has converted his father's hometown hardware store into Ashy Slashy's Hardware Store Emporium, a self-aggrandizing "shrine to a local hero" in honor of himself (Beesley).

Ash's business instincts are shown to be flawed from the beginning—he tries to integrate a pornography and sex toy emporium into the hardware store, and he gives up to 50% discounts to attractive women.

Because his manifold ineptitudes are on display at every turn, Ash usually relies on his companions' sacrifices to successfully combat evil. Throughout the franchise, he sacrifices everyone around him in the fight against evil, eventually ending up alone and on the run from the Deadite menace at the end of each installment. Despite his failures at self-reliance throughout the series, Ash espouses the classic American bootstrapping rhetoric that emphasizes individual responsibility and individual reward. As he explains to Pablo:

> ASH: At heart, me, I'm an alone wolf.
> PABLO: A lone wolf.
> ASH: Exactly.
> PABLO: Doesn't it ever get old? Bein' alone? Nobody to help you?
> ASH: No, of course not [Bassett, "Books from Beyond"].

The rugged individualist masculinity that Ash espouses here is distinctly ironic, considering that Ash frequently survives because of the sacrifice of others. The 2016 comic series, *Army of Darkness: Election Special*, comments directly on the irony of Ash's neoliberal rhetoric of self-determination and personal responsibility. Through a convoluted series of events that involves the televised slaying of a Deadite, Ash finds himself as the fictional American Patriot Party's replacement candidate in the 2016 election. He runs as the third-party contender against the Democratic nominee, the democratic socialist and Colorado Senator, Brock Anders, as well as the Republican nominee, neoconservative former Florida Governor, Valerie Sexton. Ash's platform revolves around a personal ethic of action, captured in the slogan, "Stop talking, start doing" (Serrano, *Election Special* 28). Ash expounds on this position, saying, "I've lost people I loved because too many people spent their time trying to figure out a problem instead of doing what they should have done in the first place—walk up to the problem and punch it in the f—ing face" (Serrano, *Election Special* 26). During the nationally televised presidential debate, Ash reveals the true demonic identities of both of the major party candidates. Ash, wearing a suit made from an American flag for his debate appearance, then proceeds to decapitate both demons on national television.[3] This leads to his rampant popularity and election as president. News coverage of the Ashley J. Williams administration reports: "It's being called a new era in American politics, where the common man will finally have a voice in the halls of power" (Serrano, *Election Special* 39). As a satirical Everyman character, Ash represents the irony of the American working class's embrace to the neoliberal rhetoric of individualism, personal responsibility, and private property that undermines the collective power of citizens. A direct satire of the 2016 election, the comic paints a distinctly unflattering picture of the spectrum of candidates, offering only Ash, in all his ignorant buffoonery, as a satirical remedy to the dire political choices of the 2016 election. *Army of Darkness: Election Special* ends with a metafictive question from President Ash addressed to the reader: "What? As if you've really got someone better to do the job?" (40).[4]

Key to the success of Ash's satire is Campbell's particular blend of smirking humor and pathos translated and interpreted across the franchise's various media installments.[5] Despite being an ignorant buffoon, he survives the horror of each encounter with the Deadites to live another day. Ash's ability to endure and combat evil is embodied in blue-collar American iconography: his chainsaw hand, his ever-present rifle, and the 1973 Oldsmobile Delta '88. Through the humor and irony of Bruce Campbell's performance, the values associated with these symbols of Ash's rugged masculinity are under critique. Much like the protagonists of archetypal westerns like *High Noon* (1952), *Shane* (1953), and numerous others, Ash is a modern cowboy figure, unfit for the civilized world he attempts to protect. At the end of each installment of the franchise, Ash finds himself isolated from any prior community ties, facing the uncertain future in solitude. Ash's character arc, with its curtailed economic opportunities across Ash's lifetime, symbolizes the larger labor forces at work throughout the franchise history. Even in his mid-fifties, Ash is still doing the same kind of menial work he was as a student in *The Evil Dead*. So, while Ash's competence at slaying Deadites in hand-to-hand combat is unparalleled, there is no place in middle-class America for him since the economic collapse of physically oriented middle-class industrial jobs in the mid–20th century, and his skills at violence do not contribute to the economy in a meaningful way. Ash's masculinity, expressed in his violence and rugged independence, makes him an effective warrior against the Deadites; however, those same traits cost him every potential relationship and doom him to almost forty years of labor cleaning aisles and stocking shelves in retail stores. Much like his cowboy predecessors from pulp westerns, Ash's facility with violence will always isolate him, highlighting the central irony of the lone western hero, where the hero's skills make him unfit for the civilization he seeks to protect. Unlike the classic frontier character, though, the franchise shows fans, repeatedly, that Ash's traumas and isolation are largely self-imposed, a result of his own stupidity as he repeatedly summons Deadite incursions by mishandling the *Necronomicon*.

To satirize the hypermasculine values of the dominant culture, the *Evil Dead* franchise deploys many of the tropes that mark the hypermasculine action hero of the 1980s, a genre that saw explosive growth in the era of the neoliberal turn towards Reagan's cowboy politics. As James William Gibson explains in *Warrior Dreams: Violence and Manhood in Post-Vietnam America*, the action hero that arose in the 1970s and 1980s was an archetype that was "the emblem of a movement that at the very least wanted to reverse the previous twenty years of American history and take back all the symbolic territory that had been lost" for masculine identity in post–Vietnam-era America (14). While, initially, *The Evil Dead* was an attempt to exploit the low-budget horror trends of the 1970s, by the release of *Evil Dead 2* in 1987, Ash's heroic masculine traits of toughness, chauvinism, and individuality appear custom-tailored to comment on the dominant masculine film archetypes of the day. As the stars of action films in the 1970s and 1980s, actors like Charles Bronson, Clint Eastwood, Sylvester Stallone, and Arnold Schwarzenegger redefined popular images of American masculinity. In their wake, Susan Faludi observes in contemporary culture, "manhood is defined by appearance, by youth and attractiveness, by money and aggression ... and by the market-bartered 'individuality'" (39). Her definition of contemporary manhood as aggressive, individualistic, and focused on appearance rather than intellectual depth describes the values under critique in *Evil Dead*'s continuing satire of contemporary masculinity. By the time *Ash vs. Evil Dead* appears, Ash's thought process has gotten even more anti-intellectual than ever, highlighted by his latest catchphrase, "Shoot first, think never" (Frazee). This catchphrase captures the essential link between Ash and the masculine action hero stereotype; they both value action over intellect, violence over negotiation. Again and again, Ash displays woeful ignorance on almost every subject except fighting Deadites.

The fact that Ash has remained popular throughout an almost forty-year presence in the media landscape testifies to the satire's continued relevance and resonance, as well as the creators' ability to adapt the satirical character for new audiences.[6] Recently, the patriotically themed *Army of Darkness: Ash Saves Obama* comic book mini comments on contemporary political figures directly. Here, covers by Todd Nauck and Lucio Parillo portray Ash repeatedly saving the 44th President from hordes of Deadites. The previously discussed *Army of Darkness: Election Special* comic series, as well as the "Ash for President" advertising campaign for season 2 of *Ash vs. Evil Dead* also capitalize on the linkage between patriotic imagery, politics, and the heroic buffoon. The imagery is stark and satirical, aligning patriotic values with Ash's dubious moral and ethical code, represented in typical flag-and-bunting fashion on the season 2 home-media cover, depicting Ash saluting with his chainsaw-hand. Throughout season 3, Ash uses the stars-and-stripes imagery in the advertising for his newly inherited retail business, Ashy Slashy's Hardware Store Emporium. The series culminates with Bruce Campbell's final performance as Ash in "The Mettle of Man." This season 3 finale has a moment that perfectly demonstrates the fusion of patriotism, violence, and Ash's *machismo* in a single image: Ash extending his middle finger as he stands in the hatch of a U.S. Army tank confronting the *kaiju*-sized demon, Kandar. Gibson's *Warrior Dreams* analyzes such connections between American masculinity, patriotism, and violence in a cultural movement he calls "the New War" (5), fought on screens and in the media in the decades of post–Vietnam America. Gibson explains that the "lone warrior" character from pulp westerns was reinvented as the contemporary action hero who "may fight on behalf of society, but he is not part of it" (41). Gibson continues, "Freed from the ambivalence and restraints of deep emotional relationships, freed from the boring tasks and burdensome responsibilities of everyday life, [the action hero] is reborn into the mythic world of primeval chaos, where he can develop his full powers of destruction," much like his predecessors from westerns like *High Noon* and *Shane*.

In the finale of *Ash vs. Evil Dead*, the U.S. Army officer in charge of Elk Grove's defense, Commander Gilbert (James Gaylyn), tells Ash to evacuate: "Get your ass into the transport or you're on your own, cowboy" (Jacobson, "The Mettle of Man").[7] The offhanded use of the term "cowboy" here foreshadows Ash's destiny after the final battle—Ash is repeatedly doomed to isolation because of his masculine adherence to the cowboy's violence and individualism. In the *Evil Dead* franchise, the cowboy's implements of violence, the six-shooter and the Bowie knife have transmuted into Ash's shotgun and chainsaw. The cowboy's white horse has become a cream-colored American Classic from big-auto Detroit, Ash's 1973 Oldsmobile Delta '88. The car provides the other accessories of cowboy competence, the tools of the trade. Instead of saddlebags, where any handy bit of rope or *deus ex machina* can be grabbed, the Delta boasts a trunk full of useful items, including a chemistry textbook used to make black powder in *Army of Darkness* and a portal to Hell used to dispose of the *Necronomicon* in *Ash vs. Evil Dead* (Bassett, "DUI"). At the same time, Ash frequently treats the Delta with the same loving affection a cowboy would show a trusted steed.[8] Even *Ash vs. Evil Dead*'s final shot is a blatant nod to the frontier mythos, as Ash rides off into the sunset in the Delta to fight another battle, another day.

The Delta deserves special attention throughout the series, as it is the literally the vehicle to advance the plot numerous times throughout the franchise. The Delta is a complicated symbol, as it represents the protagonist's white horse from the frontier mythos, but it also represents the optimism of industrial automotive might of America, post–World War 2. Susan Faludi explains that masculine identity in the post–World War 2 period had more constructive dimensions than it does presently, observing that in the mid–20th century "men grounded their worth and identity not in the masculine model of the warrior but in that of the builder. Being a man was ... collectively creating something tangible that was essential to a larger mission" (55). The kind of collective production exemplified in Detroit's auto-industry fit Faludi's builder model of masculinity well, and subsequently tied American masculinity to the symbol of economic prosperity for the American middle class, the automobile. But in the *Evil Dead* franchise, even the Delta itself is subject to a satirical reading because it represents a long-gone phase of American manufacturing. The Delta's appearance continuously calls to mind a bygone time, when Detroit manufacturing was the envy of the world, while continually reminding Ash and the audience of the tenuous nature of America's economic might and the decrepit nature of the masculinity represented by the car and its driver. Ash's fading masculinity is perpetually on display as compensatory swagger and overconfidence, especially in *Army of Darkness* and *Ash vs. Evil Dead*. His ruggedness is breaking down with age, and the opening scenes from *Ash vs. Evil Dead* (and numerous others) focus on his advancing decrepitude as the aging hero now needs a girdle, dentures, and black shoe polish to cover the grey in his hair (Raimi, "El Jefe"). The series catches up with Ash at age 57, living alone in a trailer, on the run for almost forty years from the Deadite menace. Ash is almost completely isolated from any sense of community, and his only regular companion at this time is his friend from work, Pablo.

The original ending to Raimi's *Army of Darkness* highlights the filmmakers' message about Ash's isolation and individualism more perfectly than any other. After leading a war against the Deadites in medieval England (a nod to Mark Twain's *A Connecticut Yankee in King Arthur's Court*), Ash takes too much of a sleeping potion to help him return to the present day, awakening in some near future to find that civilization has collapsed and that he is now utterly alone. This *Rip Van Winkle* style ending screened poorly, and was replaced with a scene of Ash successfully returning to the present day for the American theatrical release. In this version, Ash resumes his stock boy job at S-Mart, bragging about his adventures to coworkers and customers, getting one more chance to show his prowess by defeating a present day Deadite.[9] Even though the theatrical release of the film is still the most common version encountered, since the Anchor Bay home video release of the *Army of Darkness: Director's Cut* in 2000, the apocalyptic ending to the film has been widely known and available to American audiences as an epitextual artifact.[10] Although it is non-canonical in the franchise's larger story, the film's original ending succinctly demonstrates the ways in which Ash's behaviors, stupid and selfish, will always end up isolating him. Raimi's original vision for Ash's rugged individualism is reminiscent of the finale of *Planet of the Apes* (1968), where the selfishness of humans, represented by Ash, has led to complete and total collapse of society in some unknown apocalypse (probably due to a Deadite uprising that Ash slept through). Ash's rugged individualism becomes literally realized, as he is the last man on Earth. Even though we learn that Ash could have stayed in the past, could have been part of the community (the medieval warriors were willing to appoint him King), he selfishly forces the Wise Men to send him forward in time and overdoses on the time travel potion, overshooting his original destination in the 1990s. The final shot to this version of *Army of Darkness* is an image of Ash silhouetted and screaming against a blasted skyline, alone and doomed to isolation.

Ash vs. Evil Dead allowed the franchise to revisit the premise of Ash travelling forward in time to the blasted landscape of a post-apocalyptic future, as the last scene of the series has Ash awaken from a technologically induced coma at an indeterminate future date. The only remaining link to his past is the Delta, which now sports a machine gun turret and other modifications reminiscent of the vehicles in the *Mad Max* (1979) franchise. Blazoned across the front of the Delta is Ash's *Army of Darkness* catchphrase, "Hail to the King." Much like Ash himself, the Delta's modifications make it a chimeric symbol that fuses images of American industrial capitalism with violence and masculinity. In a narrative arc teeming with ironic Christ imagery, Ash finally demonstrates some small capacity for growth by embracing his role as the Chosen One (with much resistance, at first). Ash seems to grow up, at last willing to sacrifice himself to repel the Deadite incursion after running from his responsibility for more than three decades. Even in his final battle, though, Ash remains true to form.[11] Rather than killing the enormous demon, Kandar, from a safe distance with the tank he has commandeered, Ash takes a moment to taunt Kandar, a nearly fatal mistake. Kandar closes the distance and picks up the tank before Ash can figure out how to arm the tank's main cannon. When he finally does arm and fire the cannon, Kandar crushes Ash and the tank under his massive corpse. When Ash awakens in the future, the nature of his character remains stubbornly unchanged. He is greeted by a new character, the cyborg Lexx (Jessica Green), who kneels before Ash and intones, "The savior is awake" (Jacobson, "The Mettle of Man"). She throws open the gates of Ash's bomb shelter/tomb, shows him a wasteland ravaged by war, and tosses him the keys to his beloved car.[12] He asks after his missing daughter once, gets dressed for battle, and roars off into the sunset at the wheel of the Delta after leering at Lexx's body in the rearview mirror.

For all the hyperbolic masculine individualism, racism, and sexism on display, *Ash vs. Evil Dead* could easily carry the following disclaimer that once ran before episodes of *All in the Family* (1971–1979): "The program you are about to see is 'All in the Family.' It seeks to throw a humorous spotlight on our frailties, prejudices and concerns. By making them a source of laughter, we hope to show—in a mature fashion—just how absurd they are" (Kovalchik). Disclaimers like the one on *All in the Family* demonstrate what Sophia A. McClennen and Remy M. Maisel refer to as "the satire scare" in action around a piece of social commentary (175): "What if there were people out there who just didn't get the satire, and were taking all the absurdity at face value? If people are not interpreting it as satire, then not only can it not have the positive effects of satire we've described, but it could have unforeseen negative effects as well" (181). In their review of the reception to *The Daily Show* (1996–) and *The Colbert Report* (2005–2015), McClennen and Maisel conclude that, more often than not, the satire scare is much ado about nothing, as most contemporary viewers are more than perceptive enough to detect the irony inherent in even the most straight-faced satire. In contrast to *All in the Family*, it is not *Ash vs. Evil Dead*'s persistent cultural satire of racism, misogyny, and violence that made the famously strong-stomached *Evil Dead* creators blink and capitulate to the satire scare. In "Last Call," Ash drinks a potent cocktail of vodka and the animal tranquilizer, ketamine, in a recipe called "Pink Fuck."[13] The end of the episode boasts a post-credits scene where Bruce Campbell, in character as Ash, gives a public service announcement, imploring viewers to avoid the cocktail: "Hey all you knuckleheads, Ash Williams here. If someone offers you a drink of Pink Fuck, throw it away because it's bad shit. It will mess with your brain, and not in the good way. Be smart and stay safe out there" (Tilse). The voiceover plays over a two-image montage of Ash toasting a Pink Fuck cocktail and a bloody, disembodied brain in a frying pan that explodes into a bloody mess. The show regularly allows the satirical elements of Ash's character, like his violence, racism, and misogyny to air without comment, but the casual drug usage in this episode appears to merit special consideration. No matter how humorously framed, the disclaimer's singularity still manages to echo the same pedantic tone as the iconic 1987 "This Is Your Brain on Drugs" commercial it was designed to emulate (Pytka). While the more immaterial forms of social and cultural satire seem to be safe from the handwringing of the satire scare in *Ash vs. Evil Dead*, it appears the materiality of the Pink Fuck recipe and the depictions of Ash's drug usage made either the network or the creators feel the episode's disclaimer was necessary, even in a satirical show like *Ash vs. Evil Dead* in the 21st century.

The satire leveled by the *Evil Dead* franchise, and by Ash specifically, pokes fun at a set of dominant cultural attitudes regarding individualism and masculine behavior coming from the last forty years of neoliberal political belief and cultural production. Ash espouses the self-interest, anti-intellectualism, chauvinism, and thinly veiled racism associated with the individualist masculinity of neoliberalism. Ash is remarkably skilled at one thing, violence, but it is always worth remembering that violence in his life is a result of his own actions. The only reason the Deadites arise, over and over again, is that Ash never learns his lesson about meddling with the *Necronomicon*. Ash is a buffoon. He is the punchline of the whole franchise. He is a humorous, satirical character that embodies exaggerated versions of the values under critique. Campbell's smirking, self-aware performance is the audience's clue to the satire of the Ash's masculinity, defined by his extreme selfishness, anti-intellectualism, racism, and chauvinism. Despite the character's satirical edge, Ash's continual objectification of women takes on added seriousness and complexity in the #MeToo era, as the once-hyperbolic components of his exaggerated chauvinism lose critical distance from reality, and the character's actions appear more odious than humorous. Though certainly motivated by the shows' drastic ratings drop (Otterson), the network's decision to cancel the show in 2018 also reflects shifting cultural norms for humor and satire in the wake of the #MeToo movement. Campbell apparently senses opportune timing to shelve the Ash character, too. Approximately a week before the airing of *Ash vs. Evil Dead*'s finale, Campbell announced his permanent retirement from the Ash character in response to online efforts to get Netflix to save the series (Squires, "Bruce"). Campbell subsequently gave his blessing for *Evil Dead* to continue without him by turning to other characters, perhaps Mia from the 2013 reboot, or Pablo, Kelly, or Brandy from *Ash vs. Evil Dead* (Squires, "For"). Any of these characters has the opportunity to continue the legacy of *Evil Dead* and its satire of film conventions and dominant cultural values, now embodied in younger, updated characters that more directly reflect the concerns of contemporary audiences.

Notes

1. Even Fede Álvarez's *Evil Dead* (2013) nods to Campbell's iconic performance as Ash, using a post-credits tag of Ash saying, "Groovy."
2. I date the franchise history from the earliest inception of the Renaissance Pictures legal partnership between Sam Raimi, Rob Tapert, and Bruce Campbell, on 10 Aug 1979 (Warren 44–45). Since films take time to conceive, write, film, and produce, the cultural context for *The Evil Dead* (1981) begins in Carter-era in 1979 and now encompasses the entire Reagan, Bush, Clinton, Bush, Obama, and Trump administrations.
3. The reveal that the two major party candidates are evil is a not-so-subtle jab at the blurred lines between contemporary neoconservatism and neoliberalism that McWhorter describes in "When People Were Proud to Call Themselves 'Neoliberal.'"
4. Released 31 August 2016, the comic features several direct parodies of the real election's figures, including Bernie Sanders (Brock Anders), Hillary Clinton (Valerie Sexton), and the Tea Party (the American Patriot Party). Interestingly, no direct parody of Donald Trump is featured in the comic. Production lag explains such a significant omission in this piece of election satire, as Trump's rise to political prominence seemed unpredictable for many early in 2016, and he did not win the Republican nomination until the Republican National Convention, held 18–21 July 2016.
5. In 2013, Fede Álvarez's *Evil Dead* reboot without Ash became the most financially successful film in the whole franchise, at least in its cinematic run, but its critical reception continues to be mixed. *Rotten Tomatoes* reports Álvarez's adaptation scores the lowest with critics and audiences out of all four feature films in the *Evil Dead* series.
6. From its humble low-budget horror roots, at last count, *The Evil Dead* has resulted in a franchise that covers four films, a thirty-episode television series, six videogames, comic books, action figures, and innumerable other references, epitexts, and paratexts in its nearly-40-year existence ("Features").

7. Commander Gilbert's line represents an interesting coda to *Ash vs. Evil Dead*'s depiction of race because, during the climactic battle, a black character with state and military authority defines Ash's outlaw role so succinctly and precisely.

8. In "Last Call," the Delta has been stolen and demonically possessed. The episode's cold open begins with a soft-focus montage of numerous Delta appearances in the franchise, signaling Ash's deep and abiding love for the old car and everything it represents.

9. The details of the fight between Raimi and Universal over the film's ending are explained by Bill Warren (153–58), and the various versions of *Army of Darkness* are enumerated at *Book of the Dead: The Definitive Evil Dead Website* ("*Army of Darkness*: Different Versions").

10. The apocalyptic ending was also printed in the comic book adaptation of the film by Dark Horse Comics in 1992.

11. In *Army of Darkness*, Lord Arthur (Marcus Gilbert) asks Ash: "Are all men from the future loud-mouthed braggarts?" Ash replies definitively, "Nope. Just me, baby. Just me."

12. Given the filmmakers' backgrounds in Michigan and Ash's symbolic ties to blue-collar American automotive might, the post-apocalyptic landscapes at the end of *Army of Darkness* and *Ash vs. Evil Dead* are hard to read as anything but a reference to the economic devastation of contemporary Detroit.

13. The recipe for Pink Fuck is clearly visible several frames in the episode when Ash presents it to the camera. Screen captures of the recipe are widely available online.

Works Cited

Álvarez, Fede, director. *Evil Dead*. TriStar, 2013.
"*Army of Darkness*: Different Versions." *Book of the Dead: The Definitive Evil Dead Website*, bookofthedead.ws/website/army_of_darkness_different_versions.html.
Bassett, Michael, director. "Books from Beyond." *Ash vs. Evil Dead*, season 1, episode 3, Starz, 2015.
_____. "DUI." *Ash vs. Evil Dead*, season 2, episode 4, Starz, 2016.
Beesley, Mark. "Family." *Ash vs. Evil Dead*, season 3, episode 1, Starz, 2018.
Faludi, Susan. *Stiffed: The Betrayal of the American Man*. 1999, Perennial, 2000.
"Features." *Deadites Online*, deadites.net/features/.
Frazee, Damon, director. "Brujo." *Ash vs. Evil Dead*, season 1, episode 4, Starz, 2015.
Gibson, James William. *Warrior Dreams: Violence and Manhood in Post-Vietnam America*. Hill and Wang, 1994.
Harvey, David. *A Brief History of Neoliberalism*. Oxford University Press, 2007.
Hurst, Michael, director. "Fire in the Hole." *Ash vs. Evil Dead*, season 1, episode 7, Starz, 2015.
_____. "Killer of Killers." *Ash vs. Evil Dead*, season 1, episode 6, Starz, 2015.
Jacobson, Rick, director. "Home." *Ash vs. Evil Dead*, season 2, episode 1, Starz, 2016.
_____. "The Mettle of Man." *Ash vs. Evil Dead*, season 3, episode 10, Starz, 2018.
Kovalchik, Kara. "16 Cutting-Edge Facts about *All in the Family*." *Mental Floss*, 18 Nov. 2015, mentalfloss.com/article/71345/16-cutting-edge-facts-about-all-family.
McClennen, Sophia A., and Remy M. Maisel. *Is Satire Saving Our Nation? Mockery and American Politics*. Palgrave Macmillan, 2014.
McWhorter, John. "When People Were Proud to Call Themselves 'Neoliberal.'" *The Atlantic*, 30 May 2017, theatlantic.com/business/archive/2017/05/history-of-neoliberal-meaning/528276/.
Otterson, Joe. "'Ash vs. Evil Dead' Canceled at Starz After Three Seasons." *Variety*, 20 Apr. 2018, variety.com/2018/tv/news/ash-vs-evil-dead-canceled-starz-1202775341/.
Pytka, Joe, director. "This Is Your Brain on Drugs." *Partnership for a Drug-Free America*, 1987, youtube.com/watch?v=o5wwECXTJbg.
Raimi, Sam, director. *Army of Darkness*. Renaissance Pictures, 1992.
_____. "El Jefe." *Ash vs. Evil Dead*, season 1, episode 1, Starz, 2015.
_____. *The Evil Dead*. Renaissance Pictures, 1981.
_____. *Evil Dead 2*. Renaissance Pictures, 1987.
Ross, Dalton. "Ash vs Evil Dead: Sam Raimi Drops Intel on the New Show." *Entertainment*

Weekly, 9 July 2015, ew.com/article/2015/07/09/ash-vs-evil-dead-sam-raimi-bruce-campbell/.
Serrano, Elliot, writer. *Army of Darkness: Ash Saves Obama*. Art by Diego Galindo, covers by Elliot Fernandez and Pete Pantazis. Dynamite Entertainment, 2010.
_____. *Army of Darkness: Election Special*. Art by Ariel Padilla, covers by Todd Nauck and Lucio Parillo. Dynamite Entertainment, 2016.
Squires, John. "Bruce Campbell Says He's Officially 'Retired as Ash' and That's Sadly That, Folks." Bloodydisguistingwww, 23 Apr. 2018, bloody-disgusting.com/tv/3495157/bruce campbell-says-hes-officially-retired-ash-thats-sadly-folks/.
_____. "For What It's Worth, Bruce Campbell Gives His Blessing to 'Evil Dead' Continuing Without Him." Bloodydisguistingwww, 23 May 2018, bloody-disgusting.com/movie/3500583/worth-bruce-campbell-gives-blessing-evil-dead continuing-without/.
Tilse, Tony, director. "Last Call." *Ash vs. Evil Dead*, season 2, episode 3, Starz, 2016.
Warren, Bill. *The Evil Dead Companion*. St. Martin's Griffin, 2000.

Franchising Fright from Film to Game

STEFAN HALL

In 2003's "Transmedia Storytelling: Moving Characters from Books to Films to Video Games Can Make Them Stronger and More Compelling" in *MIT's Technology Review*, Henry Jenkins writes that:

> In the ideal form of transmedia storytelling, each medium does what it does best–so that a story might be introduced in a film, expanded through television, novels, and comics, and its world might be explored and experienced through game play. Each franchise entry needs to be self-contained enough to enable autonomous consumption.... Reading across the media sustains a depth of experience that motivates more consumption.... Redundancy between media burns up fan interest and causes franchises to fail. Offering new levels of insight and experience refreshes the franchise and sustains consumer loyalty.

The history of video games shows that much of the medium's production has been influenced by cinema, and perhaps nowhere is this seen more directly than in the topic of games based on movies. Functioning as franchise expansion, spaces for play, and story development, film-to-game translations have been a significant component of video game titles since the early days of the medium. As the technological possibilities of hardware development continue in both the film and video game industries, issues of media convergence and divergence between film and video games have grown in importance.

Obviously one of the key motivations for this type of franchising is economic potential, as established audiences will be more likely to seek out materials that expand upon the worlds established in films. This is particularly true with fans of particular genres—especially science fiction, fantasy, horror, and animation—that not coincidentally represent the majority of adapted films. Of the close to 700 licensed games released between 1982 and 2011 that are derived from films, only about five percent were based on horror titles;

the bulk of licensed properties come from the genres of science fiction and fantasy as well as animation. Most of the horror games, in terms of action, fall under the category of survival horror, a subgenre that focuses on character survival by limiting resources (ammunition, health, speed) as well as inhibiting player agency through reducing the visual field onscreen or actually denying interactivity at various points during gameplay. Although the term "survival horror" was first introduced in conjunction with *Resident Evil* (1996), precursors include *3D Monster Maze* (1982), *Haunted House* (1982), *Shiryou Sensen: War of the Dead* (1987), and *Alone in the Dark* (1992). More action elements were introduced in *Resident Evil 4* (2005), further changing the genre, so many game scholars look at the period from 1996–2004 as a pivotal time for survival horror where many classics were introduced such as *Silent Hill* (1999) and *Fatal Frame* (2001). This era also mostly coincides with the sixth generation of home consoles—including the Sega Dreamcast (1998), the Sony PlayStation 2 (2000), the Nintendo GameCube (2001), and the Microsoft Xbox (2001)—and horror games were able to take advantage of more data for games by using DVD drives and improvements to the CPU, GPU, and RAM to make for a more horrific visual experience and aesthetically move closer to filmic expectations.

It is in this development cycle that a notable group of games based on the *Evil Dead* films were released. Aside from an early questionable Commodore 64 release in 1984, games based on The *Evil Dead* franchise did not reappear until 2000, beginning with *Evil Dead: Hail to the King*, followed by *Evil Dead: A Fistful of Boomstick* (2003), and *Evil Dead: Regeneration* (2005). Movie properties are just one in a host of licenses sought by the video game industry—others include sports, television, comic books, cartoons, and toys—but games based on films are the most licensed source material. This franchise effect has cast some stigma on licensed property games of all kinds, devaluing their potential as media and equating them with other derivative products from their respective intellectual properties. That film-to-game titles function as ancillary marketing commodities cannot be denied in some cases, but in others they enhance, and even occasionally surpass, the source material in areas of creative expression, audience engagement, and revenue. These areas are likely, but not always, interrelated, such that a critically praised game enjoys significant sales. In a report released late in 2009, The Nielsen Company analyzed the attributes of households that purchased games based on movies. Based on a two-year study involving households that purchased at least one game based on a movie, Nielsen reported that families with children between the ages of six to twelve were the most likely to purchase games based on movies. Households likely to purchase a movie-based game also had a household income averaging over $70,000 a year and typically spent almost twice as much as average families on games and DVDs. When looking at a tendency to purchase such games by ethnic type, non–Caucasians, especially Hispanics and Asians, were most likely to purchase film-to-game titles ("Movie-based video games").

Aside from the obvious marketing tie-in, how do video games based on movies function in other ways? Given that film-to-game adaptations can cover a wide range of genres, one way to think about this question involves considering the position of the game in relation to the narrative of the film. The first category is products expressly tied to one film's narrative, such as *E.T.: The Extra-Terrestrial* (1982), *Die Hard: Nakatomi Plaza* (2002), or *Star Wars: Episode III—Revenge of the Sith* (2005). These follow the narrative of the film, either in its entirety or key scenes, and allow the user to move principal characters through recreated sets and action sequences. Since creative game play can be limited by following an established (and often linear) narrative, sometimes additional material, from narrative exposition to play spaces not seen in the source film, is added as an enticement for players as a way to enhance their filmic experience and an incentive to play a game where major plot elements could be known in advance.

The second category is products that function as sequels, prequels, or parallel/alternate narratives (sometimes using dominant points established by films). Games such as *Blade Runner* (1997), *Star Wars: TIE Fighter* (1994), *Heavy Metal: FAKK2* (2000) and *Evil Dead: Hail to the King* (2001) are positioned around the source films so that a player who is familiar with the foundational material could have a more nuanced level of play yet must be self-contained enough to offer a satisfying game experience for those unfamiliar with the referenced film(s). Eric Lindstrom, former Creative Director at Eidos Interactive, noted the creative negotiation inherent in this duality: "The biggest challenge there is with licenses is the inability to be agile when it comes to decisions that intersect with the character and presentation. If you want to make a change, and you believe it's right for the game and the franchise, you still need to go through an approval process before moving forward on the decision" ("Why do games go bad?" 21). If a game is narratively situated between two films, such as *Star Wars: TIE Fighter* or *Enter the Matrix* (2003), the films serve as anchor points for the game's design. In the case of *TIE Fighter*, since the source films had come out years before, the game play had far less constraint than *Enter the Matrix*, which was intended as a bridge between the released *The Matrix* (1999) and its theatrical sequel, *The Matrix Reloaded* (2003). As ambitious as this transmedia narrative was, technical issues with the game and major changes in protagonists between the films and the game resulted in significant confusion for both game players and film audiences, even in cases where the demographics overlapped. Because *TIE Fighter*, while serving as a bridge between *The Empire Strikes Back* (1980) and *Return of the Jedi* (1983), presented an alternate narrative not covered in the films, it was able to introduce new characters and situations while referencing film elements and plot points to drive its own design and narrative progression. During his 2001 promotional "Chins across America" tour, Bruce Campbell noted that he often had to field the question "Will there be an *Evil Dead IV?*" (Campbell 308). Campbell suggested that people wanting a sequel to *Army of Darkness* (1992) should "look to the video game," referring to *Evil Dead: Hail to the King* (2000) as the game is set after the events of that film.

The third category is products in milieu established or created by film, but not expressly related to established filmic narrative. A game like *James Bond 007: Everything or Nothing* (2004) used the current Bond actor's likeness and voice (Pierce Brosnan) as well as supporting actors from the films, the requisite Bond girls, a new title song with a credit sequence done in the signature Bond cinematic style, and the standard international action within a completely new script written just for the game. *Star Wars: Knights of the Old Republic* (2003) uses the familiar visual referents and some plot points to create an entirely new era in the *Star Wars* universe, setting the game 1,000 years before the action of the films. While this technically could be seen as a prequel of sorts, the characters and vistas are so far removed from their filmic origins that it ostensibly functions as a derivative product that is almost new in origin. Games of this type tend to be more well-received by players as there is just enough expansion of a film's universe to retain familiarity but enough expansion to permit innovation in narrative and game play. *Evil Dead: A Fistful of Boomstick* falls into this category as it is a sequel to *Hail to the King* and narratively develops this new plot, while *Evil Dead: Regeneration* is in an interesting position between the second and third categories as it is unconnected to *A Fistful of Boomstick* and instead takes place in an alternate reality from the original film trilogy, depicting what would have happened if Ash did not enter the time portal at the end of *Evil Dead 2*.

At this point it is useful to briefly outline the plot of all three of these *Evil Dead* games as they all share some similarities that appear to be core elements of the narrative as well as comparable game mechanics. *Hail to the King* game takes place eight years after the events of *Army of Darkness* (and more specifically, the theatrical ending to the film not the unused alternate). Ashley "Ash" Williams is back at the S-Mart, where he is beginning a new relationship with Jenny, a fellow employee. Ash starts to suffer recurring nightmares about the *Necronomicon Ex-Mortis*, which prompts Jenny to take Ash back to Professor Knowby's mountain cabin and begin to deal with his post-traumatic stress. Unbeknownst to them, Ash's possessed severed hand is waiting and plays Knowby's incantation tape, causing the evil force to reawaken and kidnap Jenny. Springing into action, Ash is quickly stopped by Evil Ash, knocking Ash unconscious and escaping. Upon regaining consciousness, Ash rebuilds his chainsaw hand and then goes to rescue Jenny, embarking on a mission to recover five missing pages from the *Necronomicon* and the Kandarian dagger (in the possession of a possessed Annie Knowby in the cabin's fruit cellar). Part of the action requires Ash to pursue Evil Ash and Jenny through another time portal back to a 9th century Arabian village, where Ash defeats his evil twin and frees Jenny from possession. Using another spell from the tome, Ash returns with Jenny to Dearborn, Michigan, where to his horror the *Necronomicon* is for sale as a mass market paperback and evil forces are rampant across the country. As Ash screams in horror, the game ends.

A Fistful of Boomstick begins three years after the events in *Hail to the King*, although through Ash's recounting of the story the game quickly switches to a flashback structure. Trisha Pettywood, an investigative journalist looking into the *Necronomicon* phenomenon, is interviewing Professor Alex Eldridge, a colleague of Professor Knowby, on television station KLA2. Ash is watching the interview while he drinks in a nearby bar, and the bartender is sympathetic to Ash because something bad has happened to Jenny. Eldridge is publicly discrediting Ash's claims about the Deadites and interdimensional time travel, which prompts Trisha to play Knowby's audio tape to get Eldridge's opinion about it, and this of course reanimates the evil forces. Fortunately, Ash just happens to be carrying his trusty shotgun and ventures into the streets of Dearborn to do battle. In his attempt to reach the television station, Ash secures a spellbook (which gives him various powers throughout the game, including super strength and the ability to possess different Deadites), and ultimately joins forces with Trisha and Eldridge. Through a series of adventures, they have to recover the Kandarian Summoning Stone from the local history museum only to be double-crossed by Eldridge, who wants to use the Stone to take over the world. Ash has to pursue Eldridge through another time portal, sending him back to colonial Dearborn in 1695, where Ash encounters his distant ancestor, Williams the Blacksmith, who upgrades his weapons and helps him fight the Deadites. Eldridge escapes again, and Ash pursues him through another portal, arriving in Civil War–era Dearborn circa 1863. Brokering a ceasefire between the Union and Confederate soldiers, Ash uses them to fight the Deadites. With some help from a special gun crafted by the great-great-great-grandson of Williams the Blacksmith, Ash defeats Eldridge and enters a time portal to return to present-day Dearborn. Of course, Ash's suffering continues, as the Deadites have taken over the town by acquiring the Kandarian Summoning Stone, which Ash foolishly left in the Union fort. This leads to a battle with the Deadite Queen, who upon her death is revealed to be Trisha. The framing narrative of the game then leaves the flashback structure as Ash finishes recounting his tale. Again displaying his ineptitude with magic items, Ash's attempt to use the Stone to cleanse Dearborn instead sends him to the time of what appears to be imperial Japan where he must begin to battle anew as the game ends.

Evil Dead: Regeneration is a departure from the previous two entries in that it establishes a completely new narrative. As publisher THQ switched from developer Heavy Iron Studios to Cranky Pants Studios, it is not surprising that the story linking *Hail to the King* and *A Fistful of Boomstick* was abandoned. Ignoring the time travel ending of *Evil Dead 2*, *Regeneration* begins with Ash in the Sunny Meadows psychiatric institution, committed for the horrific events at Knowby's cabin (which serves as a tutorial level for the player). Sally, Ash's lawyer, reveals that she has found Knowby's diary, corroborating some of the events from Ash's story. Shortly after she departs, Ash's psychiatrist, Dr. Reinhard, manages to activate the *Necronomicon*, which he plans on using to control the world. Ash manages to retrieve his chainsaw and shotgun and is about to leave the institution when Knowby's spirit appears and warns him of Reinhard's plan. To better confront Reinhard, Ash teams up with Sam, a diminutive victim of Reinhard, a half-Deadite man named who can be reborn from any death but remains further unaffected by the *Necronomicon* because of his liminal status. An encounter with a Deadite queen gives Ash the ability to voluntarily transform into Evil Ash and access different abilities. After several more battles and closing more portals, the spirit of Knowby reappears, tells Ash that Reinhard has acquired his diary and is preparing to make a human sacrifice (most likely of Sally), and that Ash must save the world. An infuriated Ash replies that he is focused on saving only Sally and maybe Sam, and so the duo sets off for a Deadite temple and the final encounter with Reinhard. After his defeat and closure of the final portal, it appears that Ash will finally see his romantic aspirations realized, but Sally is possessed and Ash resorts to killing her. The final portal reopens, sucking Ash, Sam, and the *Necronomicon* into parts and times unknown, ending the game.

Considering the three narratives of the games, several common elements can be easily discerned. Aside from the obvious centrality of Ash, Knowby remains a figurative and literal force in each title, similar to the way he was the story catalyst for *The Evil Dead* (1981) and *Evil Dead 2* (1987). Control of the *Necronomicon* drives a considerable amount of the plot, not just releasing the evil force but creating the various portals that are also a shared component between the titles. The portals also help to cover up, both narratively and practically, the disjuncture between different levels in the game, as the types of changes are usually disguised through some sort of transportation (one of the most popular being elevators) and help to conceal the loading screens as different segments of a game's code is activated for play. Each game also ends with a cliffhanger and references the ambiguity from the end of all three films. There appears to be no respite for Ash, and as a hero he must again and again battle the Deadites. There also appears to be no true possibility of a relationship for Ash as any romantic potential in Jenny, Trisha, or Sally is always marred by death. (Even in the 2014 comic book series, *Army of Darkness: Ash Gets Hitched*, his betrothal to Sheila is disrupted by yet another time portal accident. Clearly, Ash has a lot of problems.)

Most critical to the games is the primacy of Ash as the player avatar, complete with chainsaw hand and boomstick, and furthermore he is clearly recognizable as a character model based on Bruce Campbell. As Geoff King notes in "Die Hard/Try Harder: Narrative, Spectacles and Beyond, from Hollywood to Videogame," one of the elements needed in both narrative film and narratological video games is a "developed sense of character or personality" (64). Since all three games utilize a chase or third-person perspective, the player sees and hears Ash as he is controlled in the game. Having gamers act as characters within a specific franchise environment further heightens market awareness of such a character as product. Programmers use digital technologies, with increasing levels of precision, to reproduce likenesses in video games; recent titles where characters played by human actors have been recreated within the code of the game's engine include *The Lord of the Rings* series (2001–2004), *Batman Begins* (2005), *The Godfather* (2006), and *James Bond: Quantum of Solace* (2008). To further enhance this connection, Campbell himself provides the voice for the character (while all three games used other notable voice actors, only one other actor from the *Evil Dead* series, Ted Raimi, was brought in for *Regeneration* to play Sam).

The action in *Hail to the King* is very similar to the influential *Resident Evil* in that it uses pre-rendered backgrounds and semi-fixed camera angles as well as purposefully keeping the amount of supplies (ammunition and chainsaw fuel) low for the player so that there is always a sense of urgency when it comes to conserving resources. As Jonathan Gray notes in *Show Sold Separately*, as a player "watches the action in third-person, the stark vulnerability of one's avatar is arguably more visceral" (190). *A Fistful of Boomstick* provides more camera control for the player, and so the sense of closed framing that works to amplify the sense of horror is removed and Ash becomes more of an action hero. His transformation to a powerful champion is most fully realized by *Regeneration*; with unlimited ammunition and chainsaw fuel, Ash fights larger hordes of Deadites to fill a rage meter that allows him to go into a mode where he is much stronger, dealing more damage while becoming more resistant to damage himself. Ash can also use Sam to solve traps and to engage the enemy; as Sam will be reborn each time he dies due to his half-Deadite state, sometimes these actions are rather humorous in keeping with the more slapstick nature of the film series as it went on.

Unfortunately, the *Evil Dead* games did not find much of an audience outside the established fan base for the movies who also happen to play video games. After *Regeneration*, the franchise had periodic reappearances in other media—like the comic book series released by Dark Horse and Dynamite

Entertainment or the 2007 stage musical—but would not resurface in video games until 2011 with two mobile titles, *Army of Darkness: Defense* and *Evil Dead*. *Defense* starred Bruce Campbell reprising his role of Ash in a tower defense style game basically replicating the castle siege from *Army of Darkness*. *Evil Dead*, despite its somewhat cartoony graphics, tries to recreate the first film for one storyline before shifting into a new one for the second chapter. Statistics show that *Defense* had between 1 million and 5 million installations, and the developer Backflip Studios has continued to support the game since its release. Trigger Apps, the developers behind *Evil Dead*, had been concentrating on more current film releases, such as *The Karate Kid* (2010) or *The Green Hornet* (2011), but decided to shift to an older but (hopefully) recognizable property with *The Evil Dead*. Sales data is unclear, but given that Trigger Apps is now defunct, their film licensing strategy does not appear successful. Mobile gaming has to make adjustments for the processing power of the platforms, which are typically behind those of home consoles and computers, tends to work within genres that lend themselves to the largely touch oriented control schemes of mobile interfaces, and usually has shorter play sessions. All of these factors can impact player immersion and satisfaction with a game, and for gamers who want an experience that is more evocative of the *Evil Dead* films, the mobile titles are likely not as satisfying.

So where is an engaging, technically sophisticated *Evil Dead* game? Given how influential the film series has been and continues to be (including a remake in 2013 and *Ash vs. Evil Dead* [2015–2018]) and coupled with the meteoric popularity of horror video games, why haven't there been more (and more successful) *Evil Dead* games? The problem is likely neither technical nor economic, but lies with the narrative advanced by the games. When discussing licensed video games, especially those from horror properties, Gray notes:

> Just as nightmares induced by watching a horror film often heighten its terror by transporting the viewer-dreamer into the film's world of predator and prey, uncertainty, anxiety, and visceral fear, so too does the game create a new, arguably more direct relationship between the individual player and the storyworld [189].

The world of *The Evil Dead* is not one of the unrelenting horror of *Resident Evil* or *Silent Hill*. The dead are playfully malicious in their lethal mayhem, and only a similarly playful protagonist could hope to prevail, or at least put up with victories endlessly disrupted by setbacks and errant time portals. Bruce Campbell's work as a digitized Ash has been very true to the spirit of the character, but it is that very character that is put in an unbalanced narrative. *Hail to the King* was perhaps too close to the influential survival horror it was imitating, and *A Fistful of Boomstick* moved away from this somewhat by introducing a lot more action, but *Regeneration* is the only title so far that seems to get the irreverent tone in the face of an apocalypse correct. The time is certainly right for a new *Evil Dead* game, and with it a change in game design, moving from the more rigid, linear structure that is influenced by the cinematic origins of the franchise and into an open world, sandbox style where discovering the narrative is part of the game's challenge and reward. In this way, everyone gets to be the hero, even a battered but unbroken one like Ash, full of bravado in the face of evil. Like collecting the cursed pages of the *Necronomicon*, players will go after these objectives and assemble their own stories of adventure.

WORKS CITED

Campbell, Bruce. *If Chins Could Kill: Confessions of a B Movie Actor*. St. Martin's Press, 2002.
Gray, Jonathan. *Show Sold Separately: Promos, Spoilers, and Other Media Paratexts*. New York University Press, 2010.
Jenkins, Henry. "Transmedia Storytelling: Moving Characters from Books to Films to Video Games Can Make Them Stronger and More Compelling." *MIT's Technology Review*, 15 Jan. 2003.
King, Geoff. "Die Hard/Try Harder: Narrative, Spectacles and Beyond, from Hollywood to Videogame." *ScreenPlay: Cinema/Videogames/Interfaces*. Wallflower Press, 2002.
"Movie-Based Video Games and the Households That Buy Them." *Nielsen*, The Nielsen Company (US), 16 Dec. 2009.
"Why Do Games Go Bad?" *Game Informer* 183 (July 2008), pp. 20–22.

Repulsion and Convulsion in "The Splatter Zone"

ROB ROZNOWSKI

Combining the trilogy of the *Evil Dead* horror films into a successful stage musical seemed an impossible task. Surely the cultish fans of the iconic Sam Raimi films and musical theatre purists would never be satisfied by an attempt to fuse the expectations of both factions into one satisfying evening of theatre. But *Evil Dead: The Musical* has done something very few shows (*The Rocky Horror Show* and *Little Shop of Horrors* come to mind) have done before by successfully appealing to two usually dissimilar audiences (horror film and musical theatre fans) to create a musical that succeeds on several levels. The musical succeeds in its adaptation in three key areas—a skillfully selective book, a profane pastiche score and, most important, unparalleled audience interaction. By condensing the numerous plotlines from the three original *Evil Dead* films, the creators of the musical skillfully discard unnecessary material from the movies while highlighting the most memorable moments in a vulgarly comedic book that sates most Deadites and includes enough meta-references to win over the most jaded musical theatre fans. The score also appeals to these divergent audiences by offering simple catchy tunes with hoariest of lyrics while also cleverly mocking musical theatre conventions. The musical actually tops its cinematic predecessors in one aspect—its interactivity between audience and performer. It is the unique addition of the "Splatter Zone" to *Evil Dead: The Musical* that expands audience experience of its source material while retaining its gleeful bloodlust.

While not a financial juggernaut defined by Broadway bonanzas like *Wicked* or *The Lion King*, this modest musical has created a unique journey. The original successful 2003 Toronto production spawned a successful 2006 Off-Broadway run, a national tour, a Las Vegas incarnation and numerous sold-out national and international independent presentations. As the musical's website points out, "With the success of the show in Toronto, productions began springing up all over the world. Seoul, Tokyo, Calgary, California, Kalimazoo [sic], and so many more locations ... wherever there were theatre fans twisted enough to want some blood with their musicals, there was bound to be a production" ("History"). The show's success has paved the way for numerous imitators who have copied *Evil Dead: The Musical's* successful cult formula bringing a younger, hipper and highly desired demographic to theatres worldwide. The cult success of *The Rocky Horror Show* is clearly part of the *Evil Dead: The Musical* writing and marketing plan. In fact, one of the main quotes used to promote the musical comes from Anita Gates' *New York Times* 2006 review, "'Evil Dead: The Musical' wants to be the next 'Rocky Horror Show,' and it just may succeed."

The success of *Rocky Horror*'s midnight showings were dependent upon multiple viewings of the film or show in order to become part of the action, *Evil Dead: The Musical* allows immediate (liquid) satisfaction to first-time viewers. In the musical much of the suspense is replaced by sophomoric humor while the graphic violence is replaced by an exaggerated almost Grand Guignol glee of spurting blood. As in many Raimi films (especially the first two *Evil Dead* films) the line between humor and horror is explored where an audience revels in the disgusting while laughing at their own reaction to Raimi's sick mind. It is in this intersection of repulsion of violence and convulsions of laughter that the Splatter Zone was born.

While earlier horror musicals have crafted nifty audience interactivity including the call and response quality of *The Rocky Horror Show* or the plant overtaking the theatre at the end of *Little Shop of Horrors*; this musical trumps both of those and creates a highly theatrical innovation far surpassing any cinematic viewing of the *Evil Dead* films with the addition of the Splatter Zone. The Splatter Zone is a section of the audience cordoned off for the bravest (or most foolish) audience members who willingly offer themselves to be baptized by the buckets of blood used during the show. Fountains of plasma regularly spray these patrons during the numerous death scenes. The majority of the untouched audience members revel, as the select few are drenched in stage blood. This adds a level of immersive performance to the show that connects the entire audience to the viewing experience immediately and tangibly more compelling than even a 3D viewing of any film.

In an article on Cleveland.com, writer Andrea Simakis interviews actor Andrew Di Rosa who played Jake in *Evil Dead: The Musical*'s national tour and asked him to explain how the Splatter Zone works: "Whenever a demon is shot, beheaded or otherwise sliced, diced, chopped or amputated ... that's the cue for a technician watching on a monitor backstage to trigger the box. The resulting powerful burst of blood is 'pretty ridiculous and pretty wonderful at the same time.'" The immersive, immediate and immense amount of blood soaking the macabre members of the audience in the Splatter Zone provides an unparalleled theatrical experience. To make sure all members of the zone are equally drenched unique strategies are also employed. Simakis and Di Rosa continue, "Just in case the spray doesn't reach everyone, actors have personal, portable blood packs—'like these little water-bottle pouches that we have in our vests'—that they can use to nail drier members of the crowd. 'We try to soak everybody.'"

The creation of the Splatter Zone seems a perfect Raimi-esque theatrical solution. As mentioned, Raimi's films seem to revel in the laughter response to an especially disgusting dismemberment or outrageously violent act that allows the viewer to both recoil in horror and release in laughter. In the *International Encyclopedia of the Social & Behavioral Sciences* article about the "Psychology of Disgust," Paul Rozin writes, "Disgust appears to be a universal and basic emotion.... Disgust has been transformed, in human cultural evolution, into an emotion that promotes withdrawal from a wide range of culturally unacceptable entities; it is a major force in socialization, and has become a guardian of the soul, as well as the body." It is the actual exaggeration of the disgusting elements of the Raimi films or the Splatter Zone that allows relief despite the initial recoiling from violence and bloodshed.

The relief from the exaggerated violence is usually in the form of laughter. In the case of a film or theatrical viewing it is a communal response to regulate or moderate the experience from initial disgust or horror to a safer and more manageable tone of relief or recovery. What the Splatter Zone trades on is the curious nature of sick jokes and the people who appreciate them. In the *International Journal of Humor Research*, Vassilis Saroglou and Lydwine Aciaux write about "Liking Sick Humor." They note that there are two ways people operate in relation to sick jokes. "First, people who enjoy sick jokes may allow themselves to express publicly what others repress or express less easily. This of course could include ease in playing with disgust, an emotion that usually elicits avoidant behaviors." Avoidant behaviors are used as a way of coping or to save one from psychological distress. The avoidant behavior in relation to the Raimi phenomenon is laughter.

It is their second categorization of people who appreciate and use sick humor that makes the addition of the Splatter Zone a masterstroke that out-Raimi's Raimi. "Second, positive attitudes toward sick jokes in spite of the possible discomfort of others with the same jokes in social settings may be understood as a (successful or unsuccessful) way of trying to get attention and communicate with others" (Saroglou and Aciaux). It is in fact the communal aspect of the Splatter Zone where either baptized members of the special section of the audience or a safe and dry observer in the regular seats witness such gruesome behavior in close proximity that creates this unique experience. The authors continue with the second categorization, "Extrapolating from the second interpretation, enjoyment of sick jokes may be a sign of at least some aspects of emotional instability or difficulty with emotional regulation" (Saroglou and Aciaux). And while that may certainly be true, a collection of audience members paying to be part of literal gallows humor forces a different type of emotional regulation. The audience at *Evil Dead: The Musical* creates a societal norm where members who do not laugh at the exaggerated and ridiculous bloodbath are perceived as the emotionally unstable and are on the fringes of this new society where they are unable to be part of a common communal experience. And audiences flock to it. Like the best cult musicals, the audience endorses its appeal through repeated viewing and universal shared inside jokes. The show's numerous successful long-running productions have thrived as an audience made up of Raimi film fans, musical theatre lovers, and others returns time and time again. As the *Evil Dead: The Musical* website notes of their unique and undeniable appeal, "You don't need to be a fan of *Evil Dead* to love this show. You don't need to be a fan of horror to love this show. You don't need to be a fan of musicals to love this show. As long as you like having fun … this show is for you" ("History").

What the Splatter Zone does is trade in on the psychological interplay of disgust and dismay and depends upon its regulation through humor. A shared and common experience for that outside of the theatre would be deemed unacceptable. Audience reaction is exactly what makes the Splatter Zone work. Actor Di Rosa continues in his interview, "We just love people who embrace it—hands out and face to the heavens as we douse 'em in blood" (Simakis). The dark humor and camp mix together to create a unique theatrical experience as blood is shared in increasingly ridiculous and unique ways. In Mary Wade Burnside's "Beware the Splatter Zone," she interviews show's creator Christopher Bond who notes, "We dump gallons of blood on the audience but it's done in creative ways," he said. "We don't stand there with a hose. We have a cool blood delivery system that shoots blood off in different ways. It's all fun and the audience goes bonkers for it" (Burnside).

The Splatter Zone also adds another level of marketing savvy and cult cache to the *Evil Dead: The Musical* experience. As many audience members leave the theatre drenched in blood they are immediate publicity for the immersive experience of viewing this musical. Actor Di Rosa continues, "If you're there for the Splatter Zone, you wanna walk home looking like you've been part of a massacre" (Simakis). More than that, the addition of this section expands the cult status of the show making this premium seating for an exclusive group. Audience members pay higher prices for Splatter Zone seating and come usually dressed in white to showcase the bloodletting. The Splatter Zone has become the most compelling addition to the musical viewing experience and actually seems appropriately Raimi-esque in its ability to find glee in bloody dismemberment. In fact the long-running Las Vegas production sells these seats as part of a "4-D" experience. Actor Di Rosa states that blood/waterproof gear and more is for sale in the lobby, "We sell them at the merchandise table—we have 'Evil Dead' ponchos, and we sell towels and little face cloths and stuff like that. They've thought of everything" (Simakis). Disgust as merchandising scheme.

Evil Dead: The Musical's hybrid (horror and musical) success charted new territory beyond past similar shows like *Little Shop of Horrors* and *The Rocky Horror Show*. It has also paved the way for bloody and profanity-laced imitators like *Silence! The Musical* (the unauthorized parody of *The Silence of the Lambs*) and *Musical of the Living Dead*. These more recent shows and others have tried to imitate and follow in the footsteps of *Evil Dead: The Musical*'s writing and marketing strategies to varying degrees of success. While these newer shows aim to entice the same hip demographic that have embraced the *Evil Dead* musical, they are in most cases lesser adaptations. Despite the best efforts of these imitators, the uniqueness of the Splatter Zone of *Evil Dead: The Musical* adds up to an inimitable musical success that satisfies as it disgusts.

Works Cited

Burnside, Mary Wade. "Beware the Splatter Zone at 'Evil Dead: The Musical.'" *The Exponent Telegram*, 29 Oct. 2015, wvnews.com/theet/lifestyles/pulse/beware-the-splatter-zone-at-evil-dead-the-musical/article_f144c5ff-8441-58c9-98a8-bd056b024e3c.html.

Gates, Anita. "Music and Mayhem, Blood Trail Included." *New York Times*, 1 Nov. 2006, nytimes.com/2006/11/02/theater/reviews/02evil.html.

"History of the Evil Dead Franchise," evildeadthemusicalwww, evildeadthemusical.com/history-of-evil-dead/.

Rozin, P. "Disgust, Psychology of." *International Encyclopedia of the Social & Behavioral Sciences*, 2001, pp. 3766–69.

Saroglou, Vassilis, and Lydwine Anciaux. "Liking Sick Humor: Coping Styles and Religion as Predictors." *Humor: International Journal of Humor Research* 17, no. 3 (2004), pp. 257–77.

Simakis, Andrea. "Get Set to Get Wet as 'Evil Dead The Musical' Readies Its Famous 'Splatter Zone' for a Short Run in Playhouse Square." Cleveland.com, 16 Oct. 2014, cleveland.com/onstage/index.ssf/2014/10/get_set_to_get_wet_as_evil_dea.html.

Stage Horrality
Evil Dead: The Musical *and the Theatricality of Embarrassment*

André Loiselle

Over thirty years ago, Philip Brophy coined the now-famous neologism "horrality" to describe the mixture of body horror, violently self-referential textuality, carnal morality, and over-the-top hilarity common to a wide range of early 1980s slashers. For Brophy, horrality is perfectly embodied by Sam Raimi's original *The Evil Dead* (1981), "a gore movie beyond belief that has one simultaneously screaming with terror and laughter" (Brophy 95). When transferred to the stage and magnified by song and dance, the horrality of *Evil Dead: The Musical* veers almost entirely towards hilarity and completely jettisons horror. However, as this essay demonstrates, the crude theatricality of the musical brings to the fore a degree of discomfort, apprehension and embarrassment that destabilizes surface merriment, and creates an odd sense of dread. Most professional theater productions try very hard to minimize the risk of embarrassing mistakes endemic to live performance and keep spectators safely ensconced in their comfort zone, where they can happily enjoy competent acting and well executed stage business. Conversely, *Evil Dead: The Musical* goes out of its way to break with this tradition of theatrical professionalism and embrace the danger of failure, which exposes the spectators to the constant fear of embarrassment.

The notion of a theatricality of embarrassment has been used by critics and historians to describe the political practice of certain left-wing stage directors, such as George Tabori. Tabori used a "theatre of embarrassment" to "shock, vex and hurt" the bourgeoisie out of its complacency (Feinberg 267). There is little, if any, political purpose to the theatricality of embarrassment that I observe in *Evil Dead: The Musical*. Rather what we have here, beyond the uproariously fast-paced mixture of slapstick and satire, is a frightful predisposition for discomfiture, which infuses the play with a degree of uncertainty and trepidation that conjures up the sense of moral panic caused by the original film's excessive gore and violence (Egan 27). The play's uneven campiness, its sophomoric humor and niche cult appeal, all lend themselves to the kind of upsetting blunders and mishaps that can cause bewilderment and dismay in the audience. Failed jokes, self-consciously "bad performances" that turn out to be just bad, kitschy pieces of stage business that appear less cleverly cheesy than just incompetently executed, ironic self-references that come across as disconcertingly obtuse, all of these might generate a degree of mortification in the spectator that can produce distress and anxiety, if not full-on terror. The stage lacks cinema's ability to create terrifying special effects. However, the live show, unlike film, can inject a significant amount of fear and angst in the spectator through the ever-present potential for humiliating missteps. This is how, I would argue, *Evil Dead: The Musical* functions as an example of stage horrality: by striking a delicate balance between successful entertainment and an alarming potential for abject failure.

Evil Dead: The Musical was conceived by a small group of students at Queen's University in Kingston, Ontario—George Reinblatt, Christopher Bond, Melissa Morris, and Frank Cipolla—and had its first semi-professional production at the small Tranzac Club in Toronto, in August of 2003. The "beer-soaked collegiate sketch" inspired by *The Evil Dead*, *Evil Dead 2* (1987) and, to a lesser extent, *Army of Darkness* (1992), created enough of a buzz at the Tranzac to encourage the group to polish the turd and take the show to the largest comedy festival in the world, Montreal's Just for Laughs, in the summer of 2004. With its over-the-top combination of risqué gags, absurdist musical numbers and tacky Grand Guignol effects, *Evil Dead: The Musical* attracted the attention of several big players on the North American theater scene, including Tony Award winner Hinton Battle (Ouzounian). Battle joined forces with Chris Bond to co-direct and choreograph an Off-Broadway version of the play, which opened at New World Stages on 1 November 2006 and ran for six months.

The generally positive review from *The New York Times* compared the production to *The Rocky Horror Picture Show* and noted that the show's "most rousing number, 'Do the Necronomicon,' cheerfully evokes 'The Time Warp.'" The review observes, "Truly devoted cultists may want to sit in the splatter section, the first three rows. Those seats are covered in clear plastic, and the audience may want to be too, although apparently half the fun is to wear a clean white T-shirt and spend the next two hours being sprayed with geysers of stage blood" (Gates). Following the Off-Broadway run, the show returned to Toronto, where it became a genuine hit, and triggered a flurry of revivals across Canada and the U.S., and even all the way to Korea.

An especially popular version of the musical has been running nonstop in Las Vegas since 2012, first at V Theater and, as of 2016, at the Tommy Wind Theater. This particular variation on the original stage show goes under the title *Evil Dead: The Musical 4D*, where the fourth dimension in question is the sensory experience enjoyed by those brave souls who dare to sit in the "Splatter Zone" surrounding the thrust stage. This being Vegas, a unique feature of the V Theater production was that it regularly celebrated weddings on stage during the intermission, where diehard fans, exchanged vows in front of fellow *Evil Dead* aficionados ("Kimmy & Brent"). As would be expected, the wedding officiant used the *Necronomicon* rather than a bible to solemnize the ceremony. These cultish wedding ceremonies epitomize the general tenor and purpose of the show: a gathering of faithful *Evil Dead* enthusiasts, whose eccentric liturgy is deeply rooted in the ritualistic declamation of famous catchphrases from the films and tongue-in-cheek worship of Bruce-Campbell-as-Ash, incarnated in Vegas by adequately chinned Chris Weidman.

Like other versions of the musical, the Vegas show that I attended on Friday, 13 March 2015, does away entirely with horror in favor of parody. *Evil Dead: The Musical* thus functions as a logical successor to the three films, as each installment of Raimi's trilogy progressively moves away from terror towards caricature and satire. As Kate Egan explains in her book-length analysis of *The Evil Dead*, the original undoubtedly has the "ability to scare and disturb." But as the narrative unfolds "the main attack sequences can be seen to gradually and incrementally, become more comedic" (Egan 48, 65). Similarly, as the trilogy unfolds, Raimi increasingly removes elements of gore and horror, and puts in more "Three Stooges type gags" (Egan 50). The musical concludes this movement from fear to fun by indulging in an overwhelmingly clichéd lampoon of 1980s slashers that does not include any true moments of horror.

But as stated above, regardless of its dismissal of genuine horror in favor of hilarious mockery, there remains in *The Musical* a number of unsettling elements that can cause discomfort, anxiety and dread. These emerge primarily from the materiality and performative demands of stage parody. As the vicars of the *Evil Dead* cult, the stage actors performing the play face the significant challenge of having to be entertainingly offensive, in the spirit of the original, while avoiding turning their good humor into scorn, disdain and derision, for fans of the trilogy would not tolerate contemptuous dismissal of its fundamental value as a cult object. In the roles of stupid college kids stuck in an isolated cabin, the actors also have to appear clumsy and inept while still being able to carry a song-and-dance number. Furthermore, as the ringmasters of the show, the actors also have to be responsive to their audience and adjust their performance to the dynamic of the crowd. The delicate balance required by the live performance of a spectacle like *Evil Dead: The Musical* is difficult to achieve. There is always a strong possibility that one or several parts of the production will go horribly wrong and that the entire enterprise will fall apart.

Several gags fell totally flat during the show that I attended in Las Vegas, and at least one earnest attempt to entice the audience to stand up and dance with the actors led to an embarrassing lack of participation on the part of fans. Such failures always threaten to derail the flow of slapstick energy that drives the performance, and cause severe trepidation in the spectator (at least *this* spectator!) at the thought that the show might be caught in a downward spiral of mistakes, unrehearsed insipidity and awkward silences. An online review of the Down Stage Right production of the play in Vancouver, in the fall of 2014, insightfully highlights the very real risk of staging a parody that relies on the actors' ability to draw the audience in a self-consciously absurd game of ironic engagement:

> For an exaggerated and ridiculous show like *Evil Dead* to be cheeky and entertaining rather than silly and embarrassing, two things need to happen. First, the cast needs to be strong enough to carry their audience through outrageous plot points and musical numbers like "What the F*ck Was That?" and "All the Men in My Life Keep Getting Killed by Candarian Demons." Second, everyone involved needs to completely understand what kind of show they're in. Performers who aren't talented or don't try because it's supposed to be "funny" rely on the jokes in the script without actually doing the work required to transmit those jokes to the audience. Alternatively, an actor (or director) taking themselves too seriously would deflate every scene and pull the audience down with them ["'Evil Dead: The Musical' is Bloody Outrageous"].

Intentionally or not, the threat of failure successfully serves the purpose of re-injecting in *The Musical* a dose of insecurity, consternation, and fear.

The language used by unimpressed reviewer Justin LeClaire of *Splash Magazine*, speaks volumes on the disturbing effect of an especially bad performance, in this case at Chicago's Broadway Playhouse in the fall of 2014:

> A lot of *Evil Dead: The Musical* was seriously just hard to watch. Not because we see the characters getting butchered on stage one by one, but because of how badly they butchered this entire show. I'm not kidding. It was painful to sit through. Nothing in this badly directed, poorly acted, and cheaply conceived production was even the slightest bit amusing—it was just downright embarrassing … [Chris] Bond's production is way too self-aware of its own campiness which only adds to the awkwardness of watching it all unfold.… I had to take note that only the more inebriated members of the audience seemed to be having a good time on opening night. They were the fortunate ones. As for the rest of us we just had to sit there suffering in sober solitude until it was finally over after 2 excruciating long hours [LeClaire].

Words like "painful," "suffering," "excruciating" and of course "embarrassing" attest to the play's ability to cause visceral revulsion in the spectator and, as such, function as a true horror show. My point here is not to argue that *Evil Dead: The Musical* is or is not an atrocious piece of musical theater. Rather, I wish to suggest that LeClaire's feelings of embarrassment, humiliation, discomfort, and pain are part and parcel of the particular theatrical experience associated with this play which, regardless of the talent of the cast and crew, is always subjected to the dreadful possibility of abject failure.

In addition to the fear of failure that might lead to confusion, revulsion and embarrassment, another aspect of *The Musical*'s theatricality of embarrassment that might disconcert and mortify the audience is the materiality of the "gory" special effects, in particular the red liquid that masquerades as blood. While patrons sitting in the "Splatter Zone" might restlessly await to be splashed with gory fluid at any point in the show, the anticipated discharge only happens in the second act and takes the form of a deliberate spraying process. Indeed, rather than a scattering of blood as a result of some decapitation or hand severing, the "splatter moments" are methodical ejaculations of liquid aimed at individual audience members. What this amounts to is a peculiar golden shower where the actors—especially Greg Korin in the role of Reliable Jake in the Vegas production—motion back and forth as they squirt on the audience to explicitly evoke proudly impolite public urination. If the evocation of the golden shower was not troubling enough, the fact that the "urine" is *red* raises the level of uneasiness to the point of phallic queasiness. Crossing my legs as I imagined urinating bloody piss on an adoring audience, I experienced a level of mortification at the V Theater that was so unpleasant that it became deeply pleasurable.

This paradoxical effect is the purpose of the play's theatricality of embarrassment. This is where *Evil Dead: The Musical* reaches back to the "horrality" of the original "video nasty" in its ability to terrify, disrupt and destabilize audiences, at the same time as it causes outbursts of uncontrollable laughter Such moments of gratifyingly disorienting anxiety remind the spectator of the unsettling sensation caused by the feverishly mobile camera of *The Evil Dead*, which emulates the frantically mobile gaze of the demons (Egan 61). The theater lacks the "schizoid movement-images" that, according to Anna Powell, are so effective in disturbing and perturbing horror film audiences (Powell). But in contrast, the theater does have the uncanny ability to petrify the spectator, who is always frightened at the prospect of beholding a train wreck unfolding on stage. The pleasurable trepidation caused by the prospect of abject failure does have the potential to create memorable theatrical experiences, as is suggested by the undeniable success of the *Evil Dead: The Musical* franchise. And the theatricality of embarrassment has been employed to various degrees in other stage adaptations of horror film parodies, such as *ThanksKilling The Musical* (premièred in 2013), based on Jordan Downey's 2009 cult turkey-slasher and referred to by one reviewer as an "Ouroboros of bad" (Stanley). However, such a performative strategy will always remain the province of very few cult favorites. It is only the rare film that encourages the sort of enjoyable discomfort that Raimi's breakthrough hit triggered in spectators. Consequently, only few stage versions could ever successfully capitalize on the fear of embarrassment as a means to reconnect with the unique experience of the source material. But in some singular instances, the it's-so-bad-that-it's-good aesthetics of stage parody can indeed be productively realized at the unsettling threshold of theatrical incompetence and spectacular breakdown. In those oddly magical moments, the spectator can indulge in the cheerful pain of shameful bliss where anxiety and hilarity awkwardly mesh with jitters and horror to create a sense of pure "horrality."

WORKS CITED

Brophy, Philip. "Horrality—the Textuality of the Contemporary Horror Film," *Art and Text* 11 (1983), pp. 85–95.
Egan, Kate. *The Evil Dead*. Wallflower Press, 2011.
"*Evil Dead: The Musical* is Bloody Outrageous," *NIFTYNOTCOOL*, 26 Oct. 2014, niftynotcool.com/2014/10/26/evil-dead-the-musical-is-bloody-outrageous/.
Feinberg, Anat. *Embodied Memory: The Theatre of George Tabori*. University of Iowa Press, 1999.
Gates, Anita, "Music and Mayhem, Blood Trail Included." *The New York Times*, 2 Nov. 2006, nytimes.com/2006/11/02/theater/reviews/02evil.html.
"Kimmy & Brent Get 'Carrie-d' at Their Evil Dead Themed Wedding." *Offbeat Bride*, 8 Apr. 2015, offbeatbride.com/vegas-evil-dead-wedding/.
Leclaire, Justin. "*Evil Dead: The Musical* with Broadway in Chicago, Theatre Review—A Bloody Awful Show." *Splash Magazine*, Fall 2014, lasplash.com/publish/Entertainment/cat_index_chicago_performances/evil-dead-the-musical-theatre-review.php.
Ouzounian, Richard. "Still Dead to Us." *Toronto Star*, 5 May 2007.
Powell, Anna. *Deleuze and the Horror Film*. Edinburgh University Press, 2006.
Stanley, Alyse. "Review: *ThanksKilling*." *Geeklyinc*, 21 Nov. 2016, geeklyinc.com/review-thankskilling/.

Deadites vs. Adaptation

Valerie L. Guyant

Taking *Within the Woods* (1978) as the starting point for the *Evil Dead* franchise, rather than the release of *The Evil Dead* (1981) and accepting that *Ash vs. Evil Dead* (2015–2018) will, at the very least, see a third season in 2018[1] establishes a roughly forty year span of creation and adaptation. Leaving aside the trilogy of films for a moment, *The Evil Dead* has been adapted for different media, including video games, comic books, a theatrical musical production, a board game, and a television series. It has also been adapted for different audiences: two *Simpsons* Treehouse of Horror Halloween episodes (1992 and 2016), the *Evil Dead* (2013) reboot, *Bhayaanak Mahal* (1988) and *Bach ke Zara (2008)*, which are both Bollywood films, one a loose adaptation and the other following most of the plot from the original, *Bhayam* (2007), a nearly shot-for-shot replica of *The Evil Dead* filmed in India, "Done in 60 Seconds With Clay" (2010), a Claymation version, *Evil Head (2012)*, which is a porn-horror parody, and *Evil Dead Inbred Rednecks (2012)*. The wealth of adaptation inherent to movie franchises cannot be overstated in contemporary culture. It has become de rigueur for popular movies to release a soundtrack, to have a book crossover, to have sequels, to have a game developed if the movie encourages that form of cross-promotion, and to have promotional products such as toys and T-shirts. However, none of these were standard expectations for a film released in the 1980s unless it was a *Star Wars* (1977) level blockbuster,[2] nor were any of them expectations held by the "Michigan Mafia."[3] Why and how, then, did *The Evil Dead* become a franchise rather than a single film and what makes it freshly adaptable and yet also enduring?

My aim is certainly not to retell a story that has been told so many times, but to focus on those factors that laid the groundwork for, and fed in to, the *Evil Dead* franchise's continued adaptability across time, medium, and genres. A cornerstone of adaptation analysis is to identify the source text and analyze all adaptations and variants against that source. However, as with many aspects of *The Evil Dead*, this cornerstone is problematized in numerous ways from the very beginning and it can be seen in something as simple as our inability to clearly affix commonplace identifiers that aid in adaptation analysis. *The Evil Dead* is our source text, not an adaptation, although *Within the Woods*, as the first creation, would ordinarily be the source text.[4] As Sam Raimi explained in a 1982 interview, "we made a super 8 *pilot* [emphasis added] of the movie we intended to make ... and what I did was took the screen play for [*The*] *Evil Dead*, took a number of the elements from it and wrote a very short story."[5] For all intents and purposes, then, *Within the Woods* is a pilot that is an adaptation, created prior to the realization of the source text. This meandering cross-narrative approach that allows for continuous re-visioning of the material continues throughout the narrative life of the story. While the adaptations sometimes add layers, as many adaptations do, that later texts sometimes question what has gone before has created a unique cultural touchstone that functions alternatively as either entertainment or parody, as horror or comedy, as splatstick, as a hero quest with a decidedly unheroic hero in Ashley "Ash" Williams (Bruce Campbell), and as a postmodern reflection on the nature of horrific entertainment.

Great stories are rule breakers which "contain something indefinable that makes them more than the sum of their parts" (Harrison xv) but in the case of Raimi's "great story," it is the breaking of rules that has *made* it more than the sum of its parts.[6] According to Linda Hutcheon, one of the main features that distinguishes postmodernism from modernism is that it "takes the form of self-conscious, self-contradictory, self-undermining statement" (1) and that one way of creating this double or contradictory stance is through the use of parody, in essence, citing a convention in order to make fun of it. Parody, according to Hutcheon, "is usually considered central to postmodernism" because "through a double process of installing and ironizing, parody signals how present representations come from past ones" (93). In her interpretation, Hutcheon contradicts Fredric Jameson's argument that pastiche "offers a value-free, decorative, de-historicized quotation of past forms and that this is a most apt mode for a culture like our own that is oversaturated with images" (93). In essence, Hutcheon is arguing that self-reflection and homage are essential components of a postmodern text and that these types of texts will speak most strongly to a postmodern audience. One of the most compelling aspects of parody is that it delegitimizes the idea that meaning is natural rather than artificial or that there is a stable, coherent subjective reality. That delegitimizing of the status quo is why postmodernism and parody are "both academic and popular, elitist and accessible," (Hutcheon 44) much like the *Evil Dead* franchise.

Much of what Raimi has said and which can be witnessed in the films themselves can be analyzed from a postmodern perspective from the moment *The Evil Dead* begins until the last shot of the most recent *Ash vs. Evil Dead* episode. *Within the Woods*, in comparison, is conventional in its use of a Native American burial ground and angry spirits that hunt the friends, leaving a female as the last survivor. In comparison, it is the break from horror tropes, the upending of them, and the infusion of humor that creates a compelling story in *The Evil Dead* and leaves the creators with so many opportunities to tell additional stories without wearying the audience.

First, there is the cabin-in-the-woods trope—which was certainly not a new or unique idea when Raimi used it.[7] What makes it a postmodern take on the cabin in the woods film is that the friends are not slowly stalked and decimated by an outsider—there is no Jason Voorhees or Michael Myers picking them off. Instead, they become the evil as they are possessed by the force they have unleashed, occasionally seeming to revert to their more innocent, demon-free selves before attacking again. While certainly a fresh approach, however, causing audiences to question the nature of evil [and its permanence], alone, would not have led to a memorable enough film to maintain a following for four decades.

More important to its longevity was the choice to feature Ash rather than a woman in the survivor role. Prior to *The Evil Dead*, the protagonist of most horror films, the survivor, was female, known as the Final Girl, an archetype of the horror genre (Rasmussen 45). The image of the Final Girl is:

> The image of the distressed female most likely to linger in memory is the image of the one who did not die: the survivor, or Final Girl. She is the one who encounters the mutilated bodies of her friends and perceives the full extent of the preceding horror and of her own peril; who is chased, cornered, wounded; whom we see scream, stagger, fall, rise, and scream again. She is abject terror personified [Clover 35].

However, Raimi decided to invert the expectation of a Final Girl and instead offer a Final Guy, but not a heroic, brave, or capable Final Guy. Final Girls, in horror films of the 1970s and 1980s "had to be terrorized" (Campbell 69) but they were also "avenging hero[es]" (Clover 35). When Sam Raimi decided to problematize that archetype, he did so because he "felt that [changing the protagonist from female to male] could make it even more horrifying; if you could reduce a man to scrambling and screaming and yelling and being tormented, it would be even more horrifying than a woman doing that" (Bruce Campbell quoted in Warren 36–37).

While the novelty of a male protagonist surviving a horror film certainly attracted some interest, what it did far more was give a larger percentage of audience members someone with whom to identify. Yes, Ash is terrorized by the demons possessing his friends and he makes any number of horrible mistakes while battling them, but he is also the quintessential Everyman.[8] While the character's likeability may arguably be due primarily to Campbell's charismatic portrayal, it is his Everyman status that allows audience members to identify with him so profoundly that they *want* more story about him. Ash begins the franchise as a college student, breaking relatively minor laws (trespassing) and hoping for a fun weekend with his girlfriend Linda (Betsy Baker). He works at a menial job that most of the audience will recognize (S-Mart is an easily recognizable substitute for Walmart, Kmart, or similar franchised establishments). He is far from heroic, disfiguring himself, failing to save his friends, making mistakes along his journey that constantly make his fight harder. Yet, audiences *want* to see him succeed because they recognize aspects of themselves in his behavior, despite the fanciful nature of demon possession.

This identification is furthered throughout numerous adaptations. Ash is the Final Guy in *The Evil Dead*; he is the Final Guy in *Evil Dead 2* (1987). While others may be left behind when he comes back to the present, Ash is, in essence, the Final Guy in *Army of Darkness* (1992). However, beyond these more obvious ways that the audience is encouraged to identify with Ash, he is also the only consistent character in the video games that have been spawned throughout the past thirty years and the protagonist in a wealth of comic books that further Ash's story rather than only recounting what is known from the films.

The first video game of the *Evil Dead* franchise was *The Evil Dead* (1984), released for the Commodore 64. The game raised some initial concerns, coming as it did during the "video nasties" controversy,[9] but initial reviews stated that "there is nothing here to keep even the most unworldly 12-year-old awake at night" because the "home computer graphics were [not] capable of the sort of gory special effects" the film utilized so effectively ("Software Shortlist" 43). The game does effectively adapt the general storyline of the first film to a new medium and allows players to fill the role of Ash Williams, a maneuver that allows audiences to continue to identify most strongly with the one character who may have survived the film.[10] Ash was one of the first Everyman characters from a film that people could bring home in game form and inhabit in computerized play. This ability furthered a sense of Ash belonging to everyone as a cultural icon, which was perpetuated in later video games as well, all of which have the player inhabiting Ash's role.

Many of the comic books allow audiences to learn more about Ash, including part of his story before he went to the cabin. Additionally, the comics allow a certain level of wish fulfillment for readers who are used to inhabiting Ash's persona as he battles Jason Voorhees and Freddy Krueger and saves President Obama. Ash is involved in numerous aspects of American culture through his exploits. That cultural touchstone nature of the character has furthered the longevity of the franchise as he has become a pop culture reference point. This sense that culturally aware individuals simply know who Ash is can be seen in his continued use in other mediums. For instance, Ash is referenced in the popular YouTube series *Epic Rap Battles of History* when "Charles Darwin" slams Ash Ketchum with the phrase "the real Ash packs a much bigger boomstick" and most recently in the *Funny or Die* series video "Ash vs. Evil Pokemon" where Ash Ketchum takes on the characteristics of Ash Williams and Pikachu is characterized as a Deadite.

In addition to the Everyman status of the lead character, another important aspect of *The Evil Dead*'s adaptability is encapsulated in another aspect of its postmodern sensibilities—that is, the fine line that Raimi tightrope walks between gore, guts, gags, and guffaws—the essence of the postmodern parody form known as splatstick. Splatstick is a combination of slapstick comedy and the extreme violence and over-the-top gore associated with splatter films. While horror comedy has existed for some time, what makes splatstick unique is its pacing level and the off-the-wall ways it bends reality. It is a unique brand of hyperactive phantasmagoria.[11] The pacing and humor is similar to *The Three Stooges* but with more violence mixed in. *The Evil Dead* is far closer to a traditional horror film, with some elements of gallows humor and some initial indications of splatstick sensibilities, but *Evil Dead 2* is considered by many cineastes to be the epitome of splatstick cinema. *Evil Dead 2* is not a horror film with comedic moments or a comedy with horrific moments but a true melding of the two forms of entertainment.

Raimi's inventive willingness to create a new version of his initial story, rather than a sequel, helped cement the adaptability of the franchise. Sequels to horror films have a notorious reputation for being repetitive, derivative, stale, and often cynical. If Raimi had attempted an ordinary sequel, it risked being saddled with similar labels. Instead, what Raimi and his team created defies easy labeling, for it is not really a sequel. There is no clear demarcation between the first film and the second in its storytelling. While one reason for this disjointedness is an issue with retaining rights to the films and a desire to "recap" aspects of the first film, what occurs is a form of re-visioning that tells a tonally different story. Since the second film includes Linda (now played by Denise Bixler) and Ash reciting from the book and unleashing the evil, but in a different fashion, Campbell has suggested referring to *Evil Dead 2* as "a requel! It's whatever you wanna call it!" (Cocchini).

Although on the surface this may seem a tongue-in-cheek response to an editing error, what it allows for is one of the fundamental reasons that the franchise became so adaptable. Individuals who are more interested in experiencing an Everyman-based horror film can enjoy *The Evil Dead* and those who are more interested in the splatstick version of the story can enjoy *Evil Dead 2*. Either version, however, appeals to one aspect of the postmodern sensibility of the majority of the audience: extreme violence mixed with physical humor and destruction of the human body with a dash of absurdism reminding us that what we are watching is not real. If the horror comedy fails to do this, then it can be tonally off—either too gross or terrifying to laugh at or too tame to scare and satisfy our desire for carnage. Raimi threw reality out the window with lights, sound, timing, and physical humor in both films, thereby allowing audiences to experience a level of pure entertainment that does not pretend to be anything but the visceral encounter it is intended to be, while achieving a level of catharsis.

In comparison to these two approaches to a similar storytelling moment, *Army of Darkness* is a parody of the archetypal hero quest blended with the splattery excesses that Raimi had perfected. Ash is faced with a new swath of demons and, this time, an overwhelming number of skeletons, seeking to obtain control of the *Necronomicon*. Again, Raimi offers aspects of the same story: the book, Deadites that can possess the living or newly dead, a chainsaw wielding hero who fails to be heroic, humor, and blood. He also adds a new layer that keeps the story fresh: Ash has been transported to the 13th century and is battling to return to his own time. In essence, Raimi created a blend between medieval quest films, Mark Twain's *A Connecticut Yankee in King Arthur's Court*, and *The Evil Dead* his audience had come to expect.

In his blend of gore and camp, Raimi created three transformative works that do what so few horror-based films either before or since have done— they blend horror, humor, and a poetic sense of their own aesthetic worth, while foregrounding the need to entertain.[12] Raimi revels in mischief and humor as much as he does in blood and gore and the choice to layer these stories as he did creates a freshness to the story that leaves audiences willing to experiment further in the *Evil Dead* universe, as long as they can continue to experience that universe with Ash, the character they have been manipulated in to caring about. The continued narrative disjunctions caused (however inadvertently) by issues obtaining film rights from different production companies not only "provide a conditional revision of what came before, further dislocating ordinary reality in a playful, ad hoc manner" (Royer 46), but inspire a desire to seek out additional conditional revisions.

One such conditional revision sprang from fans of the franchise envisioning another way of entertaining with the story; *Evil Dead: The Musical* is not a Sam Raimi production but the creative endeavor of a new group of college students seeking a way to tell the story. The choice to layer music onto a story that already has gore, humor, demons, and self-awareness perfectly exemplifies the conditional revision that gives adaptations of *The Evil Dead* so much power. The horror has, for the most part, been removed from this version and replaced with a self-referential sense of campiness that amps up the entertainment in a potentially family-friendly way. The musical takes advantage of the audience participation model of theater experience embraced by audiences of *The Rocky Horror Picture Show*, with a splash zone for those wishing to be sprayed with theatrical blood and (in some cases) entrails and severed heads. One recent production even encouraged audience callbacks throughout the show to heighten the postmodern appeal. In this re-visioning, all the main characters from both *The Evil Dead* and *Evil Dead 2* make an appearance but they burst into song to give voice to aspects of the storyline, such as "Look Who's Evil Now" or "Do the Necronomicon." The popularity of this re-visioning is highlighted by its continued presence Off-Broadway and in the long running Las Vegas version.

In comparison to this lighthearted retelling, *Ash vs. Evil Dead* has chosen to primarily tell new stories within Ash's fight against the demons. All the aspects of the films that people enjoy, including the campiness, the gore, and the humor, are present in abundance. That has made it popular enough to earn a swift renewal. However, at the end of Season 2, the showrunners chose to also engage in re-visioning when Ash and his friends returned to the cabin in the woods. Having taken advantage of the temporal vortex that initially took Ash to the 13th century, they enter the cabin prior to the events of *The Evil Dead* in hopes of altering history, another conditional revision. Although it is impossible to see how this re-visioning will alter the world that Ash inhabits, clearly, it will continue to infuse life into a franchise that excels at continually adapting while maintaining its originality and its cohesiveness.

The adaptations that succeed in the franchise, such as *The Musical* and *Ash vs. Evil Dead* remember the essential aspects of adaptation that allow this franchise to thrive: Everyman Ash must be involved, conditional re-visioning must be embraced, and the balance between humor and gore must be maintained. Even *Evil Head* was considered a success in the community for which it was produced because it maintained that balance. In comparison, the adaptations that have failed, either creatively or commercially—including *Evil Dead Inbred Rednecks* and the Bollywood versions—have failed because they neglected one or more of those essential components. As Bruce Campbell explained, when discussing *Evil Dead* (2013), the movie was a commercial success, but the fans let them know that it was not what they wanted or what they had been waiting for; it was missing essential components of the recipe for *Evil Dead*–style success. While the delicate mixture of humor, gore, postmodern parody, and Everyman appeal will not work for all forms of adaptation, when it comes to *Evil Dead*, it is the only mixture that does work.

Notes

1. Numerous outlets reported that season two of the series was greenlit before season one had aired and that season three was greenlit in October 2016. Starz CEO Chris Albrecht insisted that *Ash vs. Evil Dead* has "the legs of a real series" by which he seemed to intimate a longevity beyond season three (Pena).

2. *The Evil Dead*, while a box office success, made 2.4 million by the end of 1983 (IMDb). It has since earned closer to 30 million worldwide, including re-releases.

3. This phrase is used in multiple sources to refer to the initial creative force behind

the movies, which included Sam Raimi, Bruce Campbell, Ted Raimi, Ivan Raimi, Joe LoDuca, Rob Tapert, Scott Spiegel, Josh Becker, and Ellen Sandweiss. Who is included in the list varies by source; however, Sam Raimi, Bruce Campbell, and Rob Tapert are the three who maintain creative control over the franchise and are included in every compilation of names.

4. *Within the Woods* is also not a prequel, since prequels are made after a source text and tell backstory to fill in gaps that the fans might want to know or the director might want to add.

5. *Within the Woods* has also been referred to as "a distilled version of what would eventually become *The Evil Dead*" (McDonagh 140).

6. Many of Raimi's rule breaks have now become standard-bearers in the industry, including splatstick as a genre, the use of specific camera techniques, and tropes that were introduced in *The Evil Dead* and are now referenced in myriad pop culture locations. There are hundreds of examples listed on *The Evil Dead* IMDb page, Wikipedia page, and the Evil Dead Wiki *Deadites Online*. References to *The Evil Dead* have appeared in numerous films, TV shows, and video games. One of the most recent is a shout-out in the end credits of *Ghostbusters* (2016) when Jillian Holtzmann (Kate McKinnon) says that she has been working on some "next level stuff" that likely sends the ghosts and demons to "somewhere in Michigan. Sorry Lansing." While not truly adaptations, these references are exemplary of the ways in which *The Evil Dead* has maintained cultural relevance.

7. Mathjis does argue that it is "probably the most perfect, archetypal, cabin-in-the-woods film, the one against which all others are measured" (85).

8. While the term "Everyman" derives from a 15th-century English morality play where the character imparted a moral message, a contemporary Everyman is constructed so that the audience can imagine themselves as the character.

9. The VCR came down in price during the early 1980s and opened a new avenue for movies to gain popularity: the sale and rental of video cassettes. In Britain, a campaign was orchestrated against the so-called video nasties, which resulted in heavy editing of many horror films following the 1984 Video Recordings Act.

10. Fans disagree regarding the fate of Ash in the first film, but so do the filmmakers. *The Evil Dead* ends with Ash turning as an evil force comes hurling at him. In interviews, both Campbell and Raimi have said they imagined Ash as dying in that moment but both have also stated that the ending is purposely ambiguous. In his explanation of the timeline for the films, Campbell suggests that a splicing of the films together from that moment to the moment in *Evil Dead 2* where Ash is hurtled through the woods is an effective way of "making sense" of the movies' continuity issues (Cocchini).

11. Victoria Large claims that Raimi invented splatstick, whereas Kat Ellinger claims that *Re-Animator* (1985) was the first splatstick movie.

12. Carl and Diana Royer offer a wonderful analysis that equates Raimi's skill at filmmaking to that of a master composer. A similar observation was also made by Rachel Mead. This poetic, artistic element is integral to the enjoyment of the films and to their longevity as works of art.

Deadite Porn

OLGA TCHEPIKOVA-TREON

Upon release, the campy dialogue and exaggerated amount of guts and gore in *The Evil Dead* (1981) helped market it as a splatter comedy, but did not fully prevent the notorious X and later NC-17 ratings imposed by the MPAA for explicitly violent and cruel content. Aside from its membership in club NC-17, *The Evil Dead*'s growth into a cult film was stimulated by the vast and creative ways in which other media were adopting and recycling its unique merging of horror and humor: As illustrated in this anthology, *The Evil Dead*, aside from its sequels *Evil Dead 2* (1987) and *Army of Darkness* (1992)—composing the respective "trilogy"—inspired many creative works across different screen formats and genres, as well as other media, including cinematic remakes, comic books, computer games and, most recently, television series. But in between all these formats that nod towards and expand on *The Evil Dead*'s funny or shocking features, a somewhat different type of homage emerged from the adult industry. In 2012, Burning Angel Entertainment released *Evil Head*—an adult(erated) remake or parody of *The Evil Dead*.

Because of their graphic content, low-budgeted, explicit horror and porn films were not produced to be integrated into commercial circulation and, thus, typically operated on the margins of cultural production, or as some say, under the radar of public discourse. And due to these circumstances, the adult industry has been able to sneakily popularize the idea that sexual content can be found in any given context. Throughout the last decades, pornographers and pornographiennes have produced a plethora of porn parodies inspired by screen entertainment—ranging from cinema blockbusters to television cartoons and finally, very specific niche films that have come to be seen as iconic over time. Working on the logic of intertextuality, porn parodies translate popular or otherwise accomplished (cult) films into the language of adult entertainment, and, therefore, necessarily create a recursive cross-referential dynamic of reflexivity between the original and its pornographic homage. Indeed, a film's cultural relevance has come to be measured by its potential to facilitate a pornographic spoof after the emergence of a cultural meme called Rule #34—roughly defined as "If it exists, there *is* porn of it"— while film scholarship has exemplified porn parodies as paratextual commentaries on mainstream media culture that frequently does not deliver the explicit sexual content it alludes to.[1]

Both horror and porn have been classified as "body genres" that belong to the low side of cultural production for their intense impact on the spectator's physical response to the action on screen in Linda Williams' seminal essay on film bodies (4). But what is the function of such genre classifications in a postmodern media culture that theorists like Fredric Jameson have declared to rely on repetition more than innovation? In their most basic function, genres guide the audience's speculations about a film's style and content, as well as their reactions to it, in a certain direction. As Lauren Berlant writes, "[g]enres provide an affective expectation of the experience of watching something unfold" (6). Thus, a film's success, to a great extent, depends on its abilities to show (or do) what is promised by its genre classification—a good horror film will shock or disgust while a good porn film will be used as "an incitement for erotic reverie and action" according to I.Q. Hunter.[2] However, in a situation where porn *and* horror come together under the guise of a parody film, it is necessary to ask: What are the outcomes of a trilateral low-culture excess where body genres are drenched in comedy?

Evil Head comes at us as a gory and humorous fusion of *The Evil Dead*'s most prominent features with explicit, non-simulated hardcore sex. On the one hand, it functions as a paratextual reverse-image of *The Evil Dead*'s exploitation of sex and gore *through its deliberate implementation of the original's narrative and visual iconographies*, expands on its sexual connotations and adds extensive sex scenes where dirty minds may have imagined them. At the same time, *Evil Head*'s amalgamation of porn *with* horror allows for and very much results in a self-reflexive examination of pornographic traits on both aesthetic and metatextual levels. Indeed, horror, humor, and porn appear as equally overt and intentional constituents in *Evil Head*. However, the film's classification as pornographic comedy is not an accidental outcome or "lens" that can be utilized in the watching process—rather, it is the fundamental ingredient for *Evil Head*'s success and popularity and simultaneously the most significant element that guides the film's integration into the *Evil Dead* franchise. *Evil Head* puts a new twist on *The Evil Dead*'s cult status precisely because it largely remains faithful to many audio-visual features associated with sex films that first and foremost are meant to arouse, while its very deliberate implementation of body horror defamiliarizes the common perception of pornography as a purely erotic spectacle.

As one of the leading producers of Alt Porn—a genre that differentiates itself from "mainstream" pornography through explicit associations with sub-, or possibly even anti-cultural taste and lifestyle—Burning Angel navigates a somewhat coherently defined range of film aesthetics that fit the associative cluster of punk, metal and goth subcultures who frequently also extend their sympathy for specific movie genres like the horror film.[3] Burning Angel's films feature performers with various body modifications and respectively recognizable style and fashion choices engaging in a relatively traditional repertoire of oral, anal, and genital intercourse—often of the heterosexual kind—accompanied by non-scripted comments and other verbal markers of pleasure during the sex scenes. At this point, Burning Angel has produced approximately thirteen films that are tagged as both horror and parody, where the length of the spoof films ranges from twenty-minute clips to multi-hour sex flicks. However, in addition to its clear association with the adult industry, *Evil Head*'s gory and viscerally disgusting features are largely indebted to the involvement of Doug Sakmann—a director, producer and special effects artist working primarily in the horror genre.

Sakmann's collaboration with Burning Angel resulted in three films that make a point of merging horror and pornography to equal extents, starting with *Re-Penetrator* (2004), a short film paying homage to Stuart Gordon's *Re-Animator* (1985); continuing with *The XXXorcist* (2006), a considerably longer, and more sophisticated pornographic parody of William Friedkin's *The Exorcist* (1973); and ending with *Evil Head*, the main point of discussion here.[4] Indeed, Burning Angel's collaboration with Sakmann on the production level mirrors the film's close interactions between horror and porn and has received professional acknowledgment from the adult industry itself: *Re-Penetrator* and *The XXXorcist* received the *Adult Video News* Award for Most Outrageous Sex Scene respectively in 2006 and 2008, while *Evil Head* was nominated for nine awards in 2014, winning in the categories Best Makeup, and Best Actor for Tommy Pistol's performance as Ash.[5]

Evil Head follows the general premise of *The Evil Dead* with minor narrative modifications that facilitate the inclusion of pornographic scenes: two couples, Linda (Joanna Angel) and Ash (Tommy Pistol), Shelly (Kleio Valentien) and Scotty (Danny Wylde), arrive at an abandoned cabin Ash heard about from his "friend Sam [Raimi]."[6] Exploring the interior after breaking and entering, Scotty finds the mysterious *Necronomicum Ex-Mortis*—a *Kama Sutra*–like book filled with copulating skeletons and doodles of caricatured genitals inspired by the *Necronomicon* as it appears in *Evil Dead 2* and *Army of Darkness*. Excited about the dirty drawings, the group gathers to listen to the audio recording left near the book, where one Professor Nobi (spoken by Lloyd Kaufman) speculates about the book's translation and chants the fatal spell that, as we know, unleashes evil spirits. Amused by their discovery, the clique goes about their evening, unaware that they have summoned ancient demons now lingering in the woods. Left alone while Shelly is getting ready for bed, Scotty joins Linda and Ash for a threesome and is caught red-handed by Shelly in the end. Clearly the "prude" of the quartet, she is heartbroken and flees into the woods. As she sobbingly strolls through darkness, Shelly hears a tender off-voice asking her to "fuck us." She finds the voice "kind of sexy" and is intrigued by the suggestion, allowing for the notorious tree-rape of *The Evil Dead* to be turned into a consensual sex scene where Shelly enjoys the ins and outs of "double pine-etration."[7] She returns to the cabin as a Deadite, stabs Linda's leg with a tree branch pulled from her vagina and has sex with Scotty, killing him after he fails to perform a second time. Linda, now also a Deadite, enters the scene and has sex with Shelly while Ash, in an attempt to join, penetrates Shelly with his finger, infecting his hand with the summoned evil. Ash proceeds to cut off his hand with a chainsaw, saws Shelly into pieces, and is seduced by Linda. After their intercourse, Ash cuts off Linda's head and buries her in the front yard. As Linda comes back from the grave, she is joined by two other Deadite women who turn out to be Ash's ex-girlfriends. The four characters have sex one more time, terminating in an extensive close-up shot of all three women giving Ash "evil head," after which Ash slays all three women with his arm-chainsaw.

Evil Head's narrative revolves around six sex scenes—one before and five after evil spirits take hold of the female characters. All of these scenes are modeled after the traditional sexual numbers targeting a presumably male, heterosexual audience as outlined by Steven Ziplow in Linda Williams' *Hard Core* (126): 1. "Ménage à trois" with Linda, Ash, and Scotty; 2. "Masturbation" (or "Straight Sex"?) with Shelly and the trees; 3. "Straight Sex" between Shelly and Scotty; 4. "Lesbianism" with Shelly and Linda; 5. "Straight sex" between Linda and Ash; 6. "Orgy" with Ash and three dead ex-girlfriends, including Linda. In agreement with contemporary industry standards, all scenes also include some variation of "Oral and Anal sex." Before, between and after these numbers, approximately twenty-five minutes of this almost two-and-a-half-hour film are filled with non-sexual content that facilitates smoother transitions between explicit sex.

In line with the premises of the parody genre, *Evil Head* is intended for an audience that is in on the iconography of the original film. However, due to the atypical, tri-generic structure, *Evil Head*'s intertextuality is necessarily caught up in the dissonance of putting these three seemingly opposing, but yet so frequently fused, genres together—and therein lies the greatest fun. Indeed, the experience of watching porn parodies is unlikely to be marked by surprise when explicit sex functions as a substitutive—not additive—fantasy fulfillment, only heightening the erotic content that the original nods towards within the framework of rating restrictions. Consequently, the most entertaining (and possibly also most outrageous) porn parodies might be the ones that display a high degree of creativity and surprise their audience by taking a seemingly completely unsuitable narrative for pornographic associations and soak it in sex. But unlike other horror porn parodies that draw distinct lines between horror and porn content to maintain aesthetically and narratively "pure" sex numbers,[8] there is no clear-cut division between gory and erotic elements in *Evil Head*. In other words, the film—despite its amalgamation of horror and porn—contains elements that typically force the audience into a situation of "corporeal karaoke,"[9] where spectators repeat that which is shown on screen. But how can the audience respond to pornographic retakes of a genre that frequently (mis)uses sex as a means to signify violation and abhorrence, or illustrate a monstrous character's pathological condition? Joanna Angel—*Evil Head*'s co-writer and female lead—challenges the possibility to jerk off to *Evil Head* in an interview with William Bibbiani, acknowledging that the primary motivation for watching this film might be grounded in the audience's intertextual curiosity rather than a sole desire to be aroused. Similarly, she reveals that her and the crew's shared devotion to *The Evil Dead* served as the primary motivation to create this film.[10] In that sense, *Evil Head* can be seen as a work of fan fiction or, more precisely, *slash* fiction—authored by horror enthusiasts working in the porn industry whose number one rule of creative production is camp and exaggeration gone sexy, untouched by demands for a framework that suits the *Evil Dead* "brand."[11] And precisely this dynamic of authorship within the creation of *Evil Head* allows for this porn parody to be approached as a self-reflexive evaluation of the porn genre itself.

In his theorization of postmodern cultural production, Fredric Jameson acknowledges that a good parody has "some secret sympathy" (3) for the original that becomes evident to the viewers in one way or another—but Burning Angel's sympathy for *The Evil Dead* can hardly be deemed secret. And contrary to the ironic dismissal frequently associated with parodies, *Evil Head* never mocks or makes fun of its inspiration source—at least not more than *The Evil Dead* does itself. Bibbiani even deems *Evil Head* a more superior "remake" of *The Evil Dead* than Fede Álvarez's *Evil Dead* (2013), emphasizing that Álvarez's *Evil Dead* significantly deviates from the spirit of the original through its darker story and display of more explicit and brutal violence. More specifically, Bibbiani praises *Evil Head*'s maintaining of *The Evil Dead*'s comic streak and suggests it to be enhanced by explicit sex. Indeed, the pornographic scenes add another layer of humor to the campiness of the original, first, because of their displacement in a horror story but also, because pornographic films—similar to *The Evil Dead* back in the day—are small-budgeted productions and cannot afford to rely on sophisticated special effects, stunts, and set design to create atmosphere.

In *Evil Head*, humorous horror is largely created via two channels: On the one hand, the film relies on intertextuality, where, aside from the cursory resemblances in narrative and *mise-en-scène*, it also directly quotes several (i)comic scenes from the original trilogy: having buried Linda, Ash falls into exaggerated fits of hysteric laughter when the cabin's interior comes to life—similar to *Evil Dead 2*—and excitedly murmurs "groovy" upon approaching Linda and his other ex-girlfriends for the respective orgy. Such humorous interventions, however, exist outside of the otherwise pornographic routine of the movie. On the other hand, comic relief is also granted in the film's partially non-scripted dialogue, where the actors' performance fluctuates between a somewhat coherent adaptation of *The Evil Dead*'s original characters into (Deadite) porn stars, and the performers' off-script comments and reflections on the pornographic scene they are performing—filtered through their screen character.

Like many hardcore sex films, *Evil Head* engages the same phrases and vocabulary routinely adapted into pornographic script and promotion from moral or otherwise oppositional discourses[12]: the happily bad-mouthed characters verbally stimulate themselves and each other with silly puns ("I'll swallow your pole," Deadite Shelly says to Scotty) and descriptors such as "slut" and "whore" during the sex scenes, but also make a point of including the newly demonic features as enhancements of their already dirty characteristics: Scotty demands Shelly's "demon ass," and Linda asks Ash to "come all over [her] possessed face" shortly before he slashes her. However, the trans-generic chaos of the film also facilitates the creation of spontaneous, situational humor. Indeed, *Evil Head*'s dialogue (or monologue, as phrases spoken during porn sex scenes do not always follow a dialogic response pattern of coherence) is kept deliberately alienating—especially during intercourse. Shelly moans, "I never knew a tree could fuck that good," when penetrated by tree branches in the woods, and Ash responds to Linda's enraptured "You really know the way into a girl's heart" with "Yeah, through her vagina" as both break into fake laughter. He also promises to "buy [Linda] a new dress" when getting ready to DP her with Scotty,[13] followed by Linda's amused outrage about the DP where she asks, "Is this what you like to do on vacation with your friends, you weirdo?" and, as Ash and Scotty decide to both penetrate her vaginally, comments "You guys must be very good friends." Indeed, the real time, semi-serious judgments of sexual practices as "weird" display an interesting dynamic of the actors' attempts to defamiliarize—but by no means break with—their character by pointing towards their actions' displacement in a framework inspired by *The Evil Dead*, but one that is necessary for its reappropriation into pornography. The trans-generic format allows the characters to ridicule pornographic tropes from the position of a fictional character that is familiar to the audience: No one believes that Shelly "never knew a tree could fuck that good." We have no trouble identifying these narrative inserts as absurd nonsense, but nonetheless too amusing to be offensive. In turn, the alienating character of the pornographic scenes within an otherwise familiar, fictional setting helps identify those scenes' explicit sexual activity as equally fictionalized and works against the common fear of pornography as a template for off-screen sexual practices. At the same time, it also offsets some of the horror genre's negative implications about sex.

Despite the small amount of time devoted to non-sexual content, *Evil Head*, aside from its overt references to the original, also reproduces a number of the film's underlying implications: Both narratives maintain the men's humanity while drawing the women's monstrosity though displays of heightened sexual desire as the main gory spectacle—a gender-biased pattern that Kate Egan identifies as one of *The Evil Dead*'s signature dynamics (83–84). However, in an adult film framework, female licentiousness is frequently employed as the most basic catalyst of action despite the men's equal partaking in sexual activities. More importantly, the women's perversion is widely commented on—if not celebrated—by all characters involved. Indeed, the changes that come with demonic possession in *Evil Head* enhance Linda's erotic desire and also turn Shelly's apparently uptight character into a sex-hungry monster that kills Scotty when he cannot perform a second time. But unlike the original film, the insatiable sexual desire of the possessed women in *Evil Head* is not there to signify aberrance. Following the promiscuity-positive logic of porn, *Evil Head*'s female monsters depart from the naiveté attached to romantic monogamy—that which gets Bruce Campbell's Ash into trouble in the first place, according to Egan's reading of *The Evil Dead*—and embrace the raunchiness of pornographic sex. In their monstrosity, the women are "liberated" and, in turn, also continuously "liberate everyone else's inner porn star."[14]

The increasing serialization of films meant for both cinematic and small-screen release and the plethora of remakes, sequels, and prequels characterizes many branches of contemporary cultural production. As a result, texts belonging to the parody genre become part of an original's cultural continuity that is open to imitation. Tamás Bényei calls this phenomenon the "paradox of parody" (92), where every parody not only engages the original text, but simultaneously carries a potential for self-parody—or self-reflexive commentary—as well. In the context of this essay, it is important to note that this phenomenon also becomes evident in the increase of research approaching pornography as part of popular culture (Penley 315) and mainstream culture as "pornified" (Booth 397). Indeed, porn parodies facilitate porn's extraction from its subcultural milieu of morally deviant material and raise it to be discussed in closer dialogue with the non-erotic film industry, where the attachment of an original film's pornographic parody declares a film to be popular and iconic enough to make such a spoof worthwhile. And specifically due to their similarly low cultural status, it is important to acknowledge that both horror and porn make use of the same filmic devices to cause emotional and affective responses in their viewers despite aiming at rather opposite results of the viewing experience. Both genres operate on the logic of what Williams calls "maximum visibility" (*Hard Core* 48), where the close-up or money shot serves as the peak of every narrative sequence, providing the audience with the most explicit depictions of carnal pain or pleasure. Thus, maybe it is the very same maximum visibility in both porn and horror that enables us to approach these genres as comic entertainment even if (or precisely because?) the films lack any overt or intentional comedy traits.

Our ability to laugh away the lustful moans or piecing shrieks of damsels in various kinds of distress, as well as the different fluids pouring onto and out of the characters' bodies in either porn or horror films, reaffirms the safe division between on- and off-screen worlds. But the very same laughter also guides our constant renegotiation of superiority and inferiority on all other textual levels. In horror films, laughing about the monster is, at the same time, laughing *at* its monstrosity and thereby dismissing its threat. Similarly, laughter is a means to both conceal and disarm the film's affective impact when viewing pornography.[15]

In opposition to many other porn sub-genres films like *Evil Head* extend or even reject the initial purpose of pornographic material and entertain more than they arouse. Through its adaptation of *The Evil Dead*'s own genre fusion between horror and humor, mixed with hardcore sex, *Evil Head* is situated at the crossroads of different genre traditions in low cultural production and, therefore, embodies a multi-layered paradox of parody that provides the framework for an equally diverse arrangement of self-reflexivities. Indeed, *Evil Head* praises its humorous horror inspiration source but also makes a point of caricaturing some of the sociocultural implications that drive the story. Approached from a different angle, it jokingly exaggerates the audiovisual and narrative tropes common to pornography. However, all of the modifications and innovations that mark *Evil Head* as a low-culture excess where body genres are drenched in comedy are rooted in a deep sympathy for *The Evil Dead* and, more than anything, perpetuate its insistence on not taking oneself too seriously.

Notes

1. Cindy Patton originally took up porn parodies as "an erotic and humorous critique of the mass media's role in invoking but never delivering sex" (132). This passage is further quoted in Constance Penley's and, later, also Bethan Jones's and I.Q. Hunter's writings on pornography, genre transgressions, and humor.
2. In his "user's guide" to *A Clockwork Orgy*, I.Q. Hunter also suggests the need for a genealogy of masturbation in the academic approach to pornography as it is "used" more than it is "read" (127).
3. Burning Angel's website also hosts an openly accessible, interactive forum and publishes blog editorials, music and game reviews, interviews with bands or musicians, and "Get-

ting to Know..." profiles of their new stars. The content generated by Burning Angel directly encourages their online visitors and customers to participate in the website's community and discuss non-sexual aspects of alternative subculture along with the possibility to consume pornography.

4. Sakmann has moved away from collaborations with the adult industry since—none of the titles mentioned above are mentioned in his Director/Producer resume on his personal/professional website, but remain listed in his IMDb profile.

5. The AVN Awards are an annual, industry-wide award show hosted by the *Adult Video News Magazine* since 1983. Over the course of the show's existence, more detailed achievement categories were added, where some reward filmic aspects that reach beyond the spectrum of pornographic content. In 1989, "Best Non-Sex Performance" became a category in the award show, followed by an even more specific classification of "Best Sex Comedy" in 1996. An award for "Best Parody" was introduced in 2010, justified by the sub-genre's commercial success and the parodies' increasing presence in other award categories. In 2011, "Best Parody" was split into "Best Parody–Comedy" and "Best Parody–Drama" for yet another more specific differentiation, but this opposition was discontinued in 2015. Furthermore, the categories "Best Director" and "Best Screenplay" have been extended with sub-categories for parody films in 2012.

6. My intertextual speculation.

7. Kleio Valentien's tree-sex scene from *Evil Head* is also available as a streamed clip on Burning Angel's website under the title "Double Pine-Etration." Here, contrary to its occurrence in the film, the scene has a musical underscore that is explicitly identified and hyperlinked in the video description, adding to Burning Angel's efforts to create more overlap between alternative music subcultures and pornography.

8. A good illustration of this is Zero Tolerance's *Official Friday the 13th Parody*, where the infamous Jason Vorhees story of the *Friday the 13th* franchise is rewritten into an innovatively funny and sexualized horror narrative, but the sex scenes themselves are not disrupted by visual or narrative horror elements—every murder by or battle with the monster occurs strictly after a sex number is sealed by a money shot.

9. I.Q. Hunter summarizes Williams' idea that the body of a spectator is "caught up in an almost involuntary mimicry of the emotion or sensation of the body on screen" (Williams, *Bodies* 4) as "corporeal karaoke" (134).

10. Aside from Doug Sakmann's association with horror productions, Tommy Pistol has also produced, directed, and starred in his own horror film, *The Gruesome Death of Tommy Pistol* (2010), before *Evil Head* and moved on to direct another of Burning Angel's horror porn parodies, *The Walking Dead: A Hardcore Parody* (2013), after.

11. In an essay on media subversion, hyper-articulation, and parody, Paul Booth discusses the similar ways in which slash fandom and porn parodies comment on and re-appropriate the original texts they engage, where both formats point towards the ubiquity of sexuality in mainstream media culture itself.

12. Carmine Sarracino and Kevin M. Scott write that "[t]he puritan wilderness becomes the porn playground" (6) where pornography, not without a good sense of self-irony, reproduces the public discourse's labeling of it as "sinful, nasty [and] naughty" (5) with great success.

13. DP, or double penetration, is a sexual technique that involves the simultaneous penetration of the same, or two closely aligned orifices (anus and/or vagina), typically involving three individuals. In its abbreviated form, DP can function as both a noun and a verb.

14. I.Q. Hunter notes that pornographic interpretations of film plots, especially in cases where the original displays a high degree of brutality, frequently rewrite the execution of violence into a dormant sexual force that is triggered by the respective sexual perpetrators (128).

15. As Constance Penley writes, humor and silliness have been substantial constituents of pornographic films from very early on, as the possibility to laugh discharges the erotic tension of the film, especially because these early "stag films" or "blue movies" tended to be screened in gentlemen's clubs and other, comparable social settings where the display of and acting upon sexual arousal was deemed out of place (314).

WORKS CITED

Álvarez, Fede, director. *Evil Dead*. TriStar Pictures, 2013.
Bényei, Tamás. "Ironic Parody or Parodistic Irony? Irony, Parody, Postmodernism and the Novel." *Hungarian Journal of English and American Studies* 1, no. 1 (1995), pp. 89–123.
Berlant, Lauren. *Cruel Optimism*. Duke University Press, 2011.
Bibbiani, William. "The Joanna ANGEL Interviews—Evil Head & Fuckenstein (NSFW)." *YouTube*, CraveOnline.com, Aug. 28, 2013, youtube.com/watch?v=iV4tYpxs4zw.
Booth, Paul. "Slash and Porn: Media Subversion, Hyper-Articulation, and Parody." *Continuum: Journal of Media & Cultural Studies* 28, no. 3 (2014), pp. 396–409.
Egan, Kate. *The Evil Dead*. Wallflower Press, 2000.
Friedkin, William, director. *The Exorcist*. Warner Bros., 1973.
Gordon, Stuart, director. *Re-Animator*. Empire Pictures, 1985.
Hunter, I.Q. "A Clockwork Orgy: A User's Guide." *Peep Shows: Cult Film and the Cine-Erotic*, edited by Xavier Mendik. Wallflower Press, 2012, pp. 126–134.
Jameson, Fredric. *The Cultural Turn: Selected Writings on the Postmodern, 1983–1998*. Verso, 1998.
Jones, Bethan. "Slow Evolution: 'First Time Fics' and The X Files Porn Parody." *Journal of Adaptation in Film & Performance* 6, no. 3 (2013), pp. 369–385.
Orona, Gary Dean, director. *The Official Friday the 13th Parody*. Zero Tolerance, 2010.
Patton, Cindy. *Fatal Advice: How Safe-Sex Education Went Wrong*. Duke University Press, 1996.
Penley, Constance. "Crackers and Whackers: The White Trashing of Porn." *Porn Studies*, edited by Linda Williams. Duke University Press, 2004, pp. 309–31.
Pistol, Tommy, director. *The Gruesome Death of Tommy Pistol*. Baby Yetti Productions, 2010.
Pistol, Tommy, and Joanna Angel, directors. *The Walking Dead: A Hardcore Parody*. Burning Angel Entertainment, 2013.
Raimi, Sam, director. *Army of Darkness*. Renaissance Pictures, 1992.
_____. *The Evil Dead*. Renaissance Pictures, 1981.
_____. *Evil Dead 2*. Renaissance Pictures, 1987.
Sakmann, Doug, director. "Director/Producer Resume." dougsakmannwww, dougsakmann.com/project/director-producer-resume/.
_____. *Evil Head*. Burning Angel Entertainment, 2012.
_____. *Repenetrator*. Burning Angel Entertainment, 2004.
_____. *The XXXorcist*. Burning Angel Entertainment, 2006.
Sarracino, Carmine, and Kevin Schott. *The Porning of America: The Rise of Porn Culture, What It Means, and Where We Go from Here*. Beacon Press, 2008.
Valentien, Kleio, actress. "Double Pine-Etration." burningangelwww, Aug. 5, 2014, burningangel.com/en/video/Double-Pine-etration-Scene-01/65075.
Williams, Linda. "Film Bodies: Gender, Genre, and Excess." *Film Quarterly* 44, no. 4 (1991), pp. 2–13.
_____. *Hard Core. Power, Pleasure and the "Frenzy of the Visible."* University of California Press, 1989.

Macduff vs. Army of Darkness

Erin Harrington

A little-known addition to the extended *Evil Dead* family comes in the form of an Australian mash-up of Elizabethan iambic pentameter and comic B-grade schlock horror. Just as postmodern parody novels such as *Pride and Prejudice and Zombies* and *Sense and Sensibility and Sea Monsters* combine Regency literature with popular monster narratives for a savvy audience that likes its high-brow served with a strong helping of pop culture, David Mence's 2004 script *Macbeth Re-Arisen*[1] presents an undead sequel to Shakespeare's original through the lens of Sam Raimi's three *Evil Dead* films (*The Evil Dead* [1981]; *Evil Dead 2* [1987]; *Army of Darkness* [1992]). While certainly entertaining in its own right, the play aptly demonstrates the pleasures and possibilities that might come from an emphasis upon intertextuality and cultural crosspollination. As such, it is helpful to see this play not as homage but as a cheerful and deliberate extension (or, perhaps, contagion?) of the world of *The Evil Dead* into other adjacent cultural forms, much as the Canadian stage musical version of *The Evil Dead* (2003) borrows from and expands its visual and musical languages through its pastiche of both the original film and the rock musical form.

Macbeth Re-Arisen begins shortly after the end of Shakespeare's play, which finishes when the power-mad king-slaying Scot Macbeth is decapitated by rival lord Macduff, who is bent on revenge for the death of his family. Here, the newly crowned King Malcolm decides to refuse Macbeth a proper Christian burial and instead orders that the butchered body be left out for the crows. Macduff, who is both the hero of the day and so overtly, Eeyoreishly miserable that no one wants him around, proffers a portentous warning, duly accompanied by thunder and lightning, that this transgression may let Macbeth "return to plague the sacrilegious / As a formless shade, or something worse" (Mence 6). Macduff's warning is dismissed—as is Macduff himself, for his gloominess is so profound that he is lowering the tone of the Scottish celebrations. Macbeth, then, returns for round two, magically revived by the first play's meddling witches so that he may go forth as the champion of the goddess of the underworld, Hecate, as her "principal implement in waging war" against the living (Mence 12). Macbeth's role, as "Undead Lord" (Mence 12), is to reattach his head, revive his dead wife, then take back the realm of man in the name of the supernatural by leading an undead horde against the living. Macduff's role as reluctant suicidal hero, as laid out to him by the ghost of Banquo (another character back for a reprise from *Macbeth* part one), is to retrieve *The Book of the Dead*, the *Necronomicon*, from Hecate's lair in the underworld, so that he might use its spells to cast away the army of darkness. Sounding familiar? Deep in the underworld, the ghost of the Roman poet Virgil suggests to Macduff with a wink that such coincidences are not secret knowledge, "but an understanding of literary convention" (Mence 34)—a supraliterary playfulness that the play itself is predicated on.

Macbeth Re-Arisen borrows liberally, and most blatantly, from the original three *Evil Dead* films. Obvious references litter the play: Macduff, in the underworld, is confronted with a choice of three—three?!—*Necronomicon*s; the newly revived Lady Macbeth notes that, like Sheila in *Army of Darkness*, "I feel bad, yet I feel good" (Mence 22); Virgil's description of the *Necronomicon* (Mence 33) echoes the descriptions of *The Book of the Dead* in both *The Evil Dead* and *Evil Dead 2*. These moments, and dozens of others, are couched deeply with a broad range of instances poached from popular and classical texts. Beyond looping repeatedly, if not fetishistically, back upon *Macbeth*, the play riffs on lines and scenes from other Shakespearean plays including *Julius Caesar*, *Hamlet* and *Richard III*, as well as other texts, such as various iterations and developments of H. P. Lovecraft's oeuvre (like William Browning Spencer's *Résumé with Monsters*), Virgil's *Aeneid*, and *The Wizard of Oz* (1939). Even the Massachusetts "Bill Against Conjurations, Witchcraft, and Dealing with Evil and Wicked Spirits" (1692), which marked witchcraft and associated activities as a felony, is sliced apart for comic gain, as its charges are reframed within the Scottish court as densely comic bureaucratic nonsense.

The net result—for the savvy audience member, at least—is the pleasure that comes from both recognition and anticipation. A key comic and narrative moment comes when the play summons up some of the best-known material from *Evil Dead 2* as Hecate offers Macbeth a boon:

> Before I fly, I'll leave thee with a gift,
> A weapon most potent in magic, most deadly in effect.
> 'Tis called a "chain-saw," and is a kind
> Of sword, yet it hath teeth, as does the shark,
> That mayest rend the armourer's thickest plate [Mence 35].

Macbeth, mad with power, carves his hand off and attaches the chainsaw to his arm; the severed hand comes running across the stage, past the appalled Lady Macbeth, who fails to catch it. *Macbeth*'s "Lay on, Macduff" (V.vii.33) is replaced here with "Let the slaughter begin!" (Mence 40)—a line cribbed from the 1986 animated film *The Transformers: The Movie*—as Macduff tries to balance his sword while reading from the *Necronomicon* in the final, violent battle.

These myriad cultural and literary influences are stitched around one another in an anarchic and comedic fashion, at one stage coalescing into a performance for the young King Fleance of play-within-a-play "The Tragedie of the Living Dead." In this overblown drama, performed by tragedians much like the roaming players from *Hamlet*, the "canoodling" (Mence 27) of young lovers Romeo and Juliet is interrupted by a zombie attack that even the power of love cannot overcome. As the zombie attack players dressed as king and queen, the performance is interrupted by a Shepherd who warns the assembled crowd and the actual King that Macbeth and his army of the dead are approaching. Having broken the King's newly stated ban on witchcraft and related activities the Shepherd is dragged off, crying:

> No! Pry open your ears! Macbeth is come again!
> He marches on Forres with an army of skeletal minions!
> They'll swallow your souls! [Mence 27].

This is one of the most self-referential of the play's many textual mash-ups: the postmodern cinema's zombie ur-text *Night of the Living Dead* (1968) meets a goulash of Shakespearean characters and scenarios by way of late night drive-in cinema culture, and rounded off with a line to both cast and audience that calls back to one of *Evil Dead 2*'s most recognizable moments. The Deadites might swallow the souls of the Scots, just as sure this text, and others like it, eat themselves over and over.

At the same time, *Macbeth Re-Arisen* takes full advantage of what can be considered a sort of undead cultural zeitgeist in the beginning of the 21st century—an obsession with zombies as cultural texts and agents that incorporates forms as diverse as film, television, literature, electronic and table top gaming, and activities like zombie walks, which combine performance art with culture jamming. Certainly, "the zombie's utility as metaphor is virtually without limit" (Boluk and Lenz 9), but here the pleasure is in the semiotic instability of the undead and of (post)modern texts themselves. Intertextuality, then, is not simply a tool but an end to itself. The playfulness in textual translations such as pastiche, parody, allusion and imitation, be they specific moments (Lady Macbeth punches her fist out of her grave, as in the shock ending of *Carrie* (1977), and as illustrated on the original poster for *The Evil Dead*) or more general allusive sweeps (Macduff's katabasis and his encounter with Virgil), generate their own meaning rather than impoverish the original. It is the ability to reanimate and cannibalize literary and cinematic texts, be they classical or modern, which marks this play (and other postmodern works like it) as its own form of zombie (or, perhaps, Deadite). These points teeter between ironic distance and a clear, sincere affection for the original as the work "paradoxically both incorporates and challenges that which it parodies" (Hutcheon 11).

Just before Macbeth's lumbering Deadite army arrives at the Scottish court, the peevish young King Fleance announces that he has banned witchcraft, telling his gathered subjects that "Thus I banish superstition / to th'realm of Art, that it may live on as parody" (Mence 24). Thus, *Macbeth Re-Arisen* poaches from the *Evil Dead* films, just as this expanding canon plunders gleefully from the expansive and collaborative Lovecraftian mythos and the visual language of other American horror films, just as years later a film like the comic metahorror film *The Cabin in the Woods* (2012) situates its horror in a place much like the cabin at the center of *The Evil Dead*. This titular archetypal house becomes a point in an intertextual constellation, a single mark on a broad topography of generic tropes and expressions, each point linked back to another in a gleefully immanent visual language of horror. The trapdoor of the id-basement keeps flying open: Lovecraftian Elder Gods rouse themselves in the deep "basement" beneath the titular cabin in the woods; Ash twice fails to contain the evil that's been driven into the cellar of the cabin in *The Evil Dead* and *Evil Dead 2*; Macduff makes a reluctant trip down to the underworld in *Macbeth Re-Arisen* to retrieve *The Book of the Dead*, so as to bend the source of evil against itself. Each of these merry acts of narrative vandalism pillage and recontextualize, drawing strands of meaning into a broader textual tapestry that marries low with high, the cinematic with the performative, the ersatz with the authentic, and the funny with the frightening.

Notes

1. *Macbeth Re-Arisen* was performed by independent Australian theatre company White Whale Theatre in Melbourne, Australia, in 2004 and 2008 and at the Edinburgh Fringe in 2006, each time directed by writer David Mence. Other companies have staged productions in Christchurch, New Zealand (2010), and Cairns, Australia (2015).

Works Cited

Boluk, Stephanie, and Wylie Lenz, editors. "Introduction: Generation Z, the Age of Apocalypse." *Generation Zombie: Essays on the Living Dead in Modern Culture*. McFarland, 2011, pp. 1–17.
De Palma, Brian, director. *Carrie*. United Artists, 1976.
Fleming, Victor, et al., directors. *The Wizard of Oz*. MGM, 1939.
Goddard, Drew, director. *The Cabin in the Woods*. Lionsgate, 2012.
Grahame-Smith, Seth, and Jane Austen. *Pride and Prejudice and Zombies: The Classic Regency Romance—Now with Ultraviolent Zombie Mayhem*. Quirk Books, 2009.

Hutcheon, Linda. *A Poetics of Postmodernism History, Theory, Fiction*. Routledge, 1988.
Mence, David. *Macbeth Re-Arisen*. Australian Script Centre, 2004.
Raimi, Sam, director. *Army of Darkness*. Renaissance Pictures, 1992.
_____. *The Evil Dead*. Renaissance Pictures, 1981.
_____. *Evil Dead 2: Dead by Dawn*. Renaissance Pictures, 1987.
Romero, George A, director. *Night of the Living Dead*. Continental Distributing, 1968.
Shakespeare, William. *Hamlet*. Simon & Schuster, 1992.
_____. *Julius Caesar*. Reissue edition, Simon & Schuster, 2004.
_____. *Macbeth*. Simon & Schuster, 2003.
_____. *Richard III*. Edited by Barbara A. Mowat and Paul Werstine. Simon & Schuster, 2004.
Shin, Nelson, director. *The Transformers: The Movie*. Sunbow, 1986.
Spencer, William Browning. *Résumé with Monsters*. Dover, 2014.
Virgil, and Bernard Knox. *The Aeneid*. Translated by Robert Fagles. Reprint edition, Penguin Classics, 2008.
Winters, Ben H., and Jane Austen. *Sense and Sensibility and Sea Monsters*. Quirk Books, 2009.

PART III

Testimonials

Fake Shemping

Bill Vincent

In December of 1979, Ivan Raimi came to my office at Michigan State University. "Sam and Rob are making a movie in Tennessee," he said. "You want to go?" I had read my exams. My grades were in. I did want to go.

The film was titled *Book of the Dead* (later changed to *The Evil Dead* [1981]). Sam Raimi was directing; Robert Tapert was producing; and Bruce Campbell, the third member of the partnership that was to become Renaissance Pictures and the only non–Spartan, was playing Ash, the feckless lead.

At that time, I was teaching a Western civilization course called Humanities, which was required of all MSU students. My courses were in what was called the Film Track—the basic course jazzed up with weekly movies like Pasolini's *Medea* (1969), Rossellini's *The Rise of Louis XIV* (1966), and Huston's *Freud* (1962). I also taught an occasional film class.

Sam's older brother Ivan was the first to take my classes. He recommended me to Rob who took my courses for three quarters. Sam followed for one quarter in which I remember trying unsuccessfully to get him to talk about the films we were watching. Knowing he was a would-be filmmaker, I assumed he would be happy to talk about filmic techniques. I was wrong: he did not like being put on the *spot*.

Sam had been a filmmaker from the age of thirteen or so. His parents had let him have a studio in their basement. When it came time for him to go to university, his parents supposed he would go to film school, but he preferred to come to Michigan State and learn about something other than film. At State, he met and became close friends with Tapert who was two years ahead of him. Together they made a short film, *The Happy Valley Kid* (1977), about a nebbishy freshman (Rob) who is continually tormented by an evil kid played by Sam. It was funny and fresh and began the partnership that has continued to this day. When Ivan, hoping to amp up his credentials for admission to medical school, decided to start a jogging club on campus, the other two immediately turned it into a film club (still going strong today). Among Sam's other film projects while he was at State was a project he did for his Shakespeare class—a scene from *The Taming of the Shrew* in which Katharina and Petruchio have at each other in four feet of snow.

Rob graduated with a degree in business and was admitted to State's MBA program. Ivan graduated and entered medical school. Sam finished his sophomore year. At this point, Rob came to Sam and suggested they both quit school to make a film.

They decided to make a horror film, in part at least because with horror they could get away with a low-budget look—that "drive-in-movie look" Sam called it. In the summer they made a short film—*Within the Woods* (1978)—to demonstrate that they could do horror, and they showed it around to potential investors in the Detroit area where they were from. When they raised enough money they approached various state film offices. Michigan offered them nothing. Tennessee offered them a cabin in the woods and a house to use as production headquarters/living space.

And so, having driven all night from East Lansing, Ivan and I found ourselves at dawn in a small valley with a log cabin at its center. Klieg lights were the only sign that a film was being made there. Except, that is, for Sam who was crouching on the side of the hill, staring intently at the cabin, planning, I imagined, for the next shoot—something, Rob Tapert tells me, he has always done ever since, prepared for the next day's shoot before going to bed.

The next shoot here, however, would be at night: they generally filmed until dawn and returned to the house for sleep. The women (actresses) got the bedrooms; the men—that mad bunch of childhood friends, most of them having gone to camp together—slept on the living room floor. Communal meals were served and were delicious. In the late afternoon began the transfer of cast, crew, and equipment to the cabin in preparation for the night's shooting.

I was put to work. Aside from those with specific tasks—the actors, the director of photography, the make-up man—everybody did everything. We carried and cleared. If there was a tracking shot, the D.P. lay in a blanket and six of us carried him as smoothly as we could. Usually I kept the shooting log, which was a job most of the young folk did not relish. I found it gave me the opportunity to watch the process at close quarters. What a pleasure it was to watch Sam work!

I knew before I came to Tennessee that Sam was a talented filmmaker. Within the first night's shooting I became convinced that he was a genius. Or maybe I was convinced before then, watching the footage they already had, including the extraordinary tracking shot around the perimeter of the cabin, peering in through each window at the characters that are blissfully unaware that there is Something Out There.

It occurred to me then, and I have often thought later, that a successful film director is like a good general. He must have a grasp of strategy and tactics, a clear objective, and an ability to get more out of his people than they know they are capable of. He must believe in his own vision and his abilities, and he must be able to focus and remain calm in any situation.

Sam had just turned twenty when he directed *The Evil Dead*. Yet he exhibited no sign of self-doubt. Things went wrong. Of course. But they did not shake his confidence in what he was doing, and if he got angry he did not show it. He does not get flustered. Not even during the shooting of *Army of Darkness* (1992) when the crane that was supposed to drop Ash's car off the top of a cliff followed the car to the bottom did he become unhinged. I remember watching him shooting *For Love of the Game* (1999). During a break between scenes shot in a hospital, Sam stood in the midst of seeming chaos, wearing his usual jacket and tie, Kevin Costner making extensive suggestions in one ear, the assistant director asking about placing the extras for the next scene, grips wondering whether the windows needed filters, and someone else reminding him, "Sam, we only have the babies for thirty more minutes." Throughout, Sam remained calm and seemingly focused on every one of these matters, not serially, but all at once.

That focus was always evident during the *Evil Dead* shoot. So was his ability to get the most out of people. Often, Tim Philo, the cinematographer, would say that he could not do a certain shot—after all, the equipment available was minimal and primitive. Sam would take him aside, put his arm over his shoulder and talk quietly to him, and then Tim would come back and figure out a way to do the shot.

A good example of getting more out of someone than they thought they could do involved a scene with Betsy Baker who played Linda. The scene called for Linda, who by this time had turned into Evil Linda, to crash hard into the wall of the cabin. The wall was padded; but it was still very hard, and Betsy was throwing herself into it rather gingerly. Sam kept goading her until she lost her temper and threw herself at the wall with full force. The whole cabin shook. Betsy crumpled senseless to the floor. The whole crew froze, wondering if Betsy had "bought it." Then she opened her eyes and asked sweetly, "How was that, Sam?" "Fine, Betsy," he said, "but … do it again." This time she nearly went through the wall. He had found a way to get her to do what he needed her to do.

What impressed me the most, however, was Sam's vision of what he wanted. Most young filmmakers are content to merely tell their story. Sam had both a visual style and a narrative style.

The visual style was inspired by comic book art. Sam loved comic books. (And still does, I presume. The last time I was in his office, a rack of comic books made up part of the décor.) In *The Evil Dead* and many of his subsequent films he has imposed a comic book aesthetic—extreme high and low angles, compression of space, odd compositions, coupled with highly dramatic lighting.

If the visual style grafted comic book visuals into the film, the narrative style was a hybridization of another sort. Sam fully understood that the function of the horror film is to "torture the audience": as, for example, when the protagonist drops the keys just as the monster is about to pounce. As he or she feels for the keys, finds them, drops them, and so forth, the audience is fully engaged both physically and emotionally. In his horror films, Sam misses no opportunity to torment his viewers.

He also understands that, as he later put it to me, "once the guy in the rubber suit appears, it's all over." As Val Lewton demonstrated, what is unseen is scarier than anything you can show. For that reason, Sam's favorite horror film was (maybe still is) Robert Wise's *The Haunting* (1963). So in *The Evil Dead* it was important to keep the Horror in the woods invisible until the very last.

Sam's understanding of these and the other basic tropes of the horror genre were thorough. What was new to the genre was the introduction of humor, specifically the slapstick humor of the Three Stooges.

Sam was and is a great fan of the Stooges. You can see their influence in all of the *Evil Dead* films. In *Evil Dead 2* (1987), for example, Ash is attacked by his own hand until he must cut it off, and even then it skitters after him; in *Army of Darkness,* Ash plays out a Stooges routine with his own doubles.

I have often wondered whether this mixture of slapstick comedy with horror might account for the difficulties they had in finding a distributor for the film. They shopped it for over a year before showing it outside the competition at Cannes where they picked up an endorsement from Stephen King and a foreign distributor. It might also explain the initial lukewarm reception by audiences and critics. It would take the audience a decade to catch up with *The Evil Dead.*

Did I know that we were making an iconic film? No, but I was certain that it would be a very good one. I think everyone did, judging by the high level of enthusiasm throughout the troupe of actors, technicians, and fake Shemps.

Ah, yes, Fake Shemps. In IMDB, I am in the film's cast list as a Fake Shemp, along with a host of others. If you've seen the film you would have to wonder where we are all hiding. "Fake Shemp" is simply the term Sam chose to apply to all of us do-whatevers.

When he was thirteen, Sam had an epiphany. He was watching a Three Stooges episode from 1955 when he noticed that Shemp was not Shemp, but a fake Shemp. The real Shemp had died, and Joe Palma had donned Shemp's costume and kept his back to the camera to close out the four episodes remaining on the Stooges' contract for that series. Sam explains that he realized at that moment that filmmaking is "the art of Fake Shemping"—making the audience see what they expect to see.

An example: while he was a student. Sam showed me a piece of film in which a couple is riding in a car holding a conversation. The scene is shot in a low angle from outside the car on the passenger side. The car is clearly moving: you can see trees flashing by outside. Sam asked me how he filmed the scene. I said that since I knew he could not afford back projection he must have found a way to mount the camera outside the car. But, he said, the camera was on a tripod outside the car and the car was not moving. "But I saw the trees flashing by." "What you saw was some guy crouching on the other side of the car, holding two branches, and every once in a while he would wave them past the driver's side window." Sure enough, when I rewatched the film, it was clearly some guy crouching with branches. Fake Shemping. Throughout his career Sam has loved creating such illusions.

After a week in Tennessee, the company took a break, and I returned home for Christmas. I had not intended to go back, but I found I missed the excitement, the camaraderie, the intensity, and everything I was learning about the process, so I decided to go back.

I'd had time to reflect, not only about Sam's brilliance as director but also about the comparable brilliance on the part of his two partners, Bruce Campbell and Robert Tapert.

At first I had not been impressed with Bruce's performance. I judged it fake and over the top. I came to realize, however, that it was a style of acting perfectly suited to the film. Bruce, with his comic book hero's face, devised a comic book/Three Stooges characterization—call it the feckless wiseass. In so doing I think he was a pioneer of a style of acting which became one of the dominant styles of the eighties and beyond to the present day. He does it effortlessly. You have only to watch James Franco try and fail to achieve that style in *Oz the Great and Powerful* (2013) to appreciate Bruce's sublimity.

I don't think I fully appreciated Rob Tapert's remarkable effort enabling the film to happen. Though he was constantly busy getting what was needed, he was certainly the least visible of the three partners during the shoot. He has remained the least visible. But his value to the partnership is incalculable. Every Sam Raimi needs a Rob Tapert. Both his financial and organizational skills have served them well throughout a series of projects. If Sam was astonishing in his mastery of both genre and technique at such a young age, Rob was equally amazing for his rapid mastery of film production and the film business itself. Sam has become a top director; Bruce has become a star; Rob has become a major player in the industry. During a visit I made to Los Angeles a number of years later, he complained to me, "Somewhere in this town, in an office on the thirtieth floor of some building I've never been in, there's a guy I've never met whose only function in life is to fuck me up!" It remains a favorite quotation from a man who has pretty much managed not to let anyone fuck him up.

So, anyway, I went back down to Tennessee, again with Ivan and this time with Rob's sister, Mary Beth. I don't remember exactly for how long. Eight days? Ten days? Long enough to see the breaking up of the company as the final scenes were filmed—the chainsaw in the shed, everybody nervous that something might go horribly wrong; Sam and someone else (Bruce?) on either side of the camera battering Betsy with breakaway Styrofoam two-by-fours and Sam getting into it so much that when he was left with only a small piece, he hurled it at her; Sam keeping Betsy for shot after shot as the time grew dangerously short for her to catch a flight back to Detroit and a gig at the auto show.

And then it was over.

And it wasn't over. I got bulletins from Ivan about post-production progress. Then came the premiere of *Book of the Dead* as it was still called.

For *Army of Darkness* I made some suggestions for "medievalizing" the dialogue and what kinds of "acts" might perform in a medieval setting. Over the years they have invited me to be an extra in *Army of Darkness* and *The Quick and the Dead* (1995) and gave me a speaking role in *For Love of the Game*.

Being an extra is great fun. You get to watch the creative process close up, and you get to hang out with an interesting lot of people, some of them professional extras, most of them just earning some extra money, a few of them hoping to be discovered or hoping to get a line, which would automatically "Taft-Hartley" them into the Screen Actors Guild. Some will try too hard to be noticed: one of the ladies in *Army of Darkness* would have her hair and makeup done in the grungy medieval style of the film and then go off and redo her hair and makeup in a more contemporary style, appearing just as her scene was to be shot and it was too late to change her back. I was with Sam in his trailer when she came by to give him her resume and tell him that she would "be glad to do *anything* he wanted." Another extra kept waving his head back and forth during shots, realizing, I suppose, that audiences do not notice the individual extras unless they call attention to themselves. Sam kept moving the guy back further and further in the shots but finally had to let him go.

I loved hanging out with the extras and listening to their stories. They were a mixed lot, from an ex-NFL lineman to a young composer, from students to housewives. Some were doing it for a lark, some because they needed the money. Since they lived in Los Angeles, most of them had a lot of experience as extras and many stories about the foibles of the stars they had worked with. All had dreams of the elusive "bump."

Extras are always hoping for a "bump." At that time the daily pay for extras was forty-five dollars, with extra for travel. A bump would raise that to seventy dollars. You could get a bump if you were assigned to do something special that made you "visible" to the audience or if you were subjected to something particularly onerous. In *Army of Darkness* there is a pit and at one point the pit erupts with a geyser of blood. We extras, we were told, would all be soaked with blood—a bump for everybody! The night before, however, Rob exercised his control over costs: soaking everyone with blood, he told Sam, would not only increase the daily budget for extras by fifty-five percent, it would also necessitate the overnight dry cleaning of dozens of costumes. The next day we were told to run like hell when the pit began erupting: "Anyone who gets wet will be fired."

Army of Darkness was shot in Antelope Valley, a short distance from Tippi Hedren's ranch. When the wind was right we could hear her lions roaring. My part was that of a "wise man." My first day on set Sam began a shot with a close up of me, rising on the crane to an extreme high angle of the entirety of the inside of Lord Arthur's castle and then panning as I traversed the perimeter of the walls. I thought, "Wow! What next?" That shot is in the final cut, though my close-up has been lopped off. Thereafter, I can be seen right behind Lord Arthur during the opening scene in the castle. I can also be seen, impossibly, in both sides of a shot/reverse shot. Sam asked me how I could let that happen and I told him I just went where I was told to.

To tell the truth, I was not a good extra: extras are not supposed to act, just be. I acted. Sometime after *Army of Darkness* Sam said to me, "Where did you go? We had to hire a Bill Vincent look-alike." It was years before I realized that that was not a compliment. I was, in fact, no different from the woman who rearranged her curls or the guy that waved his head.

Being an extra for *The Quick and Dead* was a much different experience. We were shooting forty miles south of Tucson, so there were far fewer of the professional extras you get shooting in or near Los Angeles. These folk had been riding the current wave of westerns, and much of their talk was of rumored productions forthcoming in Arizona or New Mexico, though sadly for them the western boom was nearly at an end.

The pleasures of being in *The Quick and the Dead* were that I got to wear a spiffy costume (long duster, leather chaps and gloves, cowboy boots), and I got to see Sam direct and to watch a host of big stars at work—Sharon Stone with her array of "people," a taciturn Russell Crowe, Leonardo DiCaprio riding high on his Oscar nomination for *What's Eating Gilbert Grape* (1993), and especially two consummate professionals, Gene Hackman and Pat Hingle.

Sam was experimenting. He used a dolly/zoom, which he called "my cheesy *Vertigo* shot," and much time was spent trying to get a shot through the bullet hole in the back of a gunfight victim's skull. This involved a dummy head, a plug attached to a fishline, and a device to produce a wisp of smoke in the hole as we look through it to the victorious gunfighter beyond.

Sam gave me a speaking role in *For Love of the Game*, but I lost my one line ("No, I'm an X-ray technician." Oh, how I had practiced that line!) when the blocking had to be changed and my part was eliminated. I did end up portraying a doctor (sans line), and I ended up in the credits. I still get the occasional residual check for five or six dollars.

After that our paths crossed less and less often. I went to Rob's wedding to Lucy Lawless, an event that did not cost a penny more than the gross national product of Paraguay. I remain good friends with Ivan who amazingly balances being an emergency room doctor and writing scripts with his brother. I have had Ivan's son Max in a Michigan State study abroad program in London. I have become great friends with Betsy who has appeared in two films based on scripts of mine. And I got one more chance at *Evil Dead* (2013).

In 2013, I got an email from Rob inviting me to come to Auckland New Zealand to be in *Evil Dead*, to be directed by Fede Álvarez. I was luckily able to secure funding for the airfare from my dean, and the University decided to send along a camera crew to record the visit.

It was a great visit. I got to spend time with Rob and Lucy. I spent some time on the film set and had a couple of good conversations with Fede Álvarez, and I got to see the astonishing production facilities Rob has created over the past twenty years for the making of the TV series *Hercules: The Legendary Journeys* (1995–1999), *Xena: Warrior Princess* (1995–2001), *Legend of the Seeker* (2008–2010), and *Spartacus* (2010–2013).

Rob and I went out to the *Evil Dead* cabin about an hour north of Auckland and reminisced about the original cabin and how much things had changed. Now there were two cabins, the one custom built in the real woods and an identical one in the warehouse cum studio amidst fake trees, the difference between the two being that that roof and the walls of the studio cabin were removable. And these days Fede directed mostly from a distance, watching two monitors, one for each camera, communicating via microphone.

Wandering around the sets for *Evil Dead* and *Spartacus*, I marveled at how far that simple decision to quit school and make a movie had brought the boys, and how far, on a much smaller but still satisfying scale, my decision to make the journey to Tennessee with Ivan had brought me.

Oh, if you are looking for me in the new *Evil Dead*, you will have to look fast: I am a hillbilly who is among the witnesses to the burning of a witch. About a third of my face is visible for a split second.

But when the film was shown as a special sneak preview at Michigan State, Ivan and I were there to present it. And when the film ended, there I was in the credits—Bill Vincent.... Fake Shemp.

Do the *Necronomicon*
Evil Dead's *Journey into the Realm of Musical Theater*

L. Michael Elliott

Campy horror films don't often slice their way onto the musical stage, but the cult classic *Evil Dead* franchise was brought to life as *Evil Dead: The Musical* in 2003, enthralling a broader audience with its unapologetically over-the-top sarcasm and gore. When I had the opportunity to music direct this cult adaptation in 2011 at Ball State University, I admit I was not initially drawn to the material because it seemed to lack substance. Although a fan of the films, I could not initially see how they could be relevant on stage. And having been raised in the 1980s and very familiar the music of that decade, I did not think a score inspired by the rock and pop music of the era could carry the weight of plot and character development. My academic musical theater mind just could not fathom the marriage of this material with the art form of Rodgers and Hammerstein and Stephen Sondheim. Once we started rehearsing, however, I began to truly see how well this show was balanced. Using the basic tenants of traditional musical theater—employing music, song and dance to further the plot or character development—*Evil Dead: The Musical's* script and score weaves the narrative of the film trilogy into one stage production, relying heavily on the dry wit and campy nature of the films.

However, the stage version is not a parody of the movies. The musical's creators George Reinblatt, Frank Cipolla, Christopher Bond and Melissa Morris bring the ludicrousness of the films to life with "splash zones" that douse audience members with gallons of fake blood during the show. For example, the opened ended Las Vegas run, billed as the "Ultimate 4D Experience," includes a 100 seat splatter zone. They also include pre-show "Deadites" wandering through the lobby, interacting with audience even before the show begins. Our production, however, was in a small black box theater. A black box theater is just that, a big room, essentially, that can be configured however you need. Our stage was raised, with seating on two sides, like and L, as opposed to a traditional proscenium stage. The special effects were simple and inexpensive as the budget was small. We provided a somewhat intimate experience for the audience, however we took out the splash zone, containing all blood onstage. This show's versatility to live in different spaces is one of the best functions of the musical.

The first act of *Evil Dead: The Musical* is essentially *The Evil Dead* movie, while the second act picks up with the second movie, *Evil Dead 2*. There's a nod to *Army of Darkness* in some borrowed dialogue, and the musical's closing scene mimics the movie's final moments in the S Mart. Dramatic liberties are taken, such as the omission of Bobby Joe, although her absence is blatantly referenced early in act two. The use of such dramatic license streamlines the two-hour show, allowing it to incorporate the best of the three movies without getting bogged down by trying to replicate the films. Attempting to recreate all the verbatim complexities of a film on stage is rarely a good idea since the audience experience is so different for each medium. The value of a musical adaptation is not in the details, but in staying true to the essence of the original. *Evil Dead: The Musical* accomplishes by maintaining the iconic moments from the franchise.

"This is my boomstick"

In true musical theater fashion, the show opens with "Cabin in the Woods," a number to familiarize the audience with the characters, style and initial setup of the piece. The music is lighthearted and fun, often reminiscent of '80s pop/rock. The show immediately begins to merge the absurdity of the forthcoming situation with the nostalgia of the films as well as that of '80s pop culture. Following the blueprint of most Golden Age musicals like *Oklahoma!* or *Guys and Dolls*, the characters initially appear as stock characters: the romantic leads, Ash and Linda; the character (or comic relief) couple, Scott and Shelly; and the quirky/nerdy sidekick, Cheryl. Their one dimensionality is highlighted at the top of the show by the use of these traditional musical theater stereotypes. This makes the introduction of the characters familiar not only to avid fans, but to the first time viewer. Audiences understand the stereotypes, so the need for elaborate introduction and backstory is negated. The relationships and archetypes are quickly established, allowing the situational nature of the ensuing plot to reach its critical points in an efficient manner without leaving the non–Evil Deadite wondering what's going on.

The show continues to employ musical idioms from the '80s, with power ballads that could have been home on any Poison album, such as Ash and Linda's duet, "Housewares Employee" and Ash's lament "I'm Not a Killer," sung as he takes the chainsaw to the head of his once beloved Linda to end the first act. Many other musical genres are sampled as well. Jake sings an arousing, pulse driven song "Good Ol' Reliable Jake" that begins with a country and western inspired introduction. Professor Ed Getley finally gets his say in a cabaret style number "Bit Part Demon." The demons get funky in "Do the *Necronomicon*" and "It's Time," both bringing in a bit of disco to help their dancing feet. Annie Knowby launches into a '60s doo-wop song, "All the Men in My Life Keep Getting Killed by Candarian Demons," chronicling the lovers and family she has lost. Even opera gets a nod in "Ode to an Accidental Stabbing," which Jake and Annie Knowby sing, blending the traditional high art form with the rock 'n roll sound of the show in a heightened dialogue between the characters. Generally, in musical theater, songs are used when mere words are not enough (i.e. the content demands more than just dialogue). Songs are also used to establish/develop characters, move the plot line along either through time or emotional connection, or to elaborate a point. *Evil Dead: The Musical* deftly utilizes these basic tenants, often punctuating the quick changes in plot and tone, as well as highlighting the obvious shifts and holes within the plot.

"Good ... bad.... I'm the guy with the gun"

What really makes the show come alive is the actors. Without their genuine dedication to the material, the show would be less engaging and entertaining. The script and score may have looked simple on the page, but this allowed the performers to more easily make the lines, lyrics, and music their own. They developed the characters and relationships necessary to tell the tale, influenced and guided by the movies, yet unique to them and the production. The show is versatile, able to be performed in a variety of venues. The previously mentioned Vegas 4D Experience boasts the 100 seat splatter zone as well as multimedia elements, state of the art effects and lighting, and copious amounts of audience interaction making the audience itself another character in the show. Our show boasted only 100 seats total, used prerecorded music accompaniment instead of live musicians, and was modest in all production elements. Both of these productions are entertaining, however very different in scope. The hyper-interaction of the Vegas production would not have been met with the same kind of enthusiasm with the audience base in our small Midwestern town, nor would the splatter zone. Overall, the show is probably best experienced in a style like the Las Vegas production, but the flexibility of the show allows it to be produced even when the budget is low and the theater is small.

For anyone who has experienced a screening of *The Rocky Horror Picture Show* on Halloween, seeing *Evil Dead: The Musical* with an audience who is intimately familiar with the films and the inside jokes, the atmosphere becomes very familiar (minus flying toast and fistfuls of rice being hurled at the screen). What makes this show successful is its balance of heart, fun and humor. The humor is campy and in your face, blending well with the theatrical fun that is musical comedy. It is a fitting salute to what has made these movies endure the test time. It is not only the avid fan who will enjoy the show, however, as it is well crafted and will be appreciated by all who attend. The musical stands not only as a tribute to the cult status of the films, but also as an evolution. For the purist wanting to see the films done verbatim, they will be disappointed. This show stands alone in the chronicles of the Book of the Dead as its own entity, bringing to life the demonic comedy that is so beloved in this franchise through song, dance, and yes, a chainsaw.

Being Linda

BETSY BAKER

In the fall of 1979, I was living in the Detroit area, working to begin a career that included commercials, industrial films, some dinner theatre, and voice-overs, when I was approached by my Detroit talent agent and was told that there were three young men who called themselves "moviemakers," who wanted to make a horror movie—and asked if I would be willing to meet with them, and talk over the possibilities of being an actress in their project. Little did I know that that chance encounter would someday, somehow, and in some strange ways ... produce a worldwide cult phenomenon that I would have small involvement in, known as *The Evil Dead* (1981).

After meeting up with these "three young moviemakers"—the director, the producer, and the lead actor—and was offered the role of "Linda," I decided (some might say against my better judgment—but what did I know about horror movies?!?) to accept the invitation, pack my bags for a trip to a cabin in Tennessee, and embark on the making of a film that included lots of Karo syrup, little to no coffee, certainly no bathrooms or heated sets, and a real adventure.

I was chosen to play the part of Linda opposite Bruce Campbell, as his character's love interest—two college kids getting away for a weekend in the woods, along with his sister (huh?), and another couple. Five of us—all alone—a cabin in the woods—for a weekend of fun ... and no doubt a little romance ... maybe. But then things went very south...

Our long shoot days quickly turned into long nights ... working in cold, winter weather ... and all the while Linda being dragged, kicked, tortured, blinded while wearing hard plastic contact lenses, stabbed in the ankle, demonized, hit over the head with wooden beams, buried alive, buried again just for good measure, and let's not forget a real working chainsaw dangling above my neck.

Over the years, while *The Evil Dead* was slowly making a formidable presence first in a few neighborhood theatres, then at remote college campus auditoriums after midnight, and then in that new business on the corner called a video store, I had moved on to other ventures—commercials, other films, an auto show narrator circling for hours on a turntable ... not at all aware of people beginning to return to the video store time and again ... to rent the same movie ... over and over. It was an interesting culture; remember—not until the video stores became a cult classic of their own, were people able to enjoy movies on a repeat basis—unless you ran back to the movie theatre another night and caught it again before it left town. Movies were not seen numerous times on television yet either, if only for the mere fact that there weren't that many channels or that many options to see something screened more than once when you flipped channels.

I had no idea that there were people from all over the world that had seen the movie—some of them hundreds of times. While they were watching it weekend after weekend, I was walking into the video store with our young family, renting children's movies for our weekend entertainment. It was only in late 2001 that, after being invited to a screening of a new and improved version, did I have any inkling that the people lined up around the corner and down the street were there waiting to see the very same movie that I was in.

Over the years, with the two other actresses from the film, Theresa Tilly (a.k.a. Sarah York) and Ellen Sandweiss, we have appeared at horror-genre conventions all over the world as "Ladies Of The Evil Dead"—and have been able to meet the fans, thank them for their loyalty, answer their questions and queries about working on such an epic classic as they fondly call it sometimes, trick them with trivia questions in panels and discussion groups ... and go away wondering ... you have seen this movie how many times?!?!?!?!?

Some of the most interesting questions we've been asked are:

Did you ever think this film would have the cult following that it has produced? No.

Did the contact lenses hurt as much as they appeared to hurt? Yes.

Did they provide you with comfortable trailers and hot food during the cold nights when you filmed in the cabin? Never.

Did you ever swear at the director and call him names? Yes.

How long did you have to train with a stunt expert when you fought with Ash, while wearing contact lenses, with a two-foot knife in your hand? Are you kidding?

Did you sustain any injuries when Ash dragged you by your feet, through the cabin, down the wooden steps, and up the hill, only to proceed to hit you over the head with so-called Styrofoam wooden ceiling beams, before beheading you? Yes.

Did you practice the kissing scene with Ash before the cameras started to roll? No, darn it.

Did you ever want to walk off the set in disgust or anger? Yes—but there was nowhere to storm off to, except deeper in the woods, and you couldn't have paid me enough money to walk out into those woods in the dark—or even in the daylight—alone. Seriously.

We have indeed met fans who have watched this movie at more than one hundred sittings, who can quote nearly every line verbatim, and at the same time, who are happy to show us their colorful tattoo of a laughing woman in a white nightgown, in the door frame of a cabin—inked all the way up their leg. We have met fans who are neurosurgeons, farmers, elementary school teachers, children of children of parents who were introduced to the film for the first time at Grandma's house, college professors, policemen, and yes—all of them ultimate horror fans.

About the Contributors

Dale **Bailey**, Lenoir-Rhyne University, holds a B.A. in English from Bethany College, an M.A. in English from the University of Tennessee at Knoxville, and a Ph.D. in English from the University of Tennessee at Knoxville.

Betsy **Baker**, an Iowan, graduated with a combined degree in theater and classical voice from Michigan State University and then embarked upon headline engagements throughout the south, including The Eden Roc in Miami Beach and other venues, with a group called Musicana. She has since honed her craft in television, radio voice-overs, industrial films, and films nationwide.

Sarah **Cleary**, Ph.D., researches the juxtaposition between children, the media, and the alleged effects of popular culture on children. She is working on her first monograph on Gothic censorship and the child. She lectures in popular culture within her capacity as an academic consultant for TV and radio and is Creative Director for Horror Expo Ireland. She has also launched Revenant Creative, which provides educational support to secondary school students.

Emily D. **Edwards**, a faculty member at University of North Carolina at Greensboro since 1987, has been a television news reporter, producer, copywriter, and television art director for NBC and ABC affiliates in Alabama and Tennessee, as well as the producer or director of more than sixteen films. She has also published articles on documentary filmmaking, the occult, and popular culture in *Journal of Film and Video*, *TDR: The Drama Review*, *Sex Roles* and *Documentary Magazine*, among others.

L. Michael **Elliott**, Ball State University, received his M.F.A. in musical theatre from San Diego State University and his Bachelor's degree from the University of Missouri. He has been an active performer across the country, including the San Diego premiere of the three-person opera *Bed and Sofa* and national tour performances of *I Love You, You're Perfect, Now Change*. In the past six years, he has music directed and/or directed over thirty productions, including the musical direction for the world premiere of *Alice* at the Christian Youth Theatre in Southern California.

Michael **Fuchs** is an assistant professor in the Department of American Studies at the University of Graz in Austria. He has coedited four books, including *Space Oddities* (2018), and (co-)authored about forty published and forthcoming book chapters and journal articles on American television, horror and adult cinema, video games, comics, and contemporary American literature. For more information on his research, visit www.fuchsmichael.net.

Valerie L. **Guyant** received her doctorate from Northern Illinois University, where she specialized in speculative literature. She is an assistant professor at Montana State University–Northern where she teaches writing, literary theory, and popular genre courses. She has published works about *Carmilla*, by Joseph Sheridan LeFanu, and the Anita Blake series, by Laurell K. Hamilton.

Stefan **Hall** is an associate professor of communication at High Point University, where he teaches courses primarily in game and interactive media design. He is also the chair of the Department of Media and Popular Culture Studies in the Nido R. Qubein School of Communication. His research interests include video games, film, comic books and sequential art, and science-fiction studies.

Erin **Harrington** is at the University of Canterbury, New Zealand, where her research and teaching focus on popular culture, visual culture, and critical theory. Her core research deals with post-1960s horror cinema, in particular its relationship to women, bodies, sexualities, and issues of gender. Her other areas of interest include: culture in digital spaces, genre and cult film and television, sex and violence in cinema, and the intersection of science and gender, among others.

Brandon **Kempner** is a professor of American literature at New Mexico Highlands University. He received his Ph.D. in English from Pennsylvania State University in 2006. He studies a broad range of popular culture topics and has written essays on *The Walking Dead, Resident Evil, iZombie, Jurassic Park*, Neil Gaiman, Terry Pratchett, and the literature of 9/11.

Michael P. **Jaros**, Ph.D., is an associate professor of English at Salem State University in Salem, Massachusetts, where he teaches courses in dramatic literature, Irish literature and culture, and works with the Honors Program and as a dramaturg to the theatre program. His research and publications focus primarily on Irish culture and performance in the 20th and 21st centuries. He holds a Ph.D. from the University of California, San Diego, and an MPhil from Trinity College Dublin.

Leon **Lewis**, Appalachian State University, has taught at Long Island University in Brooklyn, New York University in Manhattan, and University College of Wales at Aberystwyth. He is the author of several books and is the translator of Gilbert Michlin's *Of No Interest to the Nation: A Jewish Family in France, 1925–1945* and edited a collection of essays on Robert M. Young.

Alex **Liddell** is a philosophy graduate from the University of East Anglia, independent researcher, writer, and longtime fan of horror media. Their academic interests include LGBTQ studies, gender studies, film theory, and critical analysis of media representation and fandom. They have published an essay in *The Ascendance of Harley Quinn* and writes at personal website Obscuricom.com.

André **Loiselle** is Dean of Humanities and teaches film studies at St. Thomas University in Fredericton, Canada. He has published more than forty refereed articles and chapters in anthologies, as well as a dozen books, including *The Canadian Horror Film: Terror of the Soul* (2015, with Gina Freitag), and *Stages of Reality: Theatricality in Cinema* (2012, with Jeremy Maron).

About the Contributors

Robert I. **Lublin** is a professor of theatre arts at the University of Massachusetts Boston. In addition to publishing numerous essays on theatre history and dramatic literature, he is the author of *Costuming the Shakespearean Stage* and contributing coeditor of *Reinventing the Renaissance*. He has also co-authored two book chapters on *Frankenstein* in film, which appear in *Fashioning Horror*.

Michael **Phillips** is a senior lecturer in English at the University of Graz in Austria. He has coedited *ConFiguring America* (2013) and published essays on topics such as American sports and culture, *Star Wars* fandom, and postmodern theory. He is developing a project on iconic musicians.

Alex **Pitofsky**, Appalachian State University, focuses his research on the novel and on British literature, law, and history in the Restoration and the eighteenth century. His writing has appeared in *Studies in Eighteenth-Century Culture, Eighteenth-Century Life, Postmodern Culture,* and other publications. He is coeditor of *The Burney Journal* and an officer of the Burney Society.

Clayton J. **Plake** is an activist-scholar pursuing an interfield Ph.D. in English and cultural studies at Claremont Graduate University. Along with the modern horror film, his interests include visual culture, artistic production and social movements, critical race theory, revolutionary Marxism, and radical pedagogy. He teaches in Fullerton College's Department of English while simultaneously engaging in interrelated activist projects aimed at empowering local communities and taking a stand against state-sanctioned neoliberal violence.

Ron **Riekki** has an MFA in theater arts from Brandeis University, an MFA in creative writing from University of Virginia, a Ph.D. in literature and creative writing from Western Michigan University, and an MA in interreligious studies from Graduate Theological Union. He wrote *U.P.: A novel* and has edited award-winning books such as *Here: Women Writing on Michigan's Upper Peninsula* (2016) along with the upcoming *Undocumented: Great Lakes Poets Laureate on Social Justice* (2019, with Andrea Scarpino).

Rob **Roznowski,** of Michigan State University, has published *Inner Monologue in Acting* and *Collaboration in Theatre: A Practical Guide for Designers and Directors,* along with the plays *Arts or Crafts* and *Comfort Food*. He worked as the national outreach education coordinator for Actors' Equity Association and has appeared throughout the U.S. as an actor and director at Goodspeed Opera House, Long Wharf Theatre, and Pittsburgh Public Theater.

Jeffrey A. **Sartain** teaches literature and composition at the University of Houston–Victoria. He studies the culture of the digital age, posthumanism, contemporary authors, contemporary film, and literary minimalism. He is the editor of *Sacred and Immoral: On the Writings of Chuck Palahniuk* (2009), and the author of numerous pieces on contemporary American literature. He serves as the managing editor for *American Book Review*.

John **Semley** is a writer based in Toronto and the author of *This Is a Book About the Kids in the Hall* (2016). He teaches a course on horror cinema at Innis College, University of Toronto.

Haerin **Shin** received her Ph.D. in comparative literature from Stanford and is an assistant professor of English, cinema and media arts, and Asian studies at Vanderbilt University. Her focus fields are Asian American literature, issues of technology and ontology, critical theory, and visual/digital media. She has published articles on Korean science fiction, cyber-affect, techno–Orientalism, digital communities and fan culture, and state surveillance. She is working on a book about how the emergence of tele-presence technology has been reshaping our understanding of being and reality.

Olga **Tchepikova-Treon** is a Ph.D. student and graduate student instructor in the Cultural Studies and Comparative Literature Department at the University of Minnesota, Twin Cities. Her research focuses on sociocultural non-normativities, liminalities, and outsiders in independent film production and consumption. Her research investigates the merging of humor and horror in Deaf cinema.

Bill **Vincent** has a B.A. from Kalamazoo College and M.A. and Ph.D. degrees from Yale University. He has taught for over fifty years at Michigan State University, where he numbered Sam, Ivan, and Ted Raimi and Robert and MaryBeth Tapert among his students. He was instrumental in forging a film program at Michigan State and has written screenplays for several low-budget short films and features. He was an extra in four Raimi-Tapert films and has acted in countless student films.

Index

Abbey, Edward 40
Accidental Exorcist 87
Aces & Eights 58
The Addicted 61
addiction 59–69, 86
The Addiction 61
AIDS 13, 66
The Alchemist Cookbook 87
All in the Family 139–140
And Hell Awaits 87
Ann Arbor, Michigan 86
Antelope Valley 194
Argento, Dario 45, 49

Back from Hell 88
Bailey, Dale 27–33, 203
Baker, Betsy 1, 73, 83, 86, 167, 190, 200–201, 203
Barthes, Roland 42–43, 49
Bataille, Georges 41, 43, 45, 49
Battle, Hinton 159
Baudrillard, Jean 42–44, 46, 49
Bava, Lamberto 44, 48–49
Beautiful Prison 87
Becker, Josh 86, 89, 171
Benjamin, Walter 53, 54
Berkley, Michigan 86
Beyond the Black Rainbow 61
Biker Zombies from Detroit 88
The Birth of a Nation 35
black 63, 142
Blatty, William Peter 27, 32
Blind Faith 88
Bond, Christopher 156, 159, 161, 196
bootleg 44–45
Breaking Bad 57
British Board of Film Classification (BBFC) 16, 22–24
British Videogram Association (BVA) 16, 18, 19, 21
The Brood 38
Brosnan, Pierce 147
Buckwalter, Ian 55, 58

Buffy the Vampire Slayer 117
Burning Angel Entertainment 172, 174, 176
Burnside, Mary Wade 156–157
cabin 5, 13, 27, 29, 31, 33, 38–39, 47–48, 53, 55–57, 59, 62–64, 69, 74, 76, 82, 85, 90–91, 110–111, 115, 121, 123–128, 130, 147–149, 160, 166–167, 170–171, 174–175, 177, 185, 189–190, 195, 197, 200–202
The Cabin 88
The Cabin in the Woods 61, 185
The Cabinet of Dr. Caligari 34, 37
camera 8, 27–28, 31, 37, 39, 43, 46, 47–49, 51, 53, 57–58, 76–77, 86, 94, 99–100, 121–122, 127, 142, 150, 162, 171, 191–193, 195, 201
Campbell, Don 86
Cannes 20, 27, 191
Cannibal Holocaust 18
Carmen 35
Carpenter, John 28, 44–45, 47, 49–50
carpenter 56
Carrie 66, 163, 184–185
The Carrier 88
chainsaw 8, 10, 11, 12, 31, 32, 76, 77, 83, 110, 111, 114, 120, 126, 127, 129, 135, 136, 137, 147, 149, 150, 169, 175, 184, 193, 198, 199, 200
Chaplin, Charlie 35
Chasing Sleep 88
Chicago, Illinois 161
Children of the Night 88
cinematography 42, 47, 100, 190
Clawson, Michigan 86
Cleary, Sarah 15–26, 203
Clover, Carol J. 28–30, 33, 46, 48, 50, 59–60, 63, 68, 113, 119, 166
Colbert, Stephen 106–107
The Colbert Report 140
Comedown 61
comedy 6, 13, 57, 77, 103, 111, 114, 116, 126, 128, 159, 165, 168–169, 172–173, 179–180, 191, 199
Cookers 61
Costner, Kevin 190
cowboy 135, 137, 194

208 Index

Craven, Wes 28, 32, 90
Crepitus 87
Crimewave 88
Cronenberg, David 38, 44, 50
Curtis, Jamie Lee 30, 33, 116

Danse Macabre 39, 40, 54
Dark Places 61
Darkman 116
Dawn of the Dead 4, 6
Dead End 87
Dearborn, Michigan 82, 89, 148
Death Bed 88
Deliverance 85
de Manincor, Richard 86
Demon Lover 88
demons 6–7, 28, 32, 57, 60, 63–64, 67, 97, 106, 114–115, 117, 134, 161–162, 166, 169–171, 175, 198
Demons 44, 48–49
despair 111
The Despair 61
Detroit, Michigan 83–86, 89–92, 137–138, 142, 189, 193, 200
devil 63, 73–74, 82, 86
Die Hard franchise 116, 146, 150, 152
directing (film) 16, 40, 46, 55, 58, 82–83, 89–92, 94, 102–103, 105, 120, 138, 158, 161, 171, 174, 180, 185, 188–190, 192, 194–195, 200–201, 203
Di Rosa, Andrew 154–157
disability 70–79
Dr. Rat 40
Don't Breathe 87
Doviak, Scott Von 82, 92

economics 19, 36, 71–73, 79, 86, 89, 97, 133, 135, 138, 142, 151
Edison, Thomas 35
Edwards, Emily D. 59–69, 203
8989 Redstone 87
Elder Island 87
Elliott, L. Michael 1, 196–199, 203
Eloise 87
Enter the Void 61
Everyman 135, 167–168, 170
Evil Bong 61
The Exorcist 27, 174, 181

The Factory on 5th 87
faith 8, 11, 52, 96, 133, 160, 173
Fanalysis 96, 98–100
farmhouse 56, 91
father 65, 89, 101–102, 132–133
fear 4–5, 7–13, 20–21, 30–31, 40, 48, 51–52, 56, 65, 70–71, 76, 85, 94, 115, 122–123, 128, 151, 158–163, 178
"Female Prisoners: Detroit House of Correction" 90
Ferndale, Michigan 82, 83
5th Kind 87

final girl 27–32, 59, 110, 113, 116–117, 122, 166
final guy 27, 30–32, 113, 166–167
Frankenstein 38, 89, 205
Franklin, Michigan 82
Freaks 58
Friday the 13th 33, 47, 180
Friedkin, William 27, 174, 181
frontier mythos 135, 137
Frostbiter 88
Fuchs, Michael 94–108, 203–204
Fulci, Lucio 4, 13, 47

The Garden 61
gaze 28, 32, 42, 48, 51, 53–54, 71, 78, 162
gender 1, 28–33, 46, 65, 74–75, 79, 83, 104, 113, 115–116
Gerbner, George 64, 68
German 34–35, 91
ghost 82, 89, 171, 183
ghoul 6, 41, 49
The Ghoul Show 84
Gibson, William James 135, 142
Gilligan, Vince 57–58
Ginger Snaps 2 61
Gladwin, Michigan 82, 83
Godard, Jean-Luc 34–35, 40
goddess 183
The Godfather 150
gods 45, 54, 60, 99, 185
Gojira 39
Goodman, David 86
goth 4, 5, 13, 26, 45, 60, 119, 174, 203
Goth 61
gross (budget) 1, 21, 89, 195
Gunning, Tom 43, 45, 48–50
Gutierrez, Ezequiel 83
Guyant, Valerie 164–171, 204

The Hackers 88
Hall, Stefan 144–152, 204
Halloween 199
Halloween 27, 28, 30, 46, 47, 48, 50, 116
Harrington, Erin 182–186, 204
Harvard 34
Haskins, Jack 65, 68
Hearse Life 87
heavens 127, 156
Hectic Knife 87
Hedren, Tippi 194
hell 8, 47, 54, 56, 64, 71, 111, 137, 194
Hellmaster 88
heroin 59, 62–64, 66, 68–69
Hills, Matt 45, 50, 94, 100, 108
The Hills Have Eyes 27, 33, 84, 90
Hitchcock, Alfred 30, 41
Housebound 61

Iggy Pop 58
In the Mouth of Madness 45, 49–50
In the Woods 88

Infinite Jest 42–44, 50
Inside Ben 87

The Jackhammer Massacre 61
James, William 34
Jaros, Michael P. 120–130, 204
Jenkins, Henry 130, 144, 152
Joyce, James 36

Kempner, Brandon 4–14, 204
Kenner, Hugh 36, 40
kill 7–11, 63, 67, 110, 112, 116, 124–127, 129, 139, 149, 161, 175, 178, 198
killer 28–31, 45, 47–48, 92, 113, 123
The Killing Screens 64, 69
King, Stephen 20, 27, 33, 36, 39, 40, 45, 52, 54, 55, 56, 58, 82, 92, 123, 191
kissing 31, 201
Knight Chills 88
Korin, Greg 162
Kotzwinkle, William 40

Lake Eerie 87
laugh/laughter 12–13, 31, 57, 61, 65, 77, 86, 104, 118, 126, 128
LeClaire, Justin 161–163
Legend of the Night 88
Lewis, Leon 34–40, 204
Lewis, Marc 63, 69
Liddell, Alex 109–119, 204
Lindstrom, Eric 146
Little Shop of Horrors 153–154, 157
locked 29, 39, 47, 128
Locked Away 87
Lost Souls 88
love 1, 7–10, 19, 32, 61–62, 66, 91, 104, 110, 113, 125–126, 129, 134, 139, 142, 155, 184, 192, 198–200
Lovecraft, H.P. 27, 32, 45–46, 110, 118, 119, 183, 185
Lovely Molly 61
Lublin, Robert I. 120–130, 205

Mad Max 139
madness 31, 44, 46, 60, 115, 119
magic 45, 60, 82, 86, 114–115, 117, 132, 148, 163, 183
The Magic Island 7
"Male Prisoners Marching to Dinner" 90
Maltin, Leonard 36, 40
Le Manoir du diable 34, 82, 90
Marshall, Michigan 82, 85, 86, 91
Marx 73, 79, 205
Mason, John 86
Massumi, Brian 53–54
The Matrix franchise 146
McLuhan, Marshall 44, 53–54
Méliès, George 34, 82, 90
Mellen, Joan 30, 33
Men, Women, and Chainsaws 28, 46, 50, 68
Michelson, Annette 48

Michigan 56, 82–92, 133, 142, 148, 164, 188–189, 195, 203, 205–206
"Michigan Naval Reserves and the Detroit Light Guards" 90
Michigan State University 83, 90, 188, 195, 203, 205–206
Mindwarp 88
mirror 5, 59, 73, 76, 116–117, 128, 139, 174
Mirrors 61
The Monkey Wrench Gang 40
monster(s) 5, 11, 13, 39, 40, 44, 45, 47, 72, 80, 89, 105, 109, 110, 178, 179, 180, 191
Monsters Among Men 87
Moontrap 88
Moonwick Circle 87
Morristown, Tennessee 37, 55, 90
Mosquito 88
mother 62–63, 75, 125, 126
musical 1, 58, 151, 153–154, 156–164, 169–170, 180, 182, 196–199, 203

Nakata, Hideo 44, 50
National Viewers' and Listeners' Association (NVLA) 17
Native American 166
Needlestick 87
neoconservative 131–134
neoliberal 70–79, 131–135, 140
Neptune's Daughter 35
Never Mind the Bollocks Here's the Sex Pistols 55
night/nighttime 52, 85, 86, 100, 125, 161, 167, 189, 194, 200–201
Night of the Bloody Transplant 88
Night of the Living Dead (1968) 5, 6, 7, 8, 9, 12, 27, 186
Night of the Living Dead (2014) 87
A Nightmare on Elm Street 28
1980s 25, 41, 46, 59, 67, 83–84, 91, 95–96, 109–110, 116, 132, 135–136, 158, 160, 164, 166, 171, 196–198
1990s 23–24, 84, 91, 96, 116, 139
1970s 5, 30, 33, 46, 55–59, 84, 88, 110, 116, 136, 166
1960s 5, 13, 40, 84, 90, 92, 116, 198, 204
Northville, Michigan 86
The Northville Cemetery Massacre 92
The Nostril Picker 88
nurse 62

Obama, Barack 136, 167
Obscene Publications Act of 1959 18, 20, 22, 23
Odysseus 40
Oklahoma! 197
Oz: The Great and Powerful 89, 91, 192

patriarchy 30–31, 116
Pay to Play 87
Phillips, Michael 94–108, 205
Philo, Tim 85, 190

210 Index

photoplay 35–37, 39–40
Pierce, Bart 83, 86
Piranha 3D 86, 87
Pitchfork 87
Pitofsky, Alex 55–58, 205
Plake, Clayton 70–81, 205
Pleasence, Donald 30, 33
poetic 169, 171
"Police Drill" 90
Poltergeist 36
Pop Skull 61
pornorgraphy 1, 41, 43, 134, 164, 172–181
POV 31, 39, 47–48, 53–54, 74, 121–123, 128
poverty 63
prejudice 131, 133, 139
Pride and Prejudice and Zombies 182
Psycho 30, 58
psychology 21, 32, 33–35, 37, 40, 42, 46, 52, 60, 69, 80, 91, 155, 156, 157
psychopath 28–29, 47–48

Queen's University 159
queer 70–71, 73–77, 78

R-Naught 15 87
race 4, 12, 38, 99, 131–133, 142, 205
racism 63, 132–133, 139–141
Radcliffe, Ann 52, 54
Ramone, Johnny 58
Ramones 57
The Ramones 55
rape 16, 20, 26, 29, 33, 53, 63, 66, 74, 83–84, 90, 123, 175
Rapturious 61
Reagan, Ronald 71, 132, 135
Reefer Madness 67
religion 60, 99
religious 40, 60
Resolution 61, 68
Résumé with Monsters 183, 186
Return of the Dead 87
Riekki, Ron 82–92, 205
Ringu 44, 49–50
Robinson, Sally 30, 33
The Rocky Horror franchise 153–154, 157, 159, 169, 199
Romero, George A. 4, 5, 6, 7, 9, 10, 11, 13, 14, 27, 47, 52, 188
The Rosary Murders 88
Rotten, Johnny 57
Rozin, Paul 155, 157
Ruin Me 87
ruins 38

Sakmann, Doug 174
Sartain, Jeffrey 131–143, 205
Sartre, Jean-Paul 41
satire 5, 131, 133–136, 139–141
Scanners 38
schizophrenia 54, 67, 162
screenplay 21, 56, 165, 180, 206

screenwriting
Semley, John 42–50, 205
Sense and Sensibility and Sea Monsters 182
sex 16, 19, 28–29, 31–33, 38, 44, 47, 61, 65–66, 70, 74, 78, 80, 90, 103, 124, 134, 139, 172–181, 203, 204
Shin, Haerin 51–54, 206
Shrooms 61, 68
Siskel and Ebert 57, 58
60 Seconds to Die 87
Sklar, Robert 36, 40
skull 194
sleep 15, 47, 138, 189
soul 19, 45, 49, 114, 122, 155, 160, 184
Spider-Man 40, 89, 94, 116
Spiegel, Scott 46, 171
The Spiral Staircase 88, 91–92
Star Wars franchise 99, 146–147, 164, 205
Sterling Heights, Michigan 86
story 1, 21, 28, 44, 57, 59–61, 64, 89, 91, 94–95, 100–101, 103, 110–111, 116, 118, 125, 138, 144, 148, 149, 151, 164–171, 176, 179–180, 190, 197
Strain 100 87
Sullivan, Tom 83, 86

Tabori, George 158, 163
Tchepikova-Treon, Olga 172–181, 206
Tenebre 45, 49
Tennessee 33, 37, 55–56, 68–69, 82–83, 85, 91, 188–189, 192–193, 195, 203
The Texas Chainsaw Massacre 27, 33, 113
Thatcher, Margaret 16–17, 19–20
Thaw of the Dead 87
They Were Lost 87
Thomas, Dylan 39, 40
3D Monster Maze 145
The Three Stooges 8, 77, 98, 113, 126, 160, 168, 191–192
Tiger, Lionel 65, 69
To the Lighthouse 36–37
Toad Road 61
Toronto, Ontario 153–154, 159, 163, 205
The Tripper 61
Troy, Michigan 86
Trump, Donald 114, 141
Twain, Mark 138, 169
The Twilight Zone Magazine 27, 33, 36, 40

Ulysses 36
Upper Peninsula of Michigan 91, 205

Vertov, Dziga 48–49, 50
Video Recordings Act 17, 23
Videodrome 38, 44, 50
Vincent, Bill 188–195, 206
Virgil 183, 185
The Visitors 87

The Walking Dead 4, 11
Wallace, David Foster 42–44, 50

Warren, Bill 14, 27, 30, 33, 56, 57, 58, 75, 76, 77, 79, 80, 122, 126, 130, 141, 142, 143, 166
Wayne State University 85–86
werewolf 39
What's Eating Gilbert Grape 194
White Zombie 7
Whitehead, Alfred North 36
witch 68, 95, 195
witchcraft 184–185
Within the Woods 92, 94, 164–166, 171, 189
wolf 29, 134
Wolf 87
woods 29, 31, 33, 38, 47–48, 51, 55–56, 64, 66, 84, 85, 90, 94, 110, 115, 121, 123–125, 166, 170–171, 175, 177, 185, 189, 191, 195, 197, 200, 202
Woolf, Virginia 36–37
writing 11, 21, 36, 45, 86, 104, 154, 157, 179, 195, 204–205

Xena: Warrior Princess 98, 195

youth 19, 78, 85, 86, 136

Zeke 58
Zillman, Dolf 65, 69
zombie 4–14, 47